CRITICAL THINKING

CRITICAL THINKING

An Introduction to the Basic Skills

Concise Edition

William Hughes and Jonathan Lavery

broadview press

BROADVIEW PRESS — www.broadviewpress.com
Peterborough, Ontario, Canada

Founded in 1985, Broadview Press remains a wholly independent publishing house. Broadview's focus is on academic publishing; our titles are accessible to university and college students as well as scholars and general readers. With over 600 titles in print, Broadview has become a leading international publisher in the humanities, with world-wide distribution. Broadview is committed to environmentally responsible publishing and fair business practices.

The interior of this book is printed on 100% recycled paper.

Library and Archives Canada Cataloguing in Publication

Hughes, William (William H.), 1936-, author
      Critical thinking : an introduction to the basic skills / William Hughes and Jonathan Lavery. — Concise edition.

Includes index.
ISBN 978-1-55481-267-7 (paperback)

      1. Critical thinking—Textbooks. 2. Logic—Textbooks.
I. Lavery, Jonathan, 1965-, author II. Title.

BC177.H84 2015b   160   C2015-905808-2

Broadview Press handles its own distribution in North America
PO Box 1243, Peterborough, Ontario K9J 7H5, Canada
555 Riverwalk Parkway, Tonawanda, NY 14150, USA
Tel: (705) 743-8990; Fax: (705) 743-8353
email: customerservice@broadviewpress.com

Distribution is handled by Eurospan Group in the UK, Europe, Central Asia, Middle East, Africa, India, Southeast Asia, Central America, South America, and the Caribbean. Distribution is handled by Footprint Books in Australia and New Zealand.

Broadview Press acknowledges the financial support of the Government of Canada through the Canada Book Fund for our publishing activities.

Edited by Martin R. Boyne
Book design by Aldo Fierro

PRINTED IN CANADA

CONTENTS

Chapter 3: Clarifying Meaning   •   47

Chapter 4: Reconstructing Arguments   •   67

ACKNOWLEDGMENTS

Many people have helped me during the process of writing and revising this book. I am grateful to Dr. Jack Macdonald, Vice President Academic of the University of Guelph, for support from the New Initiatives Fund, which enabled me to produce the first draft of this book. I am also grateful to all the University of Guelph students in 74-210 who, through their questions and comments, gave me a better understanding of what is (and what is not) needed in a critical thinking course. I am especially grateful to those students who have changed my mind about so many matters by successfully arguing back (see Chapter 11), thereby demonstrating directly that there is something of practical importance to be learned from mastering critical thinking skills.

The following colleagues and students deserve special mention for their generosity with their time and their helpful suggestions: John-Paul Boyd, Brian Calvert, Tobias Chapman, Paul Genest, Jeff Hurdman, Susan-Judith Hoffmann, Hugh Lehman, Neil MacGill, Stella Ostick, Rob Ridley, and Brian Wetstein.

Finally, I want to acknowledge a special debt of gratitude to my family: to my wife, Daphne, for her general support as well as her efforts to clean up my prose and help me achieve a measure of clarity; and to my children, Miranda, Jeremy, Jonathan, and Anna, for putting up with so much over the years while providing grist for the mill. To them all, I dedicate this book.

—Bill Hughes, 3rd edition

Broadview Press has encouraged us to prepare this concise edition of *Critical Thinking*. It is based on the 7th edition, with no changes other than deletions and alterations to the chapter numbering.

A second kind of change, which is common to all versions of the 7th edition, is less noticeable at first glance. I have gone through the self-tests, the examples, and the exposition, improving the material as much as possible. Most of these materials remain unchanged, but instructors who have used an earlier edition of the text are warned to check carefully before they make use of a particular passage in class or in a test.

Finally, I have refined the treatment of several items throughout the book, mostly in response to generous feedback from readers.

I want to thank Stephen Latta at Broadview for his indispensable help on the present edition, Martin Boyne for excellent copy-editing, Katheryn Doran for her invaluable input for the previous edition and numerous good suggestions for the 7th edition, and Robert Martin for the countless improvements he made to the 5th edition. Everyone at Broadview deserves special commendation for their patience over the years, especially Stephen.

My work on this edition is dedicated to Bill and Daphne Hughes.

—Jonathan Lavery

ONLINE MATERIALS

Every new copy of *Critical Thinking: Concise Edition* includes a passcode granting access to the *Broadview Critical Thinking Online* website. This website provides useful review and practice materials for students of critical thinking, including

- Multiple-choice and true/false questions testing understanding of the key concepts for each chapter of *Critical Thinking*
- Interactive flashcards for use in reviewing the terminology of *Critical Thinking*
- A collection of real and realistic sample arguments (including remarks from Barack Obama and George W. Bush), accompanied by interactive questions for practice in argument interpretation
- Links to interesting and controversial media reports and opinion pieces, sorted by topic, including
  - Facebook Research
  - Feminism in the 21st Century
  - Machine intelligence
  - The death penalty
  - Marijuana Legislation
- A substantial online guide to writing, including
  - Citation style guidelines for CSE, APA, MLA, and Chicago
  - Interactive punctuation and grammar exercises

*If you purchased a used copy of this book and did not receive a passcode to the *Broadview Critical Thinking Online* website, you can purchase a passcode at little cost at www.broadviewpress.com.

Part One

INTRODUCTION

---

1. Reasoning and Critical Thinking

1.1 REASONING

The ability to reason is the fundamental characteristic of human beings. It has long been held that the capacity to reason is unique to human beings, but even if it is not—if it turns out, for example, that reasoning is a quality we share with dolphins or apes or even computers—the capacity to reason is nevertheless central to what we are and how we think of ourselves. Virtually every conscious human activity involves reasoning; we reason whenever we solve problems, make decisions, assess character, explain events, write poems, balance checkbooks, predict elections, make discoveries, interpret works of art, or repair carburetors. We reason about everything from the meaning of life to what to have for dinner.

Of course, much of the time we are not engaged in conscious reasoning; often we simply listen to what others say, take note of things around us, experience feelings, daydream, listen to concerts, tell stories, or watch television. These activities need not involve conscious reasoning, but to the extent that we understand what is going on around or inside us we are not entirely passive. Some reasoning must be taking place, even if it is at a pre-conscious level. To understand reasoning properly, however, we need to understand how it differs from mere thinking. When we are merely thinking, our thoughts simply come to us, one after another; when we reason, we actively link thoughts together in such a way that we believe one thought provides support for another thought. This active process of reasoning is termed inference. *INFERENCE* involves a special relationship between different thoughts: when we infer B from A, we move from A to B because we believe that A *supports* or *justifies* or *makes it reasonable to believe in* the truth of B.

The difference between mere thinking and reasoning or inference is easy to understand through examples. Consider the following pairs of sentences:

> *Alan is broke, and he is unhappy.*
> *Alan is broke; therefore he is unhappy.*

> *Anne was in a car accident last week, and she deserves an extension on her essay.*
> *Anne was in a car accident last week, so she deserves an extension on her essay.*

This triangle has equal sides and equal angles.
This triangle has equal sides; hence it has equal angles.

Notice that the first sentence in each pair simply asserts two thoughts but says nothing about any relationship between them, while the second sentence asserts a relationship between two thoughts. This relationship is signaled by the words *therefore, so,* and *hence.* These are called *INFERENCE INDICATORS*: words that indicate that one thought is intended to support (i.e., to justify, provide a reason for, provide evidence for, or entail) another thought. Other common inference indicators include the following:

> *since*
> *thus*
> *implies*
> *consequently*
> *because*
> *it follows that*
> *given that*

It is important to note that sometimes the inference indicator is missing; this can occur when a speaker thinks the inference is quite obvious. For example:

It's raining; I'd better take my umbrella.

The actual presence of an inference indicator is not important. What is important is the relationship of support between the thoughts of the speaker. This relationship is a defining condition of an inference: if two thoughts are linked by such a relationship, they constitute an inference; otherwise they do not.

When we express an inference in words, we do so by means of statements. A *STATEMENT* is a sentence (i.e., a set of words) that is used to make a claim that is capable of being true or false. If a sentence is not capable of being true or false, then it is not a statement. Questions (*Are you awake?*) and commands (*Wake up!*) are not capable of being true or false and, hence, are not statements. Only statements can be true or false. When an inference is expressed in statements, it is called an argument. An *ARGUMENT* is a set of statements that claims that one or more of those statements, called the *PREMISES*, support another of them, called the *CONCLU-SION*. Thus, every argument claims that its premises support its conclusion.

1.2 THE CONCEPT OF LOGICAL STRENGTH

Since a statement makes a claim that can be true or false, any statement can be assessed by asking whether it is true or false. Is Alan really unhappy? Was Anne actually in a car accident? We can assess the truth or falsity of a statement in isolation, independent of its part in an argument (or a story or list, etc.). Every statement that is assessed without regard for its part in an argument must meet the same standard: truth. The truth or falsity of the statement *Alan is unhappy* does not depend upon whether it is part of an argument. To discover the truth or falsity of statements, we examine the statement itself and look for direct evidence that will show us whether it is true or false. Often, however, without further evidence it may be difficult or impossible to determine conclusively whether an isolated statement is true or false. This is why we construct arguments: they help us assess statements when the truth or falsity of a statement is not directly evident. It is also why we must learn to assess whole lines of reasoning in addition to assessing statements.

Assessing an argument is more complex than assessing an isolated statement. Since an argument always includes a claim that its premises support its conclusion, assessing an argument means assessing this claim. Do the premises really support the conclusion, and if so, how much support do they provide? In other words, how *strong* is the inference from the premise(s) to the conclusion? We say that an argument has *LOGICAL STRENGTH* when its premises, if true, actually provide support for its conclusion.

The concept of logical strength is central in critical thinking and has two important features that need to be stressed. First, the logical strength of an argument is independent of the truth or falsity of its premises: we do not need to know that the premises of an argument are true in order to assess its logical strength. When we assess the logical strength of an argument, we are really asking, *If the premises are true, would we be justified in accepting the conclusion?* and we can answer this question without knowing whether or not the premises actually are true. Consider the following example:

> *The population of Chatham is 27,000.*
> *The population of Orillia is 26,000.*
> *Therefore, Chatham has a larger population than Orillia.*

Even if we don't know the populations of Chatham and Orillia, we can still see that the inference in this argument is a strong one. If both premises are true, then obviously the conclusion would have to be true as well. The fact that either or both premises might be false does not affect the logical strength of the argument. For similar reasons, an argument with premises and conclusion that are known to be true may be a very weak argument. For example:

> *Toronto is the capital of Ontario.*
> *Ottawa is in Ontario.*
> *Therefore, Ottawa is the capital of Canada.*

In this example, the premises and the conclusion are all true, but the facts that Toronto is the capital of Ontario and that Ottawa is in Ontario provide no support for the statement that Ottawa is the capital of Canada. The inference is therefore a bad or weak one. Only if the information contained in the premises really provides a good reason for holding that the conclusion is true can we say the inference is a strong one.

Second, the logical strength of an argument is often a matter of degree. Some arguments are so strong that the truth of the premises guarantees the truth of the conclusion. Such arguments are called *DEDUCTIVE ARGUMENTS*, and they constitute strict proofs. But most arguments are not as strong as this; usually, the truth of the premises makes it reasonable to hold that the conclusion is also true, but it does not provide an absolute guarantee. Such arguments are called *INDUCTIVE ARGUMENTS*. For example:

> *Arthur has been a moderate social drinker for 20 years.*
> *No one has ever known him to get drunk.*
> *Therefore, he won't get drunk at the party tonight.*

This is a strong argument, since if the premises are true it is reasonable to conclude that the conclusion will also be true. Nevertheless, Arthur might get drunk tonight. Given the truth of the premises this might astonish us, but it is not impossible.

Understanding the concept of logical strength is the key to developing critical thinking skills. The fact that the logical strength of an argument is independent of the truth of its premises means that in order to assess an argument we must do more than merely determine whether its premises are true. And the fact that logical strength may be a matter of degree means that we must be sensitive to the various features of arguments that affect their degree of strength. If we lack critical thinking skills, we can easily be fooled into thinking that an argument is strong when the premises actually provide little or no support for the conclusion. Consider the following inferences:

> *The Democrats won a majority of seats in the last election.*
> *So they must have received more votes than any other party.*

My sister always got better grades in school than I did.
That proves that she's smarter than I am.

Eighty per cent of those who tried Painaway said they would take it the next time
they had a headache.
Therefore, Painaway is a better headache remedy.

The city council is unfair to city employees.
Jones is a city councillor.
Hence, Jones is unfair to city employees.

A majority of the union members voted in favor of the contract.
Consequently, these people must be in favor of the 1-per-cent pay reduction in the
contract.

Whenever there is high unemployment, interest rates increase.
So high unemployment causes high interest rates.

These are all weak arguments: the conclusions are not adequately supported by their premises. This does not mean that the conclusions are false or even likely to be false. It only
means that the evidence presented in the premises, even if true, does not entitle us to draw
the conclusion. The premises do not, in other words, adequately support the conclusion.

1.3 TRUTH, LOGICAL STRENGTH, AND SOUNDNESS

In section 1.2 we drew a distinction between assessing the truth or falsity of a statement and assessing the logical strength of an inference. Although these are quite
different tasks, both are important if we want to arrive at the truth. Remember that
a strong argument is one whose premises, if true, support its conclusion. In other
words, its premises, *if true*, provide a justification for believing the conclusion to be
true. But a logically strong argument, as we saw, may have false premises. So if we
want to know whether the conclusion of an argument is likely to be true, we need to
know *both* that the argument is a strong one *and* that its premises are true. What we
want, in other words, are logically strong arguments with true premises. An argument
that has both logical strength and true premises is called a *SOUND ARGUMENT*.

It is very important to be aware of the differences among these three properties.
Truth is a property of statements and never of inferences. *Logical strength* is a property of inferences and never of statements. Logical strength refers to the inferential

connection between the premises and conclusion of an argument. *Soundness* is a property of an argument as a whole. Always keep the question of strength separate from the question of truth when dealing with any argument. Never ask simply, *Is this a good argument?* Ask two questions instead:

> (1) Is this a logically strong argument? and
> (2) Are its premises true?

The order in which these questions are asked is not important. What is crucial is that they be asked separately. Only when both have been answered are we in a position to know whether an argument is sound—whether we have a good reason to accept its conclusion.

Sometimes, however, it is inappropriate to ask whether the premises are true. We may, for example, want to explore the consequences of an assumption whose truth or falsity we cannot determine. For example:

> *No one knows for certain whether Martin Bormann died in 1945. If he did not, then he probably escaped through Switzerland and Italy to South America. That is what Adolf Eichmann and a number of other high-ranking Nazis did.*

There are even times when we want to develop an argument with premises that we know or assume to be false. Such arguments are called *COUNTERFACTUAL ARGUMENTS* because at least one premise is a counterfactual statement. For instance, we may want to explore the logical consequences of some historical event that never happened; in this case, we posit a counterfactual claim as a supposition for the sake of argument. For example:

> *If Hitler had invaded Britain in 1940 he would have succeeded, because at that time the Germans had military superiority.*

Or we may want to explore the consequences of the occurrence of some hypothetical situation. For example:

> *If the state sales tax were reduced to 5 per cent, there would not be a corresponding decrease in government revenues. This is because part of the decrease would be offset by an increase in sales as a result of the sales-tax reduction.*

We should also note a special kind of counterfactual argument called the *REDUCTIO*

AD ABSURDUM. In a reductio argument, a statement is proven to be true by assuming it to be false and then deriving a contradiction from that assumption. For example:

> *It is preposterous to claim, as some people have, that Gorbachev engineered the August 1991 coup attempt by Communist hard-liners in order to strengthen his position and stop the secessionist movements in the republics. If he engineered the coup then we would have to conclude that he is an exceptionally stupid man, for not only did the coup weaken his personal position and strengthen the position of Yeltsin, his chief rival, but it unleashed a wave of secessionism that destroyed the Soviet Union. Gorbachev may not be the smartest man in the world, but no one could have become political leader of the Soviet Union and been that stupid.*

In all these kinds of cases we want our arguments to be strong, but we cannot even pretend that these arguments are sound, since we know or assume that at least one of the premises is false.

Counterfactual arguments, however, are the exception to the rule. In almost all cases our main concern is with sound arguments. If we start with true premises, and use only logically strong arguments, we are entitled to rely on the conclusions we reach. Sound arguments expand our knowledge and increase our understanding. This is why developing the ability to recognize sound arguments is so important.

1.4 CRITICAL THINKING SKILLS

The primary focus of critical thinking skills is on determining whether arguments are sound, i.e., whether they have true premises and logical strength. But determining the soundness of arguments is not a simple matter, for three reasons.

First, before we can assess an argument we must determine its precise meaning. It would be convenient if the meaning of arguments were always clear, but unfortunately this is often not so. An argument may be unclear because the meaning of one or more of its statements is unclear or because the nature of the connection that is being asserted between the premises and conclusion is unclear. This means we have to learn how to interpret statements and arguments in a way that makes their meaning as clear as possible. The skills needed for this task are *INTERPRETIVE SKILLS*. Chapters 2 to 4 are aimed at developing these skills.

Second, determining the truth or falsity of statements is often a difficult task. Even when we are sure we know precisely what a statement means, we may be unsure about its truth and may even be unsure how to go about determining whether it is true or false. As we shall see, there are several different types of statements, and each type has its own method for determining truth and falsity. The skills needed for this task are *VERIFICATION SKILLS*. We shall deal with these skills in Chapter 6.

Third, assessing arguments is complex because there are several different types of inference, and each type requires a different kind of assessment. It is necessary to learn how to recognize these different types of inferences and to become familiar with these different methods of assessment. For this purpose *REASONING SKILLS* are needed. These skills are dealt with in Chapters 7 to 12.

These three types of skills—interpretive skills, verification skills, and reasoning skills—constitute what are usually referred to as *CRITICAL THINKING SKILLS*. Developing a mastery of them is important for several practical reasons.

First, we are inundated with information of all sorts, but this information is useless unless we know how to use it in our thinking to draw out its implications and consequences. Much of it is incomplete and one-sided in ways that are often not apparent, and if we are not on our guard, we may be misled.

Second, we are constantly presented with arguments designed to get us to accept some conclusion that we would otherwise not accept. Politicians, preachers, advertisers, editorial writers, and special-interest groups of all sorts spend a great deal of time, thought, and money attempting to persuade us to believe the things they want us to believe, and it is important to be on guard against arguments that fail to meet the appropriate logical criteria. This is partly a matter of our own self-interest. When others seek to make us believe things that are in *their* interests, it is possible, or even likely, that our interests are not being well served.

Third, mastering critical thinking skills is also a matter of intellectual self-respect. We all have the capacity to learn how to distinguish good arguments from bad ones and to work out for ourselves what we ought and ought not to believe, and it diminishes us as persons if we let others do our thinking for us. If we are not prepared to think for ourselves, and to make the effort to learn how to do this well, we will always be in danger of becoming slaves to the ideas and values of others due to our own ignorance.

And finally, critical thinking skills can make it easier for us to persuade others to change their beliefs. Many beliefs are based more on emotion than on reason, although those holding them usually believe they are based on reason. In fact, it is rare to find a person, even a complete bigot, who does not believe that his or her beliefs have a rational basis. Critical thinking skills can be effective in dislodging such beliefs and persuading others to change their views.

This last point raises a number of moral questions. Like any skill, critical thinking skills can be used for good or ill. In fact, there are many ways in which they can be abused: they can be used to make a bad argument look much stronger than it really is and to make an opponent's position look much weaker than it really is; they can be used to make ourselves look wise and to make others look foolish; they can be used to avoid having to respond to legitimate criticisms and to persuade others to change their beliefs for inadequate reasons. Every day we find ourselves in situations in which we could use our critical thinking skills for such purposes, and sometimes we may be tempted to do so. Yielding to the temptation, however, is dishonest and hypocritical. It is analogous to a medical doctor using his or her medical training not to help people but to torture them more effectively.

There are other, more difficult, moral questions that can arise. How far should we go in revealing to our opponents the weaknesses we see in our arguments? Is it always right to attack the weaknesses in the views of others? How are we to be fair to those who disagree with us? How far should we go in our attempts not to distort others' views when discussing them? How forceful should we be in attempting to persuade others to agree with our views? As we shall see, there are no easy answers to such questions. They need to be approached with an equal regard for the truth and for the feelings of others and with a proper sense of our own fallibility.

1.5 CRITICAL THINKING AND THE SCIENCE OF LOGIC

Reasoning skills involve the application of principles of logic. LOGIC is the science that studies the relationships between premises and conclusions with a view to determining when and to what extent the premises actually support the conclusion. Logic was first recognized as a science in the fourth century BCE by Aristotle, who described what he believed were the basic principles of correct reasoning. These principles were elaborated and developed by a number of medieval logicians, but the basic nature of logic remained essentially Aristotelian until the late nineteenth century. About a hundred years ago, logic entered a period of radical change when mathematicians began using logic to solve certain problems regarding the founda- tions of mathematics. More recently, computer science and artificial intelligence have contributed to further developments in logic. As a result, logic has become a highly complex and sophisticated discipline of considerable theoretical import- ance. The power and sophistication of modern logic, however, have been purchased at the price of increasing abstractness. The principles of modern logic have been abstracted from ordinary language and are considered as purely formal principles, devoid of content.

Many of the critical thinking skills described in this book are drawn from logic. Our interest in them, however, is not in their theoretical foundations or theoretical significance but in their practical application. In particular, we are interested in the way in which the principles of logic function when used in natural language—that is, the languages such as English, French, or Mandarin that have evolved organically and continue to evolve as people use them in everyday life, as opposed to artificial languages such as the symbolic logic covered in Chapter 9 in which all the elements have fixed rules for usage. When any logical principle is used in a real-life setting, we face a host of special problems that take us beyond the domain of formal logic. These problems of practical application will engage most of our attention here. The principles of formal logic have their own interest and intellectual challenge, but they lie beyond the scope of this book.

There is, however, one underlying commitment that we want to preserve from the science of logic. This is something that Aristotle, the medieval logicians who followed his lead, and modern logicians who work on mathematical logic all seem to agree upon: it is that logic, as a science, is a study of normative principles, it does not merely describe its subject. *NORMATIVE PRINCIPLES* function as standards for assessment or guides for action, whereas descriptions merely attempt to accurately represent something. Henry Gray's *Anatomy* is a great work of physiology because it *describes* its subject accurately and comprehensively. Logic, however, does not simply discover in such a descriptive manner how people happen to reason. It explores the *norms* of reasoning and discovers how people *ought to* reason. Patterns of reasoning that have been identified as inductively or deductively strong are reliable for anyone to use.

But once a pattern of reasoning is discovered to be faulty or fallacious, we ought to avoid this pattern as unreliable. This is why the critical thinking skills outlined in 1.4 are so useful. There are reliable and unreliable ways of drawing implications and consequences out of information. There are reliable and unreliable ways in which other people attempt to persuade us to accept their positions. Conversely, there are reliable and unreliable ways in which we may persuade others to accept our reasoning. Most importantly, by becoming more aware of the principles of good reasoning, we *earn* our own intellectual self-respect by thinking in ways that measure up to the normative standards of good reasoning.

1.6 SELF-TEST NO. 1

I. Which of the following passages are arguments? For those that are arguments, identify the premise(s) and the conclusion.

  1. You should go home next weekend because you promised your parents you would.

  2. You should go home next weekend and have a good time with your friends.

3. Peter took first place in the 1500 metre run at the championships last year and has been training hard ever since, so he should win the championship easily this year.

4. I will be able to visit you next month after all. The doctor just told me that a second operation won't be necessary and that I'll be able to go home this Friday.

5. His car skidded on the ice and hit a van in the middle of the intersection. The car was a write-off, and the van suffered $3,000 in damage.

6. It is obvious that no great leader ever suffered from low self-esteem.

7. The company laid off 250 assembly line workers last week. I think they were justified because their sales had declined by 23 per cent in the past three months.

8. Many people think that thunder is caused by lightning. This is a mistake.

9. Most evenings I go for a walk after dinner. Usually, I walk to the park and back, which is about two miles, but last night I only went as far as the library.

10. You're crazy if you think you can take a full course load while working 20 hours a week and pass your semester. You should remember what happened to Van and Patti when they tried to do that last year.

11. My purse with several hundred dollars in cash, my watch, and my necklace have gone missing from my hotel room. The door was locked while I was out, and there's no sign of forced entry. It looks like someone on staff at this hotel is a thief.

12. We drove to Pittsburgh to visit Sally in the morning, spent the afternoon in Latrobe with Onno and his family, and then stopped at Betty's for dinner in Greensburg. By the time we finally arrived in Philadelphia last night, we were happy about visiting friends but tired from all the driving.

II. When you know enough to judge the truth or falsity of the premises, indicate which of the following arguments are sound.

1. Albany is in New York. New York is in the United States. Therefore, Albany is in the United States.

2. Montreal is larger than Beaver Creek. Beaver Creek is larger than Vancouver. Therefore, Montreal is larger than Vancouver.

3. Shaquille O'Neal is taller than Steve Nash. Steve Nash is taller than Tom Cruise. Therefore, Tom Cruise is shorter than Shaquille O'Neal.

4. No one under the age of 18 is legally an adult. Katherine is only 15 years old. Katherine is not legally an adult.

5. Hockey is Canada's national sport. A country's national sport is likely to be very popular in that country. Therefore, hockey is likely to be very popular in Canada.

6. Fez is north of Casablanca. Tangier is north of Fez. Therefore, Tangier is north of Casablanca.

7. A cat makes a good house pet. A tiger is a cat. Therefore, a tiger makes a good house pet.

8. No human being is immortal. Even the President is a human being. Therefore, the President is not immortal.

9. Everybody loves a winner. The New York Yankees have won more games than any other baseball team since its inception. Therefore, everybody loves the Yankees.

10. At this moment, I am reading a book. If I am reading a book, I must be awake. Therefore, I must be awake.

11. The HMS Pinafore is a faster vessel than the SS Minnow. The SS Minnow is faster than the Yellow Submarine. Therefore, the Yellow Submarine is the slowest of the three vessels.

12. Dogs make excellent companions. Cerberus is a dog. Therefore, Cerberus is an excellent companion.

1.7 QUESTIONS FOR DISCUSSION

In section 1.1, an argument was defined as a set of statements that *claims* that its premises support its conclusion. Sometimes it is not clear whether a speaker intends to make such a claim. In these cases we have to rely upon whatever clues the context provides to decide whether it is reasonable to interpret what the speaker has said as being an argument rather than something else. For each of the following sentences or passages, briefly describe a context that makes it reasonable to interpret it as either an argument or not an argument.

1. The expressway was closed for three hours this afternoon because of the train derailment on the overpass.

2. When George finished speaking, Frances sat quietly for several minutes, her brow furrowed in intense concentration. Suddenly, she leapt up and ran to her room, rummaged through her desk, found a sheet of paper, and scrawled a few words on it. She crammed it in an envelope, addressed and stamped the envelope, ran out of the house, and thrust it into the mailbox. "That's done," she said. "Now I am committed, and my life will never be the same again."

3. The company laid off 250 assembly line workers last week because their sales had declined by 23 per cent in the past three months. The company seems to have had no choice.

4. Mike refuses to vote because he thinks all political parties are the same.

5. I went for a walk last evening, but when I got to London Road it started to rain, so I turned around and came home.

6. Hey, it's seven o'clock; it's time to go.

7. To get rid of hiccups, breathe into a paper bag for a few minutes.

8. By the end of the war in 1945, Churchill realized that, although Britain had won the war against the Axis powers, it was an economically devastated nation that would need massive foreign aid if it was to recover.

9. This is an important decision, obviously, and I don't want to decide in haste. I suppose, all things considered, that the best thing to do would be to resign, but I would like to have until tomorrow to think about it.

10. It is a beautiful day out, and a walk in the park will make you feel better.

Part Two

MEANING

2. MEANING AND DEFINITION

Reasoning, we have said, involves thinking. Thinking, in turn, involves language, for without language we could not express (and probably not even have) any thoughts. In order to understand reasoning, therefore, it is necessary to pay careful attention to the relationship between thought and language. The relationship seems to be straightforward: thought is expressed in and through language. But this claim, while true, is an oversimplification. People often fail to say what they mean. Everyone has had the experience of having their words misunderstood by others. And we all use words not merely to express our thoughts but also to shape them. Developing our critical thinking skills, therefore, requires an understanding of the ways in which words can (and can fail to) express our thoughts.

2.1 THE COMPLEXITY OF LANGUAGE

Language is an extremely complex phenomenon. The number of different words in any language is finite, but these words can be used to generate an infinite number of different sentences with different meanings. Many of the ordinary things we say or write have never been said before by anyone. For example:

> *Professor Sutherland reminds me of my Uncle Tony; they both have the habit of running their fingers through their hair when they are thinking hard.*

It is likely that when this sentence was first written in this book, it had never been written before. And it is not just the precise wording that is unique: it is unlikely that anyone has ever had the same thought. In fact, there is no limit to the number of new sentences with new meanings that could be created. Conversely, there are often different ways of saying the same thing. For example:

> *Anne is older than everyone else in the room.*
> *Everyone else in the room is younger than Anne.*

In addition, there are often many different words or sentences that mean more or less the same thing. One lexicographer, for example, has recorded over 2,200 synonyms for the word *drunk*.

Written and spoken language, although closely connected, are nevertheless not identical: spoken language is more flexible (and hence more complex) than written language, for we can change the meaning of words and sentences through our gestures, tone of voice, and facial expressions. Note the different meanings that arise when the underlined word is emphasized in the following sentences:

> *You shouldn't steal library books.* (But it may be acceptable for others to do so.)
> *You shouldn't steal library books.* (But I won't be surprised if you do.)
> *You shouldn't steal library books.* (But defacing books is acceptable.)
> *You shouldn't steal library books.* (But stealing books from the bookstore is acceptable.)
> *You shouldn't steal library books.* (But stealing magazines from the library is acceptable.)

Understanding spoken language, therefore, requires much more than knowing the written language. In fact, the close connection between written and spoken language that exists in European languages is sometimes absent in other languages. Chinese spoken dialects (which are as different from one another as English and German) all use the same writing system, so that people who speak different dialects can communicate through writing even though they may not understand each other's speech.

Language is always in a state of gradual change, in ways that are largely unpredictable. A single language can, in a few centuries, evolve into two languages so different from each other that those who speak one will find the other incomprehensible. Given the complexity of language, it is astonishing that we develop a facility to use at least one language before we are old enough to go to school. We are all intimately familiar with at least one language, and we therefore understand what language is, at least in the sense of knowing how to use language. But at a deeper level most of us actually have only the most elementary understanding of what language is and how it works. Even linguistic theorists are uncertain about many features of language. They do not know, for example, whether the basic structure of language (i.e., its underlying grammar) reflects certain characteristics of the human mind or is merely conventional in nature. Nor do they fully understand the relationship between language and thinking: we normally use a language when we think, but is language necessary for human thought? And if it is, do people who think in different languages think differently? When we translate a speech from Russian into English, can we be sure that we understand exactly what it meant to the original speaker or what it means to a Russian audience? The relationship between language and reality is also problematic. Does language describe the world as it really is, or do we use language to impose a structure on our experience, experience that would otherwise be chaotic and meaningless?

2.2 THE MEANING OF LANGUAGE

Usually it is not difficult to explain what a particular word or sentence means. But there is much that is puzzling about the nature of meaning itself. How do words get their meaning, and how do meanings change? Is the meaning that words have different from the meaning of sentences? In order to enhance our understanding of the nature and complexity of meaning, we will look briefly at three theories of meaning. The first two are common-sense views that have been held by many people, including many philosophers and linguistic theorists. Unfortunately, both are open to serious objections, and many philosophers now regard them as untenable. The third theory avoids the weakness of the first two and is the one we will rely upon in this book.

2.2.1 The Reference Theory of Meaning

The *REFERENCE THEORY OF MEANING* was first expounded by Aristotle in the fourth century BCE. According to this view, the meaning of a word consists in what it refers to. The word *dog* refers to all the dogs in the world, so it seems plausible to hold that the meaning of *dog* is all the dogs in the world. After all, if we know what *dog* refers to, we obviously know what the word means. Similarly, the meaning of *tree* is every tree in the world, the meaning of *automobile* is every automobile, the meaning of *joke* is every joke, and so on. The meaning of a term thus consists of its reference class, that is, the class of objects to which the word refers. At first glance, the reference theory is a plausible account of meaning, and its plausibility is enhanced by the fact that pointing to the reference class is often a good way of explaining the meaning of a word. If you don't know what *antimacassar* means, I can easily explain its meaning by pointing to an antimacassar and explaining that other antimacassars vary in size and design but have the same function as this one.

There are, however, serious difficulties with the reference theory. At the heart of the theory there seems to be a confusion between understanding the meaning of a word and having knowledge of what the word refers to. When we understand the meaning of the word *dog*, we usually have knowledge of only a small proportion of the dogs that exist, and this is puzzling if the meaning of *dog* is the reference class of the term. The fact that even small children can understand the meaning of *dog* on the basis of direct knowledge of only a few dogs cannot be explained by the reference theory. The theory encounters even more serious difficulties, however, when we consider words that have no reference class. What do the following words refer to: *unless, after, yes, unlikely, the, nevertheless, was, if, where*? Does it even make sense to suggest that the meaning of *unless* is the class of unlesses? In addition, there are certain phrases whose meaning is easily understood but whose reference is unknown. For example, we all understand the meaning of the phrase *the oldest man in the world*, even when we don't know to whom it refers. If the meaning is the reference, then we shouldn't be able to understand what the phrase means unless we know who the oldest man in the world is. The reference theory of meaning, therefore, has to be rejected. As we shall see in 2.6, it is important to distinguish meaning and reference.

2.2.2 The Idea Theory of Meaning

The *IDEA THEORY OF MEANING* was developed by John Locke in the seventeenth century. He held that the meaning of a word consists of the idea or mental image that is associated with the word. When we think of the word *dog*, it seems that we have a mental image we associate with the word, and it is plausible to hold that the meaning of *dog* is this image in our minds. This theory seems to be able to deal with phrases like *the oldest man in the world*, since it is plausible to suggest that we have a mental image we associate with this phrase.

But the idea theory also encounters several difficulties. Just as the class of unlesses seems to make no sense, the mental image of unless also seems to make no sense. But in addition, the image or idea we associate with a word like *dog* turns out on reflection to be very unclear. If we attempt to describe our image of a dog, we might describe an ordinary particular dog: one that is black, short-haired, about 18 inches high, with a short tail, etc. Of course, we know that many dogs are not black, that some are long-haired, that some are very small and some are very large, and so forth. But we cannot have an image of a dog that is both black and not black, both long-haired and short-haired, and both tall and short. It is impossible for our image of a dog to include all those characteristics that we know dogs have. How, then, can our image *be* the meaning of the word?

A final difficulty with the idea theory is that it has the consequence that we can never know what another person means by certain words. You can never see my mental images, and I can never see yours. If the mental image is the meaning, how can I know what you mean by *dog*, and how can you know what I mean by *dog*? So the idea theory is problematic for several reasons.

2.2.3 Meaning as Use

A new approach to meaning, *MEANING AS USE*, was developed more recently by Ludwig Wittgenstein (1889–1951) and John Austin (1911–60). They recognized that many words do refer to things and that many words have a mental image or idea associated with them, but they held that the primary bearers of meaning are not words but sentences. Words have meaning only when they are used in sentences; without such a context they have no meaning. When we ask what some particular word means, we seem to be asking for *the* meaning of the word itself, as if it had a meaning apart from the way it is used in sentences. In fact, the only meaning a word can have is the meaning it gains from the meanings of the sentences in which the word is typically used. Notice how the different meanings of a word are expressed by using that word in different sentences:

> *I gave him a <u>hand</u> with his baggage.* (i.e., help)
> *The crowd gave him a <u>hand</u>.* (i.e., applause)
> *Please <u>hand</u> me the scissors.* (i.e., give)

> *She is a <u>green</u> lawyer.* (i.e., inexperienced)
> *He is looking <u>green</u>.* (i.e., nauseated)
> *We had a <u>green</u> Christmas last year.* (i.e., without snow)

> *Don't <u>strike</u> that child.* (i.e., hit)
> *The <u>strike</u> was over wages.* (i.e., refusal to work)
> *<u>Strike</u> three!* (i.e., the batter is "out")

But if the meaning of sentences is primary and the meaning of words is derivative—if we cannot derive the meaning of a sentence from the meanings of the words it contains—how are we to account for the meaning of sentences? Wittgenstein and Austin held that the meaning of sentences is to be found in their use. Language is a tool, and just as we don't really know what a hammer is until we know what its use is, we don't know what a sentence means until we know what it is being used to do. In order to know what a particular sentence means we need to ask, *What is this speaker, talking to this audience in this particular context, using this sentence to do?* If someone says *Hold it*, we cannot know what the sentence means until we know what the speaker intends to accomplish by saying it, what conventions apply in the situation, and how the audience reacts to the sentence. Did the speaker say *Hold it* to get someone to stop doing something or to instruct someone to grasp hold of an object? Only when we have answered this question will we know what the sentence means.

It is important to pay attention to the context, for the context typically gives us the clues we need to determine what the speaker is using a sentence to do and thus what the sentence means. There are various contextual features we can make use of, such as the social setting, the speaker's personal goals, the nature and expectations of the audience, and what has just been said by other speakers. Changing the context of a sentence can sometimes dramatically affect its meaning. For example:

> *The queen is in a vulnerable position: (a) when said by a spectator at a chess match and (b) when said by a teacher in a lecture on the role of the monarchy in Britain.*

> *The President has been shot and died a few minutes ago: (a) when said by a character in a film and (b) when said by a radio announcer in a news broadcast.*

> *Let me go: (a) when said by a person whose arm has been grabbed by someone and (b) when said by a child whose teacher has asked for a volunteer to run an errand.*

More commonly, however, context affects meaning in less dramatic but equally important ways. Usually, there are only a few possible uses of a sentence in any particular context, and we can make a reasonable judgment of its primary or intended use. It is important, therefore, to understand the various uses or functions of language.

2.3 THE MAIN FUNCTIONS OF LANGUAGE

Whenever we use language we do so for some purpose, and if we consider these purposes, we can see that there are several different types. Language, in other words, has several functions. Language is often characterized as a means of communication, and although this view is correct, it is not very informative. When we use language we almost always communicate something to someone, but usually our purpose is much more specific, and frequently we are not primarily concerned with communicating information at all. Our purpose is usually not merely to communicate, but to communicate for a specific purpose. What we mean often reflects these purposes. Consequently, how we interpret, and therefore react to, what others say depends upon what we take their purpose to be. It is therefore important to be aware of the main purposes for which language is used and how these purposes affect meaning. Each of these purposes reflects a different function of language. These purposes are not mutually exclusive, but it is helpful to keep them distinct from each other.

1. *DESCRIPTIVE FUNCTION*: One very important function of language is to describe (i.e., to convey factual information about) something. Whenever we describe something—an object, a situation, or a feeling—we are stating facts, or what we believe to be facts. For example:

This coffee is cold.
I don't have any change for the coffee machine.
A cup of coffee would calm my nerves.

Almost every time we use language we convey factual information, even though this may not be our primary purpose.

2. *EVALUATIVE FUNCTION*: Often we use language not (or not merely) to describe something but to make a value judgment about it, that is, to evaluate it. For example:

Julie is the best student in the class.

This is different from a mere factual description, for it presents a value judgment about Julie. There are several different types of evaluations: aesthetic, moral, economic, technological, and even scientific. For example, in the order listed above:

That was the worst movie I've seen in years.
He is an irresponsible person.
The best way to get rich is by investing in real estate.
The safest way of disposing of uranium waste is to bury it in old coal mines.
The theory of evolution provides the best account of the origin of biological species.

3. *EMOTIVE FUNCTION*: Language is sometimes used to express emotions and thus has an emotive function. When you hit your thumb with a hammer, you probably say something. If you say, *My thumb hurts*, you are describing your feelings. If you say, *This is a terrible hammer*, you are evaluating the hammer. But if, like most people, you say, *Damn!* (or worse), you are not describing or evaluating anything but are simply expressing your feelings or emotions. Almost any emotion can be expressed in words. For example:

I love you.
You are a loathsome creature; go away.
I shall die of unrequited love.
Thank heavens that's over.

Note that these sentences also convey factual information about the speakers' feelings, but in most contexts this function would be secondary.

4. *EVOCATIVE FUNCTION*: Language can also be used for the purpose of evoking certain emotions in an audience. If we want someone to feel sad about something, we can try to evoke that emotion through the careful choice of words and images. Poets are especially concerned with this function of language. Consider, for example, the line from T.S. Eliot's "The Love Song of J. Alfred Prufrock," which beautifully evokes the feeling of a meaningless life:

I have measured out my life with coffee spoons.

W.B. Yeats, in "The Lake Isle of Innisfree," evokes a feeling of peacefulness:

And I shall have some peace there, for peace comes dropping slow.

Advertisers frequently use language to evoke certain feelings. For example:

At Speedy You're a Somebody.

And everyone from time to time wants to evoke certain emotions in their audience. We want others to feel pity for someone, to feel anger at some situation, or to approve of something, and we use language for this purpose. Threats are usually intended to evoke fear in the victim. Political speeches are often aimed at making voters feel that a government is trustworthy or untrustworthy. Sermons often are designed to make us feel ashamed of the mean things we do.

5. *PERSUASIVE FUNCTION*: One of the most widespread uses of language is to persuade people to accept something or to act in a certain way. For example:

You shouldn't take astrology seriously. There is no scientific basis for it.

I know you don't like parties, but I hope you'll come anyway. There will be several people there that you have been wanting to meet. I know you will enjoy yourself once you get there.

Every argument is an example of the persuasive use of language: we try to persuade people to recycle waste, that the government's budget is likely to increase unemployment, that the police officer should not give us a speeding ticket, or that lotteries are a waste of money. There are two ways in which language can be used to persuade. Sometimes our purpose is to persuade by means of rational arguments, even if we often fail to achieve our purpose. But often we abandon this restriction and use anything we think might succeed in persuading our audience. This is the case with propaganda and most advertising.

6. *INTERROGATIVE FUNCTION*: In order to elicit information we usually need to ask for it. Most often this is done by asking a question. For example:

What is the due date for the essay?

But asking questions is not the only way to elicit information. For example:

Tell me your age.
I won't lend you $20.00 unless you explain why you need it.

Whatever form of words we use, we are not describing, evaluating, expressing, or evoking anything, or attempting to persuade, but seeking to gain information.

7. *DIRECTIVE FUNCTION*: We sometimes use language to command others to do something or to provide advice. For example:

Go to the principal's office immediately.
Take these pills twice a day.

These sentences would normally be used to tell someone to do something. They do not describe or evaluate anything, express or evoke an emotion, or seek information, nor, usually, do they attempt to persuade us of anything. They simply tell us what to do. The directive use of language covers ordering, commanding, directing, advising, requesting, and similar types of actions.

8. *PERFORMATIVE FUNCTION*: There is an interesting class of sentences that are known as performative utterances, i.e., utterances that are not descriptions, evaluations, directives, and so on, but are themselves to be regarded as actions. They are actions that consist of saying certain words; that is, in uttering a performative, the speaker performs some action *in addition to* merely saying a sentence. If a question arises of whether someone actually performed such an action, the only relevant evidence would consist of showing that the person uttered certain words under appropriate circumstances. For example:

I find the accused guilty of murder.

If these words are uttered by Judge Bean at the conclusion of a trial, they constitute the action of finding someone guilty of murder. If someone asks for proof that Judge Bean found the accused guilty of murder, it would be sufficient to quote the judge's words. It would make no sense to suggest that Judge Bean might have been mistaken or lying. If he said the words at the conclusion of the trial, then he did find the accused guilty of murder. On the other hand, if I say,

Judge Bean found the accused guilty of murder,

I could not appeal to the fact that I said it as proof that it is true, since I might be mistaken or lying. It is not a performative utterance, but a description: it is true only if it correctly states or describes a fact. Similarly, if after the trial Judge Bean says,

I found the accused guilty of murder,

this would not be a performative utterance, for we could not appeal to the fact that Judge Bean uttered this sentence as proof that it is true, since he might be mistaken or lying. Here are two more examples of performative utterances:

I now pronounce you husband and wife.
I resign, here and now.

When uttered under the appropriate circumstances, each would constitute an action.

9. *RECREATIONAL FUNCTION*: Finally, we should not overlook the fact that language is often used to amuse ourselves and others. We tell jokes and stories, write novels, invent puns, do crossword puzzles, play guessing games, make up limericks, sing nursery rhymes, and write rude things on washroom walls. When language is used in any of these ways it serves a recreational function. People who tell jokes, write stories, or sing nursery rhymes usually do so out of simple enjoyment.

There are other functions of language, but these are the main ones, and all others can be fitted into at least one of the above categories. For example, we sometimes use language to hurt others' feelings, but this can be regarded as an evocative use of language. It is important to understand that these categories are not mutually exclusive: most of the time language serves more than one function. Often we intend to use a sentence for two or more purposes. We tell a joke in order to make someone relax (i.e., we amuse in order to evoke a feeling). We describe an automobile accident in hopes of persuading someone to drive more carefully. We evaluate a murder so as to express our abhorrence. We order someone to do something in order to evoke in them a feeling of respect for our authority.

The functions of language can be viewed from both a subjective and an objective point of view. From the subjective point of view, we regard the speaker's intention or purpose as primary. Did Sally intend to express her feelings or to convey information? Did Todd really intend to say something funny or was he just trying to be helpful? Was the doctor just describing the options or was she trying to persuade me to have the operation? From this point of view what is important is the speaker's intentions. From the objective point of view, on the other hand, we disregard the speaker's intentions and consider how the audience is affected by what is said. From the objective point of view every utterance always has several functions, even when the speaker has only one purpose. The other functions go beyond what the speaker intends. For example, we always convey some information to our audience whenever we speak, even when conveying information is not our purpose. Again, it is sometimes difficult, or even impossible, to describe certain things in a way that avoids expressing our emotions. (Try to describe a rape in a way that expresses nothing of your feelings.) Sometimes when we intend to describe something we inadvertently amuse others, as in *We had chork pops for dinner*. Frequently, there is an unacknowledged persuasive or evaluative function in what people say. From the objective point of view, we can often draw out levels of meaning in what someone says which the speaker is not only unaware of but may even refuse to admit are present.

The difference between these two points of view is important. To understand the meaning of what someone says, we must give priority to the subjective point of view. As we shall see later, when we assess an argument it is important to pay careful attention to what the speaker means, i.e., to the subjective meaning.

2.4 SELF-TEST NO. 2

Using the contextual clues provided, which of the nine functions listed in 2.3 is the most likely primary purpose for each of the following sentences?

1. If you want to succeed in life you need a good education. (Said by a father to his 17-year-old daughter who has just told him she wants to drop out of school.)

2. Retail clothing stores can increase sales by about 30 per cent through

advertising in local media. (Said by a teacher in a business class at a community college.)

3. You can increase your sales by 30 per cent through advertising in local media. (Said by an advertising salesperson from a local TV station when talking to the manager of a clothing store.)

4. I love you more than anyone else I've ever known. (Said by a young woman to a young man.)

5. She loves him more than anyone she's ever known. (Said by a father about his daughter and her boyfriend.)

6. Peter Piper picked a peck of pickled peppers. (Said by a father to his four-year-old daughter.)

7. Your essay must be at least 1,500 words and must include a full bibliography. (Said by a professor to a class.)

8. I now declare this building officially open. (Said by a politician when cutting the ribbon at the opening of a new school building.)

9. Pedestrians Cross Here. (A sign at a crosswalk.)

10. Reading an old copy of a Dickens novel is like spending an afternoon in the attic of an old house: the feel of the old paper, the look of the dated typeface, and the musty smell all take you back to the days when even your grandparents were still children. (From an article by a literary critic entitled *Why Reading Literature Is Important*.)

11. Cloven Pickard, stop, in the name of the law. (Said by a police officer to a fleeing suspect.)

12. Cloven Pickard, you are under arrest and being charged for the murder of Oma Sage. (Said by a police officer to Cloven Pickard.)

2.5 QUESTIONS FOR DISCUSSION

Unlike the self-test questions above, the contextual clues provided here allow more than one reasonable answer. Suggest additional contextual details that would support attributing at least two plausible purposes to the speakers.

1. Why can't you pay attention? (Said by a Grade 6 teacher to a student who frequently daydreams.)

2. The next car I buy will definitely be a Volvo. (Said by someone in a TV ad for Volvo.)

3. Military intelligence is a contradiction in terms. (Said by a historian in a course on the history of World War II.)

4. Frankly, Scarlett, I don't give a damn. (Said by Clark Gable in the film *Gone with the Wind*.)

5. Like, wow, man, what a blast. (Said by a teenager after a rock concert.)

6. Can you imagine what it must have been like, having to care for two small children in a Nazi concentration camp? (Said by a woman about her grandmother.)

7. Your time is now up. (Said by a teacher at the end of an examination.)

8. Most of the time he's a real jerk. (Said by a girl about her brother.)

9. I have often wondered what became of him. (Said by a middle-aged woman about a childhood friend.)

10. The best way to remove chewing gum from a carpet is to rub it with an ice cube for a minute or so. (An excerpt from a book of household hints.)

11. You've just proven that billboard advertising works! (Written on a billboard.)

12. Read me another story, grandma. (Said by a child at bedtime.)

2.6 DEFINITION

In section 2.2.3 we noted that words often have more than one use or meaning. It is important to understand that not all the different uses of a word need have anything in common; for some words there may be a common element, but for many there is not. As long as we know how to use a word for some particular purpose, we know what the word means when used in that sense. Indeed, it is often difficult to enumerate all the different accepted uses of a word. But this is not a problem for the meaning-as-use theory, for it denies that words must have a single meaning. Since words typically have several different uses, it follows that there will be several different meanings, and as long as we understand a particular use (i.e., know how to use the word for that purpose), we understand the meaning of the word when used in that way.

The meaning of language thus depends upon its use and context, and it is often very difficult to say precisely what a word means if we ignore these factors. Normally this is not a serious difficulty, for we can usually get by with a rough idea of what words mean as long as they are being used in ordinary contexts. But sometimes this casual approach is inadequate, and it becomes important to focus on the precise meanings of a word. When a lawyer explains what constitutes an assault, or a sales clerk says the microwave oven is under warranty, or a scientist talks about energy, we run the risk of misunderstanding if we fail to pay careful attention to the precise meanings of their words. These are the kinds of occasion when definitions are important; without them we may misunderstand what is being said. Of course, we also need definitions when we come across a word we are unfamiliar with or when a familiar word is being used in an unfamiliar way. In these cases, it is not misunderstanding that we want to avoid, but rather not understanding at all.

To understand how definitions work, we need to note the distinction between the sense of a term (sometimes called its *connotation* or *intension*) and its reference (or *denotation* or *extension*). The *SENSE* of a word is what we understand when we understand its meaning, and the *REFERENCE* is the class of things to which the word refers. The sense of the term *bachelor*, for example, is the concept of an unmarried male, and the reference of the term is the class of all bachelors in the universe, not only those who now exist but those who have existed in the past and will exist in the future. All words must have a sense, although some words, as we saw in section 2.2.1, have no reference.

2.7 THE PURPOSES OF DEFINITION

In order to understand how definitions work, we need to be aware of the different purposes for which definitions may be put forward. There are three main types.

2.7.1 Reportive Definitions

The most common purpose of definitions is to convey the information needed to use a word correctly. The correct use of a word consists of its standard usage—how the word is in fact used by those who make regular use of it. When we want to know the meaning of a word in its standard usage, we need a *REPORTIVE DEFINITION*, i.e., one that reports its standard usage. Standard dictionaries give reportive definitions.

Reportive definitions can sometimes be troublesome, because it may not be clear whether a particular use can be regarded as part of the standard usage. For example, years ago the word *cohort* was standardly used to refer only to a group of persons banded together. (This reflected its original meaning in Latin, where it referred to a military unit roughly akin to a platoon.) Now, however, it is usually used to refer to a friend or associate. The sentence *Fred arrived with his cohort*, if used to mean that Fred arrived with his friend, would have been incorrect 50 years ago, but is now usually accepted as correct. This shift in meaning was probably brought about by people who did not understand the old usage and who were therefore using the word incorrectly, but the mistake has become so widespread that it is no longer regarded as incorrect; this shift in meaning is often explained by the term *folk etymology*. Only dedicated linguistic reactionaries, also known as purists, continue to regard the new usage as incorrect. Except for cases where a meaning shift has not yet been accepted as standard usage, however, reportive definitions are usually quite straightforward.

2.7.2 Stipulative Definitions

Sometimes it is useful to be able to create a new, more precise meaning. For example, a report on land use in Ontario would find it necessary to define the categories of land use that are being employed, using a *STIPULATIVE DEFINITION*. The report would therefore stipulate how the words *agricultural, residential, industrial, recreational*, and so forth are being used. When we do this we are not attempting to report the standard usage, although it would clearly be foolish to depart radically from it. For many specific purposes, such as doing research or enacting legislation, it makes good sense to stipulate the precise meaning that is to be attached to key words. As long as this stipulated meaning is explicitly stated, there is no risk of misunderstanding, and there is an obvious gain in clarity and precision.

There is nothing to prevent us from inventing a new word by using a stipulative definition. For example, we might invent the word *spinge* to refer to the deposit that builds up between the bristles on a toothbrush, or the word *tele-nuisance* to refer to solicitation phone calls from marketers. We can also stipulate a new meaning for an old word: for example, using *bubble* to refer to a promise made by a politician. There is, however, no guarantee that these new words or uses will become part of the standard usage. This is likely to happen only when there is a need (or a perceived need) for the new term. If enough people think it is important to be able to talk about a new object or phenomenon or to refer to something in a new way, then a new word will usually be forthcoming, and will soon become part of standard usage. Until this happens, however, new words depend for their meaning upon stipulative definitions.

2.7.3 Essentialist Definitions

Some words—such as *justice, truth, love, religion, freedom, deity, death, law, peace, health*, and *science*—refer to things or qualities that have considerable importance. When we ask *What is justice?* we are not asking for a reportive definition, since such a definition might reflect a widespread misconception about the essential nature of justice. Nor would we be asking for a stipulative definition, since we can invent these for ourselves as easily as the next person. We are asking for a definition that reveals the essential nature of justice.

The correctness of an *ESSENTIALIST DEFINITION* cannot be determined merely by an appeal to standard usage, like a reportive definition, nor by an appeal to its usefulness, like a stipulative definition. Essentialist definitions really need to be understood as compressed theories; they attempt to express in succinct form a theory about the nature of what is being defined. Thus, assessing an essentialist definition involves assessing a theory, and this goes far beyond questions about the meaning of words.

These three purposes of definition are important since when we want to determine whether a definition is acceptable we must first decide its purpose. Good stipulative definitions and good essentialist definitions are usually inadequate reportive definitions, and good reportive definitions are usually unsatisfactory essentialist definitions.

2.8 METHODS OF DEFINITION

There are several different methods that can be used to define words. These methods can be used for reportive, stipulative, and essentialist definitions.

2.8.1 Genus-Species Method

A common method of defining a word referring to a kind of thing is to mention a larger category (a genus) to which that kind of thing belongs, and then to specify what makes that particular kind (that species) different from the other species in that genus. (Note that this is not the more particular meaning of the words *genus* and *species* in biology.) For example:

> *A sea-plane is an airplane that is adapted for landing on and taking off from a body of water.*

The definition states that a sea-plane is a member of the class of airplanes (i.e., it is a type of airplane) that is distinguished from other airplanes by being adapted for landing on and taking off from a body of water.

Most words can be defined using the *GENUS-SPECIES METHOD*. Some, however, cannot because they lack a genus of which they are a member. A sea-plane is a member of the class of airplanes; an airplane is a member of the class of machines; a machine is a member of the class of...? At this point we have to look hard to find an appropriate class. We might use the class of systems:

> *A machine is a system of interacting parts.*

But then what is the appropriate class for systems? At some point, the process of finding a genus-class must end, and at this point we can no longer use the genus-species method.

2.8.2 Ostensive Method

Sometimes the meaning of a word can easily be conveyed by giving examples, either verbally or by pointing. If someone wants to know what a bassoon is, it may be sufficient to hold one up and say,

> *Here is a bassoon.*

Or we may point one out by saying,

> *The bald guy in the third row of the orchestra is playing a bassoon.*

Sometimes it is necessary to give several examples in order to ensure that the meaning is clear. If we try to define *vehicle* ostensively, we will need to point to more than cars; we will also need to point to vans, trucks, buses, tractors, motorcycles, bicycles, and so on. If the range of examples given is too limited, we will have conveyed only part of the meaning of the term.

Using *OSTENSIVE DEFINITIONS* for general terms can be problematic. If we attempt to define ostensively terms such as *fairness* or *truth*, it may be difficult for someone to grasp what the different examples have in common. It is difficult to point to or give examples for some words: for example, *neutron*, *space*, or *history*. And words that have no reference (for example, *very*, *where*, and *forever*) simply cannot be defined ostensively because there is nothing to point to.

2.8.3 Synonym Method

Often all that is needed to define a word is to give a *SYNONYM*. For example:

> *Effulgent* means the same as *radiant*.

Obviously, this method works only for words that have more or less exact synonyms. Words that lack a synonym have to be defined using one of the other methods. And, of course, such definitions will only be helpful for someone who understands the meaning of the synonym.

2.8.4 Operational Method

Sometimes a term can be defined very precisely by specifying a rule or operation. In science, for example, it is essential that each concept be defined in a way that specifies exactly when it can be applied and when it cannot. One way of achieving such precision is to establish a rule that the term is to be applied only when a specified test or operation yields a certain result. For example:

A genius is anyone who scores over 140 on a standard I.Q. test.

OPERATIONAL DEFINITIONS are commonly used outside science when defining terms that are used to distinguish things that form a continuum, such as the quality of meat, student performance, or degree of drunkenness. Thus we have operational definitions for such terms as *Grade A beef, honors standing,* and *legal intoxication.* Operational definitions often arise initially as stipulative definitions but may later become part of the standard usage.

2.8.5 Contextual Method

Some words can best be defined by using the word in a standard context and providing a different sentence that does not use the word but has the same meaning. For example, the concept of *logical strength* used in this book can be defined as follows:

This argument has logical strength

means the same as

The premises of this argument, if true, provide a justification for believing that its conclusion is true.

2.9 ASSESSING REPORTIVE DEFINITIONS

A good stipulative definition is one that fixes a precise meaning of a term in a way that will be useful for some specific purpose. A good essentialist definition is one that reflects a true or reasonable theory about the essential nature of the phenomenon to which the term refers. But what is a good reportive definition? The short answer to this question is that a good reportive definition of a word is one that tells us what others mean when they use the word and what others will understand us to mean when we use it. In other words, it will accurately describe the actual standard usage of the term. There are several ways in which a reportive definition can fail to be a good definition.

2.9.1 Too Broad a Definition

A definition is too broad when the defining phrase refers to some things that are not included in the reference of the term being defined. The definition

> *A typewriter is a means of writing*

fails as a definition because the defining phrase (*a means of writing*) refers not only to typewriters but also to chalk, pens, and pencils, among other things. The definition is too broad because it includes more than it should. Here are some other examples of definitions that are too broad:

> *Soccer is a game played with a ball.*
> *A beaver is an amphibious rodent, native to northeastern North America.*
> *A sofa is a piece of furniture designed for sitting.*

If we regard these not as definitions, but as statements, they are all true. Soccer is, obviously, a game played with a ball. In a sense, therefore, definitions that are too broad do not say anything that is actually false. It is when such statements are put forward as definitions that problems may arise.

2.9.2 Too Narrow a Definition

A definition is too narrow when the defining phrase fails to refer to some things that are included in the reference of the term being defined. The definition

> *A school is an institution that aims at teaching children how to read and write*

is a bad definition because the defining phrase fails to refer to schools that do not aim at teaching children how to read and write, such as medical schools and dance schools. It is too narrow; it excludes these other kinds of schools. Here are some other examples of definitions that are too narrow:

> *A parent is a person's biological mother or father.*
> *A farm is a place where crops are grown.*
> *A bigamist is a man who is married to two women at the same time.*

As with definitions that are too broad, definitions that are too narrow do not say anything that is obviously false. What they say may be true for a large portion of the class of things being defined, but because they are not true for *all* of the things being defined, each is a bad definition.

2.9.3 Too Broad and Too Narrow a Definition

A definition can sometimes be too broad and too narrow at the same time. This happens when the defining phrase refers to some things to which the term does not (too broad) and also fails to refer to some things to which the term does (too narrow). For example:

A pen is an instrument designed for writing words.

This definition is too broad because it includes pencils and typewriters as well as pens, and it is too narrow because it fails to include pens that are designed for drawing pictures.

In order to determine whether a definition is too broad or too narrow, it is necessary to compare the reference of the term being defined with the reference of the defining phrase. Two questions need to be asked: (1) does the reference of the defining phrase include things that are not included in the reference of the term being defined? If it does, then the definition is too broad. And (2) does the reference of the defining phrase exclude things that are included in the reference of the term? If it does, then the definition is too narrow.

Here are some examples of definitions that are both too broad and too narrow:

Hockey is a game played on ice in Canada.
A doctor is a person who treats physical ailments.
A professor is a teacher who does research.

2.9.4 Circular Definition

A *CIRCULAR DEFINITION* is one that includes the term being defined (or its cognate) in the definition. For example:

A golf ball is a small spherical object used in the game of golf.

The problem here is obvious: anyone who does not already know what golf is will not be enlightened by the definition. Circular definitions are therefore usually useless.

When a definition uses a cognate of the term being defined, the circularity may be less obvious. For example:

A surgeon is a person who practices surgery.

This definition is circular because *surgeon* and *surgery* are cognates (i.e., they come from the same root). Circular definitions involving cognates may not always be useless, however, since a person may know the meaning of one and not the other.

People do not often put forward circular definitions that are as blatant as these examples. But sometimes a pair of definitions, neither of which is itself circular, can lead to a kind of circularity when taken together. If someone defines *freedom* as *the absence of coercion*, and then defines *coercion* as *the absence of freedom*, the definitions taken together are circular and therefore likely to be useless.

2.9.5 Obscure Definition

A definition can also be useless when it fails, through the use of vague, obscure, or metaphorical language, to express clearly the meaning of the term being defined. Consider the following definitions:

A marathon is a long foot-race.
A grampus is a kind of blowing, spouting, blunt-headed, dolphin-like cetacean.
A fact is anything that rubs the corners off our prejudices.

The first of these definitions uses a vague expression (*long*) that leaves the meaning of the term somewhat obscure, and if we read it charitably as "longer than 1 mile," say, that only makes it too broad. The second uses a scientific term (*cetacean*) that is likely to be unenlightening (to non-biologists, at least). The third is likely to be uninformative because it uses a metaphor (*rubs the corners off*). In most circumstances these definitions will be unsatisfactory. However, a definition that uses an obscure technical term may nevertheless be correct (for example, the second of the above definitions); if we want to have a precise understanding of the term, we will have to look for a definition of the obscure term and hope that it is not equally obscure.

2.10 ASSESSING STIPULATIVE AND ESSENTIALIST DEFINITIONS

The errors in section 2.9 describe five different ways in which a definition can fail to convey adequately the standard usage of a term. Stipulative and essentialist definitions, however, are not intended to convey the standard usage of a term. As we saw in section 2.7.2, stipulative definitions are intended to establish a new or restricted meaning for a term and cannot, therefore, be criticized for failing to convey adequately the standard usage of the term. Essentialist definitions, as we saw in section 2.7.3, are intended to describe the essential nature of something, and since there is no guarantee that the standard usage of a term will reflect a correct understanding of its essence, we cannot criticize an essentialist definition for failing to convey the standard usage of the term. How, then, are such definitions to be assessed?

Stipulative and essentialist definitions are always put forward for a specific purpose. Whatever their purpose, they must enable the audience to know how to use the term in accordance with its stipulated or essential meaning, and this means that they should not be obscure or circular. For example, if a report defined an offensive weapon as

anything that can be used to inflict harm on another person,

we could criticize it for being vague, even though we recognize that it is intended as a stipulative definition. Similarly, the definition

love is essentially a mutual loving dependency between two people

is clearly circular. Except in contexts where a definition has a humorous purpose, obscurity and circularity will be grounds for criticism.

A more serious problem can arise when a stipulative or essentialist definition of a term is significantly different from the standard usage of the term. The fact that the two meanings are different is not by itself a problem, but it can lead to misunderstanding and confusion. It might be reasonable for some purposes to stipulate the meaning of heat wave as a period of at least three successive days in which the high temperature exceeds 90 degrees Fahrenheit. But if the high temperatures over the past week were 89, 95, 95, 89, 95, 95, and 89, we would be puzzled if someone denied we were in a heat wave. Anyone who uses such a stipulative definition should remind us of this fact, for example by saying, *Technically, this doesn't count as a heat wave.*

The possibilities for misunderstanding are increased when the term being given a stipulative or essentialist definition lacks a clear and precise usage, since the discrepancy between the ordinary usage and the defined meaning may not be immediately apparent. Worse, terms whose ordinary meaning is somewhat vague often stand in the greatest need of a more precise definition; for example, *conflict of interest, sexual harassment, potentially violent offender, dangerous level of PCBs, mental abnormality, pollutant,* and *national security.* For bureaucratic or legal reasons, such terms may need to have a precise meaning assigned, and it is extremely important to be aware of the possible meaning shifts that may deliberately or inadvertently be involved.

These meaning shifts can best be described by reference to the concepts of too broad and too narrow. We have seen that in order to determine whether a reportive definition is too broad or too narrow, we compare the reference classes of the defining phrase and the term being defined. This same comparison allows us to determine whether the reference of a stipulative or essentialist definition of a term is broader or narrower than the standard usage of the term. Consider the stipulative definition of an *adult* as *a person 18 years of age or older,* which is the legal meaning of the term in the majority of North America. This definition is narrower than the standard usage of the term, since it regards a person as an adult simply on the basis of being 18. We must be careful, however, in making claims about standard usage. Do those who commonly use this term in fact agree that anyone who is 18 is an adult? Most people would probably want to say that only some 18-year-olds are adults. If this is the standard usage of the term *adult,* we can conclude that the legal definition is a narrow one.

If we want to criticize such a definition, however, we must do more than point out that it is broader or narrower than the standard usage. The question is whether the broader or narrower definition has desirable or undesirable consequences. In some cases it may be desirable to broaden or narrow the scope of a term and in other cases not. There is nothing sacred about standard usage, so such questions are always debatable. These debates sometimes raise important questions of social policy. More commonly, however, it is only necessary to remember that a stipulative or essentialist definition of a term gives a *different* (i.e., broader or narrower) meaning than the term has in its standard usage. For example, when the theologian Paul Tillich defines *atheist* as a person who lacks what he calls ultimate concern, it is important for the reader to be aware that Tillich's definition is significantly different from the ordinary usage of the term; he is trying to provide an essentialist definition. And when a piece of legislation defines a terrorist as "anyone who belongs to a terrorist organization, whether or not they commit or plan a terrorist act," it is important to be aware that this definition is much broader than standard usage for reasons that have to do with the enforcement and administration of the law.

What is suggested by these special considerations for stipulative or essentialist definitions is that we must first identify whether a definition is reportive, stipulative, or essentialist. Then, if it is stipulative, we must identify the purpose for which the definition is formulated, and assess whether it fulfills this purpose. (Of course, we should think critically about this purpose, too, but for the moment we are concentrating on definitions.) And if it is essentialist, we must do the hard work of understanding the theory within which the definition is set; then we can assess whether all the appropriate essential details are included within the definition as the author has formulated it. (Again, of course, we should think critically about the entire theory, but for the moment we are concentrating on definitions.) In these cases, we cannot appeal to standard usage to assess the definition, but we can assess them on rational grounds according to the purposes associated with stipulative and essentialist definitions.

2.11 A WARNING

Defining words is an art. It requires good judgment to know what kind of definition is appropriate in any particular context. Compilers of dictionaries attempt to provide definitions that can serve in a very broad range of contexts, but even they make no claim to give a full and complete account of the meanings of words. They do not, for example, attempt to cover every slang, dialect, or metaphorical use.

Most of us are not writers of dictionaries, and we attempt to provide definitions only when a particular need arises. Sometimes we are asked what a word means: a friend asks what the difference is between *disinterested* and *uninterested*; a German tourist asks what *street* means; a child asks what *obstetrician* means. In such circumstances, there is no need to give a full definition: we need only provide enough information to remove the questioner's ignorance. The friend may need only to be told that *disinterested* means the same as *impartial*. The German tourist needs only to be informed that *street* means *Strasse*. The child will be content if told that *obstetrician* means *a doctor who treats pregnant women*. The appropriate kind of answer is one that meets the needs of the questioner, and this is usually less than a full reportive definition.

Sometimes, however, we need to define a word because we want to increase or deepen our understanding. This is likely to arise with terms that are abstract or stand for a complex object or phenomenon; we often have a general idea of what they mean and can point to examples, but we find it very difficult to say precisely what they mean. For most people, the following terms fall into this category: *energy, classical, crime, psychiatry, nation, pornography, religion, imagination, evil, illness, cause,* and *trust.* These are important matters, and if we want to increase our understanding of them we must attempt to ensure that we have a clear understanding of the words. But even here we do not usually want a full reportive definition. Often we are interested in only one sense of the word (for example, *energy* as a scientific term), and sometimes we want only to be able to distinguish between similar things (for example, between *psychiatry* and *psychology*).

2.12 SELF-TEST NO. 3

What errors are committed by the following definitions? (Assume a context in which they have been put forward as reportive definitions.)

1. A supreme court is the highest court in the United States.

2. Poetry is an art form that uses words to communicate ideas and images.

3. A snowplow is an implement designed to remove snow.

4. Restoration is the process or activity of restoring something to its former condition.

5. A tritone is the musical interval of an augmented fourth or a diminished fifth.

6. A stapler is a device for fastening pages together.

7. A nurse is a woman who is trained to look after the sick.

8. A bungalow is a one-story building.

9. The United Nations is an organization aimed at fostering co-operation and peace between nations.

10. A sport is any activity involving competition between individuals or groups of individuals.

2.13 QUESTIONS FOR DISCUSSION

In light of the purposes and methods of definition covered in this chapter, assess the following definitions:

1. A psychological disorder is any personal way of perceiving or interpreting events which is used repeatedly in spite of its consistent failure (from G.A. Kelly, *Personality Theory and Research* [Toronto: John Wiley and Sons, 1970], p. 240).

2. The term suicide is applied to all cases of death resulting directly or indirectly from a positive or negative act of the victim himself, which he knows will produce his death (from Émile Durkheim, *Suicide: A Study in Sociology*, tr. Spalding and Simpson [New York: Free Press, 1966], p. 44).

3. Under the *M'Naghten* rules a person is insane if at the time the act was committed, the party accused was laboring under such a defect of reason, from a disease of the mind, as not to know the nature and quality of the act he was doing; or, if he did know it, that he did not know he was doing what was wrong (from *A Concise Dictionary of Law*, 2nd edition [Oxford: Oxford UP, 1983]).

4. Socialism. Principle that individual freedom should be completely subordinated to interests of community, with any deductions that may be correctly or incorrectly drawn from it, e.g. substitution of co-operative for competitive production, national ownership of land & capital, State distribution of produce, free education & feeding of children ... (from *Concise Oxford Dictionary* [Oxford: Oxford UP, 1934 edition]).

5. A student is considered a full-time student when he or she regularly attends a college, university, or other educational institution that offers courses at a post-secondary school level and the student takes, during a semester, 60% or more (typically four or more full courses) of the usual course load for the qualifying educational program in which the student is enrolled (Canada Revenue Agency, P105(E) Rev 13).

6. Poetry is the spontaneous overflow of powerful feelings ... recollected in tranquility (from William Wordsworth, Preface to *Lyrical Ballads*, 1800).

7. A cynic is a person who knows the price of everything and the value of nothing (attributed to Oscar Wilde).

8. Liberty is the right to do whatever the law permits (Baron de Montesquieu, *The Spirit of the Laws*, book XI).

9. TERRORISM: an ideologically motivated unlawful act or acts, including but not limited to the use of violence or force or threat of violence or force, committed by or on behalf of any group(s), organization(s), or government(s) for the purpose of influencing any government and/or instilling fear in the public or a section of the public. (Widely used home-owner's insurance-policy definition for the purpose of a terrorist exclusion clause.)

10. A material witness is someone who has information that is essential to a factual claim made by the prosecution or defense in a legal action (*A Concise Dictionary of Law*, 2nd edition [Oxford: Oxford UP, 1983]). [A material witness can be detained by authorities if he or she is deemed to be a flight risk, even if that person is not suspected of committing a crime. Numerous people were detained as material witnesses after the attacks of September 11, 2001, even when there were no charges against them.]

3. CLARIFYING MEANING

The failure to understand the meaning of what others say and the failure to understand how others can misunderstand the meaning of what we say are the seeds of much frustration, resentment, and discord. In this chapter we examine some of the ways in which misunderstanding can result from a lack of clarity in the language we use. Our purposes here are (1) to develop the ability to recognize obscurity in what others say, and (2) to learn how to say clearly what we mean. For both aims the standard of assessment is precision. In formulating statements that purport to be true and definitions that specify the meaning of terms, we think more clearly when our points are put as precisely as possible. Even when we disagree with someone, there is more hope of a resolution if the disagreement can be focused on something precise. So it is helpful to learn how to diagnose ways in which points are formulated imprecisely and to identify strategies for clarifying points so that they are as precise as possible.

3.1 THE PRINCIPLE OF CHARITY

Often we are confronted by a choice between two or more interpretations of what someone has said, and sometimes these interpretations have different degrees of plausibility. If we adopt the least plausible interpretation, it is often easy to show that the statement is false. On the other hand, if we adopt the most plausible interpretation, it is usually more difficult to show that the statement is false. It is tempting, therefore, when faced with a statement we disagree with, to adopt the least plausible interpretation of it. After all, if we can get away with foisting an implausible view on our opponents it makes it easier to show that they are wrong (or stupid, irrational, foolish, etc.). It is especially tempting to do this when the most implausible interpretation is the literal one. For example:

> *The worst thing that can happen to a mother in this country is to fall into the clutches of the Women, Infants, and Children program.*

> *The only difference between an amateur and a professional musician is that the amateur performs for personal satisfaction while the professional performs for money.*

> *Doctors who perform abortions are guilty of first-degree murder.*

We all recognize that the literal interpretation of such statements is unlikely to be what the speaker intended. They are exaggerations or overstatements. If the speaker is present we may want to have a bit of fun by pointing out the absurdity of what was actually said. Sometimes this is legitimate, for example when debating in congress. However, when there is an important issue at stake, we should not let our desire to poke fun at our opponents prevent us from listening to what they are really trying to say. When our opponents are not present and cannot clarify what they have said, we ought to be prepared to do so on their behalf. It is up to us to find the fairest interpretation of their words that is available, the one that best represents their presumed intentions.

Thus, in any discussion we have a moral obligation to treat our opponents fairly. When they are present, we ought to give them the opportunity to clarify what they have said. When they are not present, we have a moral obligation to follow the *PRINCIPLE OF CHARITY*, that is, to adopt the most charitable interpretation of their words among the possible interpretations suggested by the context. The most charitable interpretation is the one that makes our opponent's views as reasonable, plausible, or defensible as possible. According to the principle of charity, whenever two interpretations are possible, we should always adopt the more reasonable one (unless something in the context suggests that another interpretation is what the person meant).

Why should we be charitable to our opponents? After all, it might be argued that if the purpose of engaging in a debate is to win, the principle of charity will make our task more difficult. But winning is not the primary purpose of rational discussion. The primary purpose should always be to discover the truth and to develop views and positions that are as reasonable and defensible as they can be. It is always possible that our opponents are right and we are wrong, or that our opponents are partly right and our position needs to be amended in some way; in either case, we stand to benefit from discussion. Even if our opponents are totally wrong, it is a useful test of the strength of our own position to be able to show their errors. In any case, we owe it to our opponents to interpret their words in a reasonable manner. Anyone who has ever been involved in a discussion with an opponent who persistently violates the principle of charity will understand the unfairness of such treatment and will appreciate the importance of observing the principle.

The principle of charity should be followed not only when we are interpreting single statements, but also when we are interpreting longer passages and even entire books. Throughout this book we shall often find it necessary to invoke the principle of charity. Being charitable to our opponents should eventually become second nature.

3.2 LINGUISTIC AMBIGUITY

3.2.1 Ambiguity and Vagueness

Some sentences are ambiguous. Some sentences are vague. But ambiguity and vagueness are not the same. An *AMBIGUOUS SENTENCE* is one that has two or more different but possibly quite precise meanings. A *VAGUE SENTENCE* is one that lacks a precise meaning. Ambiguous sentences should be avoided whenever there is a risk of misinterpretation—whenever there is a risk that the hearer will select the wrong meaning. Except in jokes and when it serves a clear literary purpose, ambiguity is something we must avoid. Vague sentences, however, are necessary if we are trying to express a vague thought or feeling. For example:

> *I don't care much for Beethoven's early string quartets.*
> *That was a noisy party they had last night, and it went on until all hours.*
> *Lots of people own two television sets.*
> *Joyce Carol Oates's novels have a disquieting effect upon the reader.*

These sentences are vague, but they are not ambiguous. In most contexts, there is no need for greater precision about such matters. If challenged, we could easily be a little more precise, but it would be very difficult (and usually pointless) to attempt to remove the vagueness altogether. There is nothing wrong with vagueness when we want to express a vague thought or when there is no need for precision.

In contexts in which precision is needed, however, we sometimes come across sentences that look quite precise but that turn out to be extremely vague. For example:

> *Applicants must hold a diploma in early childhood education or have equivalent work experience.*

The phrase *equivalent work experience* sounds quite precise, but without further information it is impossible to tell what kinds of work experience are going to count as equivalent. Does raising three children of one's own count? What about occasional baby-sitting over a period of six years? A half-time job as a helper in a nursery school for three years? Two years' experience as a kindergarten teacher? Potential applicants need a precise statement of the minimum qualifications for the position, but the sentence fails to provide it.

Those who use vague sentences when precision is needed, or who use vague sentences that look precise, should be challenged. Sometimes it is quite easy to see precisely what needs to be challenged. For example:

The fact that the Democrats won more seats in the electoral college than any other party in the 1992 federal election shows that the voters wanted a Democratic government.

The vagueness here arises with the phrase *the voters*. We need to ask, *How many voters?* We know that *the voters* cannot refer to all the voters, since other parties also received votes. Does it mean most of the voters? This may well be the speaker's intent, but, if so, the claim is false since in fact fewer than half of the votes cast were for Democratic candidates in that election (not an unusual situation for any federal government in the United States). The Democratic victory did not result from the support of the majority of voters. This example shows the importance of asking for quantifiers: *Do you mean all, most, or just some?* and *Do you mean always, usually, or just sometimes?*

In other cases, however, the vagueness arises from the use of terms that are inherently vague. The committee chair who says,

My officials are monitoring this situation very closely, and I can promise that we shall take all appropriate measures to ensure that the situation is resolved in a way that is fair to all the parties involved

should be challenged on grounds of vagueness. Despite the appearance of having promised to do something specific, the chair has not really promised to do anything at all. What are *appropriate measures?* They could be anything or nothing. What does *fair to all the parties* mean? We have no clear idea. Such phrases are inherently vague and can mean almost anything. People who use them should be challenged to say more precisely what they mean.

It is important to understand that ambiguity and vagueness arise from the use of words within sentences and not properties of the words themselves. This is because, as we saw in section 2.2.3, words typically have more than one meaning, and the context in which they are used usually tells us which meaning is the intended one. It is the context that makes sentences vague, and it is when the context lets us down that sentences become ambiguous. Of course, the ambiguity or vagueness of a sentence often rests upon the meaning of a word or phrase, but the ambiguity or vagueness arises only at the level of the sentence.

Here are some other sentences that should be challenged on grounds of vagueness, at least in normal contexts:

Essays for this course should be long enough to deal adequately with the assigned topic.
You should sign our petition to protest against the violation of our rights by the
government.
If you persist in this course of action, all hell is going to break loose.

3.2.2 Referential Ambiguity

REFERENTIAL AMBIGUITY arises when a word or phrase could, in the context of a particular sentence, refer to two or more properties or things. Usually the context tells us which meaning is intended, but, when it doesn't, we may choose the wrong meaning. If we are not sure which reference is intended by the speaker, we will misunderstand the speaker's meaning if we assign the wrong (i.e., the unintended) meaning to the word. If someone tells you that Pavarotti was a big opera star, you will have to guess whether *big* refers to *fat* or to *famous*. Sometimes, however, it is the context that creates the ambiguity. If someone is comparing the merits of two universities and says, *It is quite a good university*, the context may not tell us which university is being referred to.

Referential ambiguities are usually easy to spot and, once recognized, are easily avoided. This is especially true in conversation, since we can ask for clarification: *Do you mean that Pavarotti was fat or famous?* Or, if we select the wrong meaning, it will not be long before we discover our mistake: *Oh, I thought you meant he was famous!* There is, however, one type of referential ambiguity that deserves special mention: that between the collective and the distributive use of a term. Most nouns refer to a class of individual objects: *dog*, for example, refers to the class consisting of all dogs, and *book* refers to the class of all books. Usually when we use such nouns we do so in order to say something about each and every member of the class. When we use a term in this way it is being used *DISTRIBUTIVELY*. But sometimes we use terms to say something not about each and every member of the class but about the class as such. When we use a term in this way it is being used *COLLECTIVELY*. Consider the following:

> *Our university has a large wrestling team.*

If we interpret *wrestling team* distributively, the statement means that the individual members of the team are large. If we interpret the term collectively, the statement means that the team has a large number of members. Usually the context makes it clear whether a term should be interpreted distributively or collectively, but sometimes it does not, and we can mistakenly assume the wrong interpretation.

It is useful to develop the ability to recognize referential ambiguities even when they are unlikely to cause misunderstandings, for then we are less likely to assume a wrong interpretation inadvertently. Here are some more examples of sentences containing referential ambiguities:

> *Tom gave Ted's skis to his sister.*
> *Harold told me that he would do it next week.*
> *Americans make more telephone calls than Canadians.*
> *The government has provided constant funding for post-secondary education over the last three years.*

3.2.3 Grammatical Ambiguity

GRAMMATICAL AMBIGUITY arises when the grammatical structure of a sentence allows two interpretations, each of which gives rise to a different meaning. A few years ago a British newspaper reported that

> *Lord Denning spoke against the artificial insemination of women in the House of Lords.*

The grammar makes it unclear whether it was the speech or the insemination that took place in the House of Lords. This is because the phrase *in the House of Lords* could modify either *insemination* or *spoke*. Of course, which meaning applies in this case is clear despite this ambiguity, but that is not always the case.

Here are a few examples:

> *He promised to pay Stephanie and Michael $50 to clear all the junk out of the basement and take it to the dump.*
> *Ashley strode out of the studio with Nikki following her, saying, "I'll never give him up."*
> *Daphne decided to quit smoking while driving to New Denver.*
> *Jim and I have suffered tremendously; often I wake up in the morning and wish I were dead, and I know Jim does too.*
> *Women with babies who attend college encounter all sorts of exceptional challenges.*

3.2.4 Use and Mention

Another type of linguistic ambiguity arises through the failure to distinguish between *USING* a word or phrase and *MENTIONING* a word or phrase. Consider the following sentences:

Tom said I was angry.
Tom said, "I was angry."

Clearly these sentences have different meanings, even though the words are identical. The difference in meaning arises because the phrase *I was angry* is being *used* in the first sentence but is only *mentioned* in the second. Quotation marks or italics are commonly used to mark the difference. But direct quotation is not the only occasion when we want to mention a word, and in these cases we should also use italics or quotation marks to make our meaning clear. For example:

Paddy is Irish.

As it stands, this sentence means that a particular person, called Paddy, is an Irishman. But if we put quotation marks around "Paddy" it would mean that "Paddy" is an Irish name. Here are some more examples of sentences whose meaning would change if the word or phrase that is mentioned (as indicated by quotation marks) were being used instead:

The word "itself" is hard to define.
"John Smith" was placed on the ballot.

The ability to detect linguistic ambiguities is an important skill, for undetected ambiguities can create misunderstandings that lead to those frustrating discussions in which everyone seems to be at cross-purposes. On the other hand, people who delight in finding linguistic ambiguities that do not in fact mislead anyone may be amusing for a time but can become extremely annoying. Since our interest is in clarifying meaning, we are concerned only with ambiguities that do or may mislead.

3.3 SELF-TEST NO. 4

Identify the kind of ambiguity in each of the following sentences and state the different ways in which each sentence can be interpreted.

1. Billy gave his sisters a box of candy for Christmas.

2. He's a chicken.

3. Melissa only has one dress.

4. The General loses battle with nurses. (A newspaper headline)

5. Conversational German is extremely difficult.

6. Children need discipline to become responsible adults.

7. If, after you think it over, you still decide to drop out of school, I promise I won't say another word to you.

8. In multi-section courses, the instructors should be free to choose the text.

9. Eighty per cent of the stores tested illegally sell cigarettes to minors with no questions asked.

10. She arrived at the theater in a white limousine with a bright red hood.

11. The apartment superintendent came to our door during the party last night to complain about the noise in his pyjamas.

12. Tell me where she hit you.

3.4 ANALYTIC, CONTRADICTORY, AND SYNTHETIC STATEMENTS

Often, when we know what a statement means we still do not know whether it is true or false. If I say, *I was born on October 22*, you understand the meaning of what I have said, but you do not know whether what I have said is true or false. The sentence is one of a large class of sentences for which the truth or falsity is not determined by its meaning. There are, however, certain statements whose truth or falsity is determined by their meaning. Consider the following examples:

> *All bachelors are unmarried adult males.*
> *Some bachelors are married.*

Once we understand the meaning of these statements, we know that the first is true and the second is false. They are true, or false, by definition. We do not need to investigate the facts in order to know whether they are true or false. Someone who tries to discover their truth or falsity by sending a questionnaire to a group of bachelors asking whether or not they are married obviously does not understand the meaning of the statements.

A statement that is true by definition is called an *ANALYTIC STATEMENT*. A statement that is false by definition is called a *CONTRADICTORY STATEMENT*. A statement whose truth or falsity is not solely dependent upon the meanings of the words in it is called a *SYNTHETIC STATEMENT*. All statements can be placed in one of these three categories.

These distinctions are useful in clarifying the meaning of certain statements whose meaning is imprecise. When a statement seems false, we can ask whether it is a false synthetic or a contradictory statement. When a statement seems true, we can ask whether it is a true synthetic or an analytic statement. For example, if someone claims that every successful person is wealthy, it is useful to know whether they are interpreting the word successful as meaning financially successful. If so, their claim becomes analytic, for it really means that all wealthy people are wealthy. In a case such as this, it may seem to be a waste of time arguing against an analytic statement, but it is helpful to identify *that* it is analytic rather than synthetic; it helps clarify what is at stake in a disagreement. In practice, people do not usually approach discussions with precise definitions of the key terms. It is when they are challenged—for example, when someone says, *I know several very successful poets and artists who are not wealthy*—that the temptation arises to define words in a way that makes their claim analytic. Since analytic statements are true by definition, such a move seems calculated to ensure victory in the debate.

But such victories are usually hollow, for analytic statements are always in a sense trivial. Obviously, all successful people are wealthy—if, by *successful*, you mean *wealthy*. But why should anyone think it interesting to claim that all wealthy people are wealthy? It is true, but trivially true. The interesting question in such a debate is whether one should regard financial success as the only kind of success, and this cannot be determined merely by defining words. In practice, people who attempt to win a debate by making their claim analytic usually shift back and forth between analytic and synthetic interpretations in the course of the debate. To show that their claim is true they adopt the analytic interpretation; to show that it is important they adopt the synthetic interpretation. In this way they convince themselves that their claim is both true and important, but the true meaning is trivial and the important meaning is unproven and possibly false.

Sometimes a claim is made into an analytic one in ways that are indirect, and it may take some perseverance to uncover these moves. Usually, these indirect moves arise from arguments that are used to defend a claim. The claim that a free-enterprise system is superior to a socialist system, in its most plausible interpretation, is a synthetic statement. But suppose the following argument were put forward to support this claim:

(1) In a free-enterprise system, market forces determine how resources are allocated within the society.
(2) It is more efficient to allocate resources through market forces than through decisions by government officials.

(3) An efficient system is superior to an inefficient system.
(4) In a socialist system, decisions by government officials determine how resources are allocated within society.
(5) Therefore, a free-enterprise system is superior to a socialist system.

This is a logically strong argument, in the sense that, if the first four statements are true, then the conclusion must also be true. Premise (4) is unproblematic as a characterization of socialism. The danger arises when attempting to show that premises (2) and (3) are true. It is all too easy to assume their truth by regarding them as analytic. Premise (2) becomes analytic if it is assumed that an efficient allocation of resources is by definition one that is produced by market forces. Premise (3) becomes analytic if it is interpreted to mean that an economically efficient system is economically superior to an economically inefficient system. But if the premises are interpreted in this way, then the conclusion needs to be re-interpreted to mean that a system that allocates resources efficiently is more efficient than one that does not allocate resources efficiently. In this way, the conclusion itself becomes analytic. It is true, but trivially so, since its truth depends not on the facts but only on the way the key terms are defined. The real argument will, of course, resurface as an argument about the truth or adequacy of the interpretations of premises (2) and (3).

3.5 SELF-TEST NO. 5

For each of the following sentences, determine whether it is best interpreted as analytic, synthetic, or contradictory.

1. A full deck of playing cards contains 52 cards.

2. A yard is longer than a foot.

3. It is better to be free and unhappy than to be a contented slave.

4. No one has ever run the marathon in less than two hours.

5. Death comes for us all, sooner or later.

6. I'm not saying that postal workers should not have the legal right to strike, but the postal service is so vital to the economy, and postal strikes cause so much personal inconvenience to so many people, that I think the government should enact legislation banning strikes in the post office.

7. In the southern hemisphere, the sun rises in the west and sets in the east.

8. All parents love their children, when they are newborn.

9. A rose by any other name would smell as sweet.

10. A rose is a rose is a rose.

11. You can't fit a square peg into a round hole.

12. My bicycle is in excellent condition, once both wheels are straightened out, the broken frame is welded, the tires are patched, the handlebar gets replaced, and a seat is put on it.

3.6 DESCRIPTIVE AND EVALUATIVE MEANING

In section 2.3 we characterized the main uses of language. The first two of these—the descriptive and the evaluative—are probably the most common uses of language and probably also the most fundamental. As a result, we find that many words have come to have meanings that are both descriptive and evaluative. When someone says that Fritz Kreisler was a renowned violinist, the word *renowned* has a double meaning. First, it means that Kreisler was well known as a violinist. Second, it means that he was an excellent violinist. The first meaning is descriptive, since it refers to the fact that Kreisler was well known. If there is a disagreement about this fact, it can be settled by looking for historical evidence regarding how widely known he was during his lifetime. The second meaning, however, is evaluative; the speaker is giving his or her opinion that Kreisler was an excellent violinist. This opinion is not factual, since if there is a disagreement over whether Kreisler was an excellent violinist, it cannot be settled by consulting the facts. Someone who thinks that Kreisler was not an excellent violinist would be able to accept the *DESCRIPTIVE MEANING* but would have to reject the *EVALUATIVE MEANING* of our statement.

There are many descriptive words and phrases that also have an evaluative meaning. It is common to find two or more words or phrases that have more or less the same descriptive meaning but different evaluative meanings. We have seen that *renowned* and *well known* have the same descriptive meaning, but the former has a positive evaluative meaning that the latter lacks. The word *notorious* has the same descriptive meaning but has a negative evaluative meaning. The evaluative meanings of *renowned* and *notorious* convey an evaluation of the person as being good or bad, whereas *well known* conveys nothing about the speaker's evaluation. Notice the shift in the evaluative meanings in the following pairs of sentences while the descriptive meaning remains more or less unchanged:

He is very self-confident.
He is arrogant.

She is sexually liberated.
She is promiscuous.

He is a dedicated conservative.
He is a fanatical conservative.

They are freedom fighters.
They are terrorists.

It is important to be aware of such differences in meaning, since we can sometimes be led to accept a particular evaluation through a failure to distinguish descriptive and evaluative meanings. The facts that would show that someone is very self-confident and the facts that would show that someone is arrogant are very similar, and a skilled arguer can easily create the impression that someone who is self-confident is really arrogant (or vice versa). But the same facts can only be used to justify two statements with different evaluative meanings if the evaluative meaning is ignored and they are regarded as purely descriptive statements. The evaluative part of the meaning requires a separate justification.

3.7 SELF-TEST NO. 6

The italicized word or phrase in each of the following sentences has both a descriptive and an evaluative meaning. Indicate whether its evaluative meaning is positive or negative and briefly paraphrase its descriptive meaning in non-evaluative terms. Suggest a descriptive synonym or equivalent phrase that has a neutral (or no) evaluative meaning but preserves the descriptive meaning of the sentence.

1. There is *vicious* competition among students at the Juilliard School of Music.

2. Jennifer is a *compulsively* tidy person.

3. This year Mark has been a very *responsible* student.

4. During the last 30 years the moral standards of ordinary people have *declined*.

5. Simon is one of those people whose main motivation in life is *greed*.

6. The Governor announced that the budget for social services would be *slashed* by 12 per cent over the next three years.

7. I think your doctor is being *excessively* cautious in his approach to treating your illness.

8. Jon was *suckered* by the salesman into buying the car.

9. Beethoven's Ninth Symphony was composed during his *mature* years.

10. So we have a deal, then. I'll get my *girl* to type it up and send it to you for signing.

3.8 NECESSARY AND SUFFICIENT CONDITIONS

A special kind of ambiguity can arise when talking about the conditions that have to be met in order for a claim to be true or for something to occur. Referring to such conditions is common when we are talking about the causes (i.e., the causal conditions) of certain events: for example, *Under what conditions would a major economic depression occur again?* It is also common when we are talking about entitlements or justifications for certain actions: for example, *What are the conditions for graduating with distinction?* It seems that all we need to do to answer such questions is to list the conditions that, if they existed, would lead to a depression or to graduating with distinction. Unfortunately, the relationships between conditions and what they are conditions for are often a great deal more complex than they seem, and, in order to clarify these relationships, philosophers and scientists have developed a distinction between two types of conditions, necessary conditions and sufficient conditions. Much confusion and ambiguity can result when these two types of conditions are not clearly distinguished.

To understand the ambiguity that results when the two types of conditions are not distinguished, consider the following:

> (1) Being at least 18 years of age is a condition for being eligible to vote in federal elections in the United States.

This could mean either of the following:

> (2) Anyone who is at least 18 years of age is eligible to vote in federal elections in the United States, or

> (3) Anyone who is not at least 18 years of age is not eligible to vote in federal elections in the United States.

These sentences have different meanings. We can see the difference by asking what each says about a particular case, for example, a 57-year-old prison inmate. According to (2) such a person is eligible to vote, but (3) makes no such guarantee. In fact the correct interpretation of (1) is (3). By law, every eligible voter must be at least 18 years of age—that is, if you are not 18 you can't vote—but the law also states that a person serving a sentence of two or more years in a correctional institution is not eligible to vote. So not everyone who is 18 years of age is eligible to vote, which means that (2) is false. Being at least 18 years of age is *a* condition, but it is not the only condition that has to be satisfied for someone to be an eligible voter. To avoid this ambiguity, we should revise (1) to read:

(4) Being at least 18 years of age is a necessary condition for being eligible to vote in federal elections in the United States.

A *NECESSARY CONDITION* is defined as follows: X is a necessary condition for Y if, and only if, when X is false Y must also be false (or, when X is absent Y cannot occur). In other words, unless the necessary condition X is true, Y will not be true; but the truth of X does not guarantee the truth of Y. This yields a simple test for the truth of a necessary-condition statement: look for an instance of Y that is not also an X. If we can find one such case, then the statement must be false, since we have discovered an instance where X is not a necessary condition for Y. If we cannot find such a case, then we should accept the statement.

A sufficient condition is quite different from a necessary condition. Consider the following:

(1) Holding a B.A. from the University is a condition for being a member of the University Alumni Association.

This is ambiguous between:

(2) Anyone holding a B.A. from the University is a member of the University Alumni Association, and

(3) Anyone not holding a B.A. from the University is not a member of the University Alumni Association.

Obviously, (2) is the most likely interpretation of (1), for someone with a B.S. or any other degree from the University is an alumnus. Notice the structural difference from our first example, where (3) was the correct interpretation. This is because here we are dealing with a sufficient condition. A person who holds a B.A. from the University does not need to meet any additional conditions in order to be a member of the University Alumni Association, although obviously holding a B.A. is not the only way one can become a member of the University Alumni Association. To remove the ambiguity we need to revise (1) to read:

(4) Holding a B.A. from the University is a sufficient condition for being a member of the University Alumni Association.

A *SUFFICIENT CONDITION* is defined as follows: X is a sufficient condition for Y if, and only if, when X is true Y must also be true (or, when X is present Y must occur). In other words, a sufficient condition for Y is something whose truth or presence guarantees Y, but whose falsity or absence does not prevent Y. This yields a simple test for the truth of a sufficient-condition statement: look for an instance of an X that is not also a Y. If we can find one such case, then the statement must be false, since we have discovered an instance where X is not a sufficient condition for Y. If we can find no such case, then we should accept the statement.

The difference between a necessary and a sufficient condition is subtle but important. Essentially, it's a question of what kind of guarantee is being made. When the condition is necessary, the author is asserting that its falsity or absence *guarantees* whatever it is a condition for won't be true. On the other hand, when the condition is sufficient, the author is asserting that the condition is something whose truth or presence *guarantees* that whatever it is a condition for will be true. Chapter 9 introduces some concepts from deductive logic that will help make this difference clearer, but until then we can focus on the nature of these two guarantees: a necessary condition guarantees that Y won't be true unless X is true, whereas a sufficient condition guarantees that Y will be true if X is true.

Sometimes, a condition can be both necessary and sufficient at the same time. Consider the following:

It is a condition for a candidate being declared the winner in an election for the Ohio legislature that the candidate received more votes than any other candidate in the election.

In this example, receiving more votes than any other candidate is a sufficient condition for being declared the winner (since anyone who receives more votes than any other candidate must be declared the winner), and it is also a necessary condition (since every candidate who is declared the winner must have received more votes than any other candidate). Another example of this sort is the relationship between *Today is Tuesday* and *Tomorrow is Wednesday.* Each of these statements is both a necessary and sufficient condition for the other.

Now, just to make things more complicated, we need to note what can happen when two or more conditions for the same thing are joined together. Being at least 18 years of age is not the only necessary condition for being eligible to vote in federal elections in the United States; we have already noted that one must not be a prisoner or an insane person, but in addition one must also be an American citizen. We can set out these necessary conditions as follows:

> *The necessary conditions for being eligible to vote in federal elections in the United States are:*
> *(1) being at least 18 years of age,*
> *(2) not being an insane person or a prison inmate, and*
> *(3) being a US citizen.*

These constitute all the necessary conditions for being eligible to vote in federal elections in the United States. But notice that these three necessary conditions are, *when taken together*, a sufficient condition. This is because any person who satisfies all three of these conditions is eligible to vote. Whenever we can list all the necessary conditions for something, we will have listed the conditions that are *JOINTLY SUFFICIENT CONDITIONS.* So, in this case, (1), (2), and (3) are individually necessary and jointly sufficient conditions.

In a similar way, we can sometimes find two or more different sufficient conditions for something. For example, according to the Texas Penal Code Sec. 19.02, a murder is committed when someone

> *(1) intentionally or knowingly causes the death of an individual;*

> *(2) intends to cause serious bodily injury and commits an act clearly dangerous to human life that causes the death of an individual; or*

> *(3) commits or attempts to commit a felony, other than manslaughter, and in the course of and in furtherance of the commission or attempt, or in immediate flight from the commission or attempt, he commits or attempts to commit an act clearly dangerous to human life that causes the death of an individual.*

This section states three sufficient conditions for the crime of murder. If, in a particular case, any one of these conditions is met, the accused person will be found guilty of murder. If we take all three conditions together, that is, if we take section 19.02 as a whole, we can say that it states the necessary condition for murder in the sense that at least one of these conditions must be met by every case of culpable homicide. This is because the absence of all three conditions means that an accused person would not be found guilty of murder.

So far, all our examples have dealt with criteria or entitlements. When dealing with causes, necessary and sufficient conditions work in the same way. When scientists search for a *full* account of the causes of some phenomenon, they are looking not only for the conditions that are individually sufficient, but also for the conditions that are individually necessary and jointly sufficient. However, if our sole interest is in controlling some phenomenon, all we need is a partial account of the causes of that phenomenon. If we want to prevent something from happening we don't need a full account of its causal conditions, since if we can eliminate one necessary condition, then we can prevent the event from occurring. For example, if we want to prevent a disease from spreading all we need to do is find and eliminate one of the necessary conditions for the spread of the disease. On the other hand, if we want to produce a certain effect, all we need to do is to find one (or one set) of its sufficient conditions that we can bring about. For example, if we want to lose 20 pounds, we need to find only one way (for example, exercise) that works (i.e., is sufficient), and can ignore all the other ways (for example, dieting, diet pills).

3.9 SELF-TEST NO. 7

State whether the italicized phrase in each of the following sentences identifies a necessary condition or a sufficient condition or a combination of the two. (*Note*: Once you understand the two different meanings of each sentence, you will have to use your common-sense knowledge to decide which is the more likely meaning.)

1. To bring down a fever, *apply a cloth dampened in cold water to the patient's face, arms, and legs.*

2. *Any student who has not paid his or her tuition fee by the first day of the term, or who has not made arrangements with the bursar's office for delayed payment,* will be automatically required to withdraw from the university.

3. To be admitted as a graduate student, *applicants must have a four-year honors degree with a 75-per-cent average on all courses taken in their last two years.*

4. You cannot get an A average unless *you work hard throughout the whole term.*

5. Essays will be returned to the student without being graded, if *they are submitted without a proper bibliography.*

6. The Bruce Prize of $500 will be awarded to *the graduating student who has the highest cumulative average in all his or her philosophy courses.*

7. In the US *only US citizens* can be elected president.

8. For the business community to regain confidence in the economy, *interest rates must come down.*

9. *You have to have good physical coordination* to be a good skier.

10. No one can become a university professor these days unless *he or she has a Ph.D. degree.*

11. You can't watch television tonight, Sarah, until *your homework is done and you've had a bath.*

12. The results of a departmental vote are valid if, and only if, *at least 25 per cent of members are present at the meeting in which the vote took place.*

3.10 QUESTIONS FOR DISCUSSION

In light of the distinctions and concepts outlined in this chapter, discuss the following passages:

1. We hold these truths to be self-evident, that all men are created equal, that they are endowed by their Creator with certain unalienable Rights, that among these are Life, Liberty, and the pursuit of Happiness (from the *Declaration of Independence*).

2. No rational person ever commits suicide.

3. To assure the maximum effectiveness in teaching, it is sometimes necessary to place limits on the enrollment in courses. Some courses have enrollment limits because of limited laboratory or studio space. Others have limits to enable instructors to incorporate additional papers and examinations, small group discussions or special projects. A writing-

intensive course, for example, is normally limited to 20 students, and a seminar is normally limited to 12 (from the 2007 *Hamilton College Catalogue*, p. 4).

4. *Politician*: As far as we are concerned an impartial dispute-settling mechanism is an essential precondition for any free trade deal between Canada and the United States.
Interviewer: So you are saying, then, that you would support a free trade deal as long as the Americans accept an impartial dispute-settling mechanism.

5. Suppose someone is drowning 20 feet from shore. We throw him 10 feet of rope and he drowns. It would be illogical to conclude: "Rope is useless in the prevention of drowning." But this is the logic of the Governor's claims that most government-funded social assistance programs are "based on the assumption that any social problem can be solved simply by throwing enough tax dollars at it." No one with any understanding of our social problems has ever made such a stupid and simplistic assumption, yet the Governor persists in spreading the myth that only such an assumption can justify social assistance programs.

6. For years, the United States government has persisted in lecturing other countries about their records on human rights. But why should another country pay attention to the carping of foreigners whose own country still follows racist policies and practices? I refer, of course, to the large number of subtle ways in which our government discriminates against our native people. The overall effect of these policies is to bring about a slow cultural genocide.

7. Thou shalt not kill.

8. The Association for the Mentally Retarded recently changed its name to The Association for Community Living. The Association felt that "retarded" was a derogatory term and that dropping the term was an important step in their fight to change public attitudes towards a social group that has often suffered in the past from cruel and hostile treatment at the hands of the more unenlightened members of the community.

9. For many years public opinion polls have shown that about two-thirds of those polled support capital punishment for premeditated murder. Year after year the fluctuation has never been more than 2 or 3 per cent. Last year, however, a pollster who was surveying public opinion on a range

of social issues inadvertently changed the wording of the question about capital punishment and used the term *death penalty* instead. The results were astonishing. Forty-seven per cent of the respondents agreed that the death penalty should be used for premeditated murder while 48 per cent disagreed. It is possible that some people who were asked the old question confused capital punishment with corporal punishment and thought that they were supporting the use of corporal punishment for murderers. It is more likely, however, that the image conjured up in their minds by the term *death penalty* is much more vivid and violent than that of *capital punishment*, which has a more bureaucratic or clinical connotation. If this is a correct explanation for the difference in the impact of the two terms, then *death penalty* should be the preferred term, for it is surely closer to the reality of what happens. This would mean that the results of the poll are not a fluke, and that public opinion is actually evenly split on the question.

4. RECONSTRUCTING ARGUMENTS

4.1 RECONSTRUCTION

Unfortunately, the arguments we encounter in real life do not come with their premises and conclusions neatly labeled. Even worse, they are usually embedded in extraneous material that, although it may aid in interpreting the argument, is not actually part of the argument itself. Before we can critically assess an argument, therefore, we have to determine what the actual argument is. What is its conclusion, what are its premises, and what is the precise relationship between them? The process of eliciting this information is called *RECONSTRUCTING THE ARGUMENT*. The aim of reconstructing an argument is to produce a set of statements that represents the actual argument—the premises, the conclusion, the relationship between premises and conclusion—the author intended to present. The specific words used in the reconstruction need not be the actual words used by the author, for, as we have seen, it may be necessary to revise the words used in order to clarify the meaning or to remove ambiguities. What is important is to ensure that as far as possible the reconstruction does not violate the author's intent, and where this is unclear, does not violate the principle of charity.

Reconstructing an argument involves two phases. In the first, the premises and the conclusion of the argument must be identified. In the second phase the structure of the argument must be identified. When identifying the premises and conclusion of an argument that is presented in written form we will use the following conventions:

(1) The conclusion is underlined and labeled by C.

(2) Premises are enclosed in brackets and labeled by P1, P2, P3, etc.

(3) Missing premises or a missing conclusion are labeled by MP1, MP2, MP3, etc., or MC.

To see how this works in practice we will reconstruct the following argument:

The most important challenge facing educators today is to teach students how to write decent prose. By "decent prose" I do not mean elegant writing: I mean simple straightforward writing that conforms to the rules of English grammar and clearly conveys its meaning. The ability to write decent prose is important because those who lack it will be unable to understand the great achievements of our cultural heritage—whether of Homer or Hemingway—and, perhaps even more important, will be unable to communicate effectively in today's world.

The first step is to identify the conclusion. What is the author's main point? What is the author trying to get the reader to accept? It seems quite clear that the conclusion is the first sentence: that the most important challenge facing educators today is to teach students how to write decent prose. We should always be careful at this step. It is extremely important that the conclusion be correctly identified, for if we mis-identify the conclusion, whatever we say about the argument will almost certainly miss the point and be a waste of everyone's time.

The second step is to identify the premises. What reasons does the author present to support the conclusion? There are two: (1) those who lack the ability to write decent prose will be unable to understand the great achievements of our cultural heritage, and (2) those who lack the ability to write decent prose will be unable to communicate effectively in today's world. The second sentence in the passage, it should be noted, is not a premise, since it cannot plausibly be regarded as providing a reason in support of the conclusion. Its function is to explain in more detail the meaning of the conclusion. So in reconstructing the argument within the passage, we can set this sentence aside.

Following the suggested conventions, the passage should now look like this:

> <u>*The most important challenge facing educators today is to teach students how to write decent prose*</u> *(C). By "decent prose" I do not mean elegant writing: I mean simple straightforward writing that conforms to the rules of English grammar and clearly conveys its meaning. The ability to write decent prose is important because [those who lack it will be unable to understand the great achievements of our cultural heritage](P1)—whether of Homer or Hemingway—and, perhaps even more important, [will be unable to communicate effectively in today's world] (P2).*

Before moving to the second phase in reconstructing an argument, that is, identifying its structure, we need to consider how to deal with missing premises and conclusions.

4.2 MISSING PREMISES AND CONCLUSIONS

Many of the arguments we encounter in real life are incomplete, in the sense that if we consider only what the author says, we will be forced to assume that the speaker has left something out. Consider:

P. Doug's birthday is tomorrow.
C. Therefore, Bob should buy him a present.

If this is the entire argument, it is quite weak. The mere fact that tomorrow is Doug's birthday is not by itself a good reason for Bob to buy him a present. Either the speaker is quite stupid, or something is missing, such as the fact that Bob and Doug are brothers or are close friends. The principle of charity requires us to consider whether something is missing. If the author is present, we need only ask; once we learn that Doug and Bob are brothers, we have the missing premise that makes sense of the argument:

MP2. Bob is Doug's brother.

If the author is not present, we have to use whatever knowledge we possess and whatever clues the context provides to supply a missing premise that makes the best sense of the argument. If, however, we lack the knowledge that would allow us to supply the missing premise, we can make only a tentative assessment of it. We should say that, unless there is some special relationship between Doug and Bob, the argument is a weak one.

Supplying missing premises is not always as simple as this. Consider the following argument:

P1. High crime rates are caused by the widespread use of probation and suspended sentences.
C. Therefore, we should amend the criminal law to provide for mandatory minimum prison sentences for all crimes.

A fair interpretation of this argument shows that there are two missing premises. The first is the relatively obvious one, that we are experiencing higher crime rates; clearly, this is something the author believes. Thus, we need to add the following:

MP2. Crime rates are high.

The second missing premise is a little less obvious. On reflection, however, it seems likely that the speaker is also assuming the following:

MP3. Crime will be deterred more effectively by a new policy of mandatory imprisonment than by the current one that allows for suspended sentences or early parole.

MP4. We should lower crime rates.

Supplying these three missing premises increases the strength of the argument. The strength of this reconstructed argument, it should be noted, is its logical strength: if its premises are true, then its conclusion is likely to be true. (It is probably not a sound argument, however, since it is unlikely that P1 and MP3 are true.)

There is an important difference between MP2 and the other two missing premises. MP2 supplies some missing information that presumably the speaker knows or believes. MP3 and MP4, on the other hand, are assumptions or *PRESUPPOS-ITIONS*. A presupposition is not simply missing information; it is a statement that is logically required by the argument in order for one of its stated claims to be true. In this case, the argument draws a conclusion about the relationship between mandatory sentences and lower crime, even though the premise makes no mention of either of these things. What's missing after P1 has been identified and MP2 supplied is not simply something of the argument's factual content; rather, what's missing is something indispensable for its logical strength. In reconstructing the argument, we needed to ask, (1) what must be logically presupposed about mandatory sentences in order for the conclusion to be true? and (2) what must be logically presupposed about what attitude we ought to adopt toward crime? MP3 answers the first question, and MP4 answers the second question. Finding the presuppositions that underlie an argument can often be quite difficult and usually requires considerable care. Such presuppositions are important because frequently they are the real bone of contention between the two sides of an issue.

Let us return to the argument we started to reconstruct in section 4.1. We have already established the premises and conclusion:

> *P1. The ability to write decent prose is important because those who lack it will be unable to understand the great achievements of our cultural heritage.*
> *P2. The ability to write decent prose is important because those who lack it will be unable to communicate effectively in today's world.*
> *C. The most important challenge facing educators today is to teach students how to write decent prose.*

Is there a missing premise in this argument? It is clear that the author is making the following assumption: that educators have a responsibility to give students an understanding of the great achievements of our cultural heritage and to teach students how to communicate effectively. On the basis of what the author has said, it is almost certain that he or she is making this assumption. Otherwise, it is difficult to imagine why the author thinks that the conclusion is supported by the given premises. So we must add the following premise:

MP3. Educators have a responsibility to give students an understanding of the great achievements of our cultural heritage and to teach students how to communicate effectively.

How can we be sure that this is the actual presupposition of the author? If the author is available, we can ask whether he or she accepts this assumption. If the author is not available, there may be other of his or her writings we can consult. Otherwise we will have to follow the principle of charity and attempt to work out the most plausible assumption and add it as a missing premise.

When we are eliciting assumptions of this sort, there are two factors to be considered. We need to find a premise that, if true, actually provides support for the conclusion, and the premise should be as plausible as possible. Often these two factors pull in opposing directions: a premise that gives the argument logical strength may be less plausible than another premise that provides less logical strength to the argument. We might, for example, have tried another version of MP3:

MP4. Educators have the sole responsibility for giving students an understanding of the great achievements of our cultural heritage and for teaching students how to communicate effectively.

This, however, is less plausible than MP3, since it denies that parents, for example, have any responsibility in these matters. But if we use it instead of MP3 in our reconstruction, the argument would have greater logical strength. The choice between MP3 and MP4 should be made on the basis of the principle of charity: which version of the missing premise yields the more reasonable interpretation of the argument? In this case MP3 seems a much more reasonable presupposition than MP4.

Sometimes we encounter an argument with a missing conclusion. Usually it is easy to figure out what the conclusion should be. For example:

People who want to see the death penalty reintroduced in Canada should look at the United States. In the US, the death penalty is routinely applied for first degree murder, yet their murder rate is much higher than the murder rate in Canada.

The most likely interpretation of this passage is: this is an argument whose conclusion is that the death penalty should not be reintroduced in Canada. It is difficult to imagine a context in which the speaker would not intend his or her comment to be a reason for not reintroducing the death penalty. When reconstructing an argument with a missing conclusion, we should follow the guidelines suggested above for dealing with missing premises.

4.3 SELF-TEST NO. 8

Supply the missing premises or conclusions in the following arguments.

1. It is after midnight and the gas stations are all closed, so I won't be able to drive you home.

2. Whenever your car's engine is flooded, you should put the accelerator right to the floor and then try to start it. So floor it and try again.

3. But you are still a Catholic, and Catholics are supposed to make a special effort to attend church at Easter.

4. Living in a large metropolis is much more stressful than living in a small town. So Jennifer is going to be even more uptight when she moves to Chicago next year.

5. He skipped more classes than he attended, so it will be no surprise when he fails his mid-term.

6. Children whose parents are extremely strict usually turn into teenage rebels, and Todd's father was tougher on him than any parent I know.

7. You broke my hearing aid, you clumsy oaf. Now I'll have to get a new one.

8. The high school drop-out rate in our district is about 15 per cent higher than the provincial average. Clearly, the school board ought to introduce programs to persuade students not to drop out, as well as programs designed to make it easier for those who have already dropped out to resume their education.

9. I deserve a much higher grade on my essay than a D+. I worked really hard on it.

10. There ought to be a law prohibiting the use of animals in research. After all, we would not tolerate that kind of treatment of humans.

4.4 SPECIAL CASES

The examples we have been considering so far contain arguments in which there is an inference from the premises to the conclusion that attempts to show that the conclusion is true. The truth is transmitted, so to speak, from the premise(s) to the conclusion. But not everything that contains premises and a conclusion follows this pattern, and there are two special cases that we should keep in mind as we go on.

Sometimes we encounter passages that contain arguments but are not arguments themselves. These are called reports of arguments. And sometimes we encounter explanations in which the inference from the premise(s) to the conclusion is not a transmission of truth, because the truth of the conclusion is not at issue; rather, explanations outline the logically prior principles that specify *why* a state of affairs is as the conclusion describes it.

4.4.1 Reports of Arguments

A *REPORT OF AN ARGUMENT* is a statement that says that so-and-so argued in a certain way. For example:

> *John refuses to vote in elections because he believes that all politicians are dishonest.*

This statement tells us that John refuses to vote in elections and that his reason for not voting is his belief that all politicians are dishonest. But the statement itself is not an argument: it simply tells us that John reasons in a certain way. A report of an argument is no more an argument than a photograph of an accident is itself an accident. Of course, since it is a statement, we can ask whether or not it is true, that is, if it correctly reports some facts about John. It may be false because John's refusal to vote may rest on his belief that despite their promises, all political parties behave the same if they win. Or it may be false because, although he believes all politicians are dishonest, he votes anyway. If the statement is true, however, that does not make it an argument, because its truth consists only in the fact that it reports correctly how John reasons. Here are two more examples of reports of arguments.

> *According to an editorial in* The Chronicle, *standardized, nation-wide scholastic achievement testing will improve the quality of education because it will enable us to learn what works and what doesn't work in the classroom.*

> *In 1851 John Stuart Mill argued that we should never restrict freedom of expression because in the long run complete freedom of expression has beneficial social consequences, even if in some particular cases the consequences are harmful.*

These are both reports of arguments put forward by someone other than the speaker. We may agree that *The Chronicle* and John Stuart Mill did say what the speaker claims they said, but this does not mean that we agree with the arguments that are being reported.

Of course, the arguments that are reported can be considered as arguments in their own right. But to do this we must no longer regard them merely as reports of what others have said: we must view them as arguments that claim to give us good reasons for accepting their conclusions. Now we must ask ourselves whether standardized testing will improve the quality of education and whether complete freedom of expression will in the long run have beneficial social consequences. What *The Chronicle* and John Stuart Mill believe is now irrelevant. What is relevant is only the argument itself.

It is sometimes difficult to know whether a report of an argument is intended by the speaker to be taken as an argument. Some people seem to prefer to take part in discussions by citing other people's arguments; they are inclined to agree with the arguments they report, but if they meet serious criticism they can easily back off by claiming that they don't fully agree with *The Chronicle* or John Stuart Mill. But often people who introduce another person's argument into a discussion clearly do mean to stand by it; they report the argument precisely because they think it is a sound argument. In these cases, we are entitled to interpret a report of an argument as itself an argument. There is no easy test to decide when we should treat a report of an argument as itself an argument. We can only rely upon the context and the principle of charity to help us decide.

4.4.2 Explanations

The second kind of special case consists of *EXPLANATIONS* or explanatory arguments. An explanation is an attempt to show *why* or *how* something happens (or has happened) when there is little reason to doubt the truth of the conclusion. For example:

> *My car won't start because it is out of gas.*

> *The reason the Republicans lost the last election is that they were perceived by the voters as arrogant and uncaring.*

> *Teachers, who in recent years have become increasingly sensitive to public criticism, are opposed to nation-wide scholastic achievement testing since they fear that the results could be used or misused in attempts to criticize them as poor teachers.*

> *The Penguins got a penalty because they had too many players on the ice.*

There are several different types of explanations. Many explanations are causal: they explain an event by reference to its causes. But some explanations are non-causal. We explain how volleyball is played not by reference to the causes of volleyball, but to the rules of volleyball. We explain how to register as a university student by reference to the university's registration procedures. We explain people's behavior by reference to their motives and goals. We explain what a hammer is by reference to its function.

The purpose of an explanation is to make explicit why or how some phenomenon occurred or some event happened; as we said above, explanations are appropriate when the event in question is taken for granted and we are seeking to understand *why* it occurred. Thus, when I say that my car won't start because it is out of gas, I am not trying to find support for my belief that my car won't start. I know this already. What I want is an explanation for the fact that it won't start. Is it because the engine is flooded, or because of an electrical fault, or because the car is out of gas? If the gas gauge indicates "empty" and I accept this as accurate, I can say *My car won't start because it is out of gas.* The stated premise *It [my car] is out of gas* and the missing premise *A car without gas will not start* explain why *My car won't start.* In this case, there is no doubt about the truth of the stated premise, nor the missing premise (a presupposition), nor the conclusion. It is not that the mere truth of the premises is transmitted to the conclusions, but their intelligibility; that is, we seek explanations not because the truth of the conclusion is in question, but because our understanding of it is incomplete.

By contrast, with the arguments we have been considering up until now, what is at issue is primarily whether the conclusion *is* true; the function of the premises is to supply reasons for believing that the conclusion is true or correct. Because these arguments purport to *prove* that their conclusion is true, they may be described as *PROBATIVE ARGUMENTS.* Consider the following argument, which might look at first like an explanation:

> *Susan, you should visit your parents more often, because it gives them such pleasure when you do.*

Here the speaker is trying to persuade Susan to do something she is reluctant to do by providing a reason for doing so. It would make little sense to interpret this passage as an explanation, that is, that the speaker and Susan both agree that she should visit her parents more often and are discussing why this is so. More plausibly, the speaker has some doubt as to whether Susan believes she should visit her parents more often, and this person offers a reason for Susan to accept it.

When we read a passage that cites evidence in support of a conclusion, we should first ask whether the conclusion is presented as (1) a statement that is true but is more clearly understood in light of the evidence provided in the premise(s), or (2) as a statement whose truth is in question but is purported to be true on the basis of the evidence provided in the premise(s). If the answer to (1) is "yes," then it is an explanation; if the answer to (2) is "yes," then it is an argument in the usual, narrow sense of the word that we have been using in this book; i.e., it is probative.

There are, however, cases where only the context can tell us whether we should treat a passage as an explanation or as an argument in the narrow, probative sense of the word. For example:

Jim's health is good because he has a healthy diet and gets plenty of exercise.

We can imagine a context in which both the speaker and the audience know that Jim's health is good, and the speaker wants to explain why this is so. But we can also imagine a context in which they know that Jim has a healthy diet and gets plenty of exercise, and the speaker wants to argue that Jim is in good health. Usually, the context makes it clear whether it is an argument or an explanation that we are dealing with.

Explanations are of course subject to debate, and there are many disagreements as to what is the correct explanation for some phenomenon or event. This means that sometimes explanations themselves become the subject of an argument. For example:

Women are economically disadvantaged in our society not because they have traditionally been socialized into accepting passive and supporting roles, but because they have been and still are excluded by men from economic power. The effects of traditional socialization on women's attitudes are still very real in many cases, but it does not account for their economically disadvantaged position, since when women do seek careers in business, which is where the real wealth is to be made, they are systematically excluded by men from the corridors of real power and influence.

This is an argument about what is the correct, or best, explanation of the fact, which is not at issue, that women are economically disadvantaged in our society. The speaker is, however, not merely asserting an explanation, but attempting to argue that his or her explanation is correct. Arguments about explanations, like this one, can sometimes be difficult to distinguish from the explanations themselves. For now, the best we can do is rely upon the context to help us decide, bearing in mind, as always, the principle of charity.

4.5 SELF-TEST NO. 9

For each of the following passages, indicate whether it is an argument in the usual, probative sense, an explanation, or a report of an argument.

1. I find it extremely difficult to perform for an audience. When I was a child, my parents used to brag all the time about what a prodigy I was, and they used to get so upset when I played badly that I was always terrified that they would stop loving me if I didn't play well. Consequently, I still imagine all sorts of things going wrong, like having a memory lapse, or dropping my flute.

2. David was so upset at what he had done that he ran all the way home to fetch the first aid kit and tried his best to bandage up the cut on Michael's foot. Then he helped Michael walk home and explained to his mother what had happened. The fact that it was really Michael's fault—as even his mother realized—didn't make any difference to David at all; he felt responsible for his friend.

3. We'd better watch Mary closely for the next 24 hours. She has had a nasty knock on the head, and there could be a concussion. If we see any signs of grogginess or disorientation, then we'll take her to the hospital.

4. There are several reasons why a child's school performance can suddenly deteriorate. Sometimes it is because a physical problem, which may be caused by a virus or a poor diet, affects the child's concentration. Sometimes it is because of a problem at school, such as an inexperienced teacher who has not learned how to recognize when children are only pretending they understand their lessons. Most commonly, it is because of a problem at home, such as the parents getting a divorce.

5. The reason your local taxes go up when you make improvements to your home and property is that the tax rate is based upon the value of your property. The more your property is worth, the higher your local tax. It may not be fair, but that is how the system works.

6. In most states the previous sexual conduct of a victim may not be introduced by the defense in sexual assault cases. The central argument is that information about specific instances of the victim's prior or subsequent sexual conduct is irrelevant to the particular charge before the court, and may prejudice jurors against the plaintiff.

7. You should never turn off your computer without following the exit procedure for your software program. This is because you will lose the files you have been working on, unless you save them before you exit.

8. I have consulted my lawyer, and he advised me that unless you refund the entire purchase price, I could take you to court and get my money back. And he says that if I complain to the Better Business Bureau, you could lose your membership.

9. Using juries in criminal trials is a stupid system. When there is only a judge trying the case, the prosecution has to persuade only one person that the accused is guilty. But when there is a jury, the prosecution has to persuade all 12 members of the jury that the accused is guilty. If only one juror has a grudge against the police, or has sympathy for the accused, or is just too dumb to understand the evidence, then a guilty person will go free. The jury system works to the advantage of criminals. We should abolish it.

10. Americans really don't understand how political parties operate in Canada, for they fail to realize the tremendous power that the leader of the party has over rank-and-file party members and especially over the elected members of the legislature. In the United States the party leader's power is much more limited, even when the leader becomes president. This is because their constitution is based upon the separation of powers between the legislative and executive branches of government.

4.6 THE STRUCTURE OF ARGUMENTS

The structure of an argument is important because it can tell us how the premises are intended to support the conclusion and can give us some of the information we need in order to undertake a critical assessment of the argument. The easiest way to see the structure of an argument is to represent it graphically using what is called a tree diagram. A *TREE DIAGRAM* is a schematic representation of the structure of an argument using letters (P1, P2, MP3, C, etc.) to represent the premises and conclusion, and an arrow to represent *therefore*. There are three basic argument structures.

4.6.1 Simple Arguments

In section 1.1 we saw that every argument must have a conclusion and at least one premise and that the premises and conclusion are connected by an implicit or explicit *therefore*. The simplest type of argument consists of a single premise and a single conclusion. Such arguments have a structure that we will call a *SIMPLE ARGUMENT* structure. For example:

> P. When Jim quit playing the trumpet, he gave it to his younger brother.
> C. Hence, Jim won't be able to lend his trumpet to Andrew.

The tree diagram for such simple argument structures is:

4.6.2 T Arguments

When we consider arguments with two premises, there are two possible structures the argument might have, and it is important to be aware of how they differ. Consider the following argument:

> P1. Every medical doctor has had to tell someone that a loved one has died.
> P2. Beth is a medical doctor.
> C. Therefore, Beth has had to tell someone that a loved one has died.

This argument has the following structure:

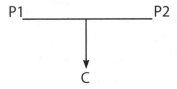

Notice that each premise, considered by itself, provides little or no support for the conclusion. By itself, the fact that every medical doctor has had to tell someone that a loved one has died provides no support for the conclusion. Similarly, the fact that Beth is a medical doctor does not by itself provide any support for the conclusion. If either premise were false, the remaining premise would provide little or no support for the conclusion. It is only when both are true that they provide support. An argument with this structure is called a *T ARGUMENT*, because the lines joining the premises to the conclusion form a T.

T arguments may sometimes have three or more premises. Consider the following argument:

> *P1. Every physically handicapped person who has tried to find employment knows the anguish of rejection.*
> *P2. Jody is physically handicapped.*
> *P3. Jody has tried to find employment.*
> *C. Therefore, Jody knows the anguish of rejection.*

The tree diagram for this argument is:

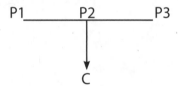

4.6.3 V Arguments

The third basic structure can be seen in the following argument:

> *P1. Frances is very successful in her career.*
> *P2. Frances has a secure and supportive marriage.*
> *C. Therefore, Frances is a happy person.*

This argument has the following structure:

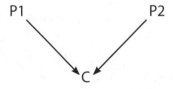

Notice that two separate reasons are offered in support of the conclusion. Each operates independently of the other. If either premise is missing or false, the remaining one still provides support for the conclusion. We shall call arguments with a structure of this sort *V ARGUMENTS*, because the lines joining the premises to the conclusion form a V.

Like T arguments, V arguments can have three or more premises. For example, the argument above would be strengthened by adding another premise that functions in the same way as the first two:

P3. Frances had a stable and secure childhood.

Our argument now has the following structure:

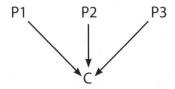

Obviously, the diagram now looks more like a W than a V, but to keep things simple we will continue to call it a V argument.

The distinction between T and V arguments is important because they represent two different ways in which two or more premises can combine to support a conclusion. To distinguish the two types of argument structure, it is necessary to ask whether the premises have to work together in order to provide support for the conclusion or whether they work independently of each other. The premises of a T argument work as a team, and both must be true to provide support for the conclusion; if either premise is false, then the other by itself would provide little or no support for the conclusion. On the other hand, each of the premises of a V argument provides independent support for the conclusion: if either premise is false, the other would still provide independent support for the conclusion. We shall see the importance of the distinction when we come to the assessment of arguments. If one of the premises of a T argument is false, then the argument is weak even if the other premise or premises are true. But if one of the premises of a V argument is false, the argument may still be strong if the other premise or premises are true. It is important, therefore, to pay careful attention to the structure of arguments.

4.6.4 Complex Arguments

The above are the three basic structures out of which more complex structures are constructed. Consider the following argument:

P1. Max was born in the US to American parents.
P2. This means that Max is an American citizen.
C. Therefore, Max can vote in federal elections.

This argument has the following structure:

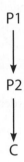

Note that the tree diagram contains two arrows. This is because the second premise is really a sub-conclusion that is supported by the first premise. In reality, there are two arguments here; P2 is the conclusion of the first argument and the premise of the second. The first argument is P1 therefore P2, and the second is P2 therefore C. The combined argument does not, however, present two separate reasons to support the conclusion, but only one. P2 presents a reason for C directly, whereas P1 presents a reason for C indirectly by providing a reason for P2.

When reconstructing an argument that has two conclusions, it is necessary to determine which is the main conclusion and which is the subordinate conclusion. Sometimes the argument makes this quite clear. When it does not, we should ask which is best regarded as a premise for the other. Taking account of all the contextual clues and the principle of charity, which of the following makes better sense of the argument?

C1 therefore C2, or
C2 therefore C1.

Consider the following argument:

City Council should approve the proposed arts center without delay, for several reasons. The need for a center has been demonstrated many times; anyone who examines the evidence will agree that existing facilities are woefully inadequate. The financial benefit to the community is harder to pin down precisely, but no one can deny that local merchants and the city's tax base will benefit. The only question is whether the city can afford to make a reasonable contribution to the annual operating costs. It is foolish to expect a consensus *on this question: after all no one likes higher taxes, no matter how worthy the cause. But the fact is that Charlottetown has a lower tax rate than most cities its size and is in excellent financial shape. And the proposed increase in taxes would amount to only $2.00 per year. It is clear, therefore, that the city can afford the arts center.*

This passage has two conclusions. The opening sentence is a conclusion, which the passage goes on to give reasons for. But the final sentence gives another conclusion. We determine which is the main conclusion by asking which of the following makes the best sense of the whole passage:

(1) City Council should approve the proposal for an arts center. Therefore, the city can afford an arts center.
(2) The city can afford an arts center. Therefore, City Council should approve the proposal for an arts center.

It is obvious that (2) makes good sense while (1) does not. This means that we should regard the opening sentence of the passage as the main conclusion. The other is a sub-conclusion or the conclusion of a subsidiary argument that has been included to support one of the premises of the main argument.

Some arguments, however, are much more complex than these examples suggest. Here is another argument with a complex structure:

P1. When the North American Free Trade Agreement was negotiated, it had the support of the President and all the governors.
P2. In several states the opposing parties voted to ratify the agreement.
P3. So politicians of both political parties across the United States strongly supported the agreement.
P4. However, the vast majority of Americans were strongly opposed to the agreement.
C. Therefore, the politicians were out of touch with the views of the people.

In this argument P1 to P3 constitutes a sub-argument: it is a V argument with P1 and P2 as premises and P3 as its conclusion. P3 is then used as a premise in a second argument: it is a T argument with P3 and P4 as premises and C as its conclusion. The tree diagram for this argument is thus a combination of a T and a V structure:

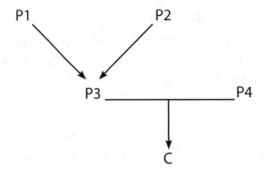

4.7 SELF-TEST NO. 10

Label the premises and conclusion and draw a tree diagram for each of the following arguments. Where appropriate, supply missing premises or conclusions.

1. Anyone who has brains and ambition will go far in this world. Carla has certainly got plenty of both, so she will go far.

2. I have never had any problems with the last four Fords I've bought, so I don't think I'll have any problems this time.

3. The Mets should win the National League pennant this year. They have solid depth in their pitching staff, their hitting has been consistently good this year, their coaching is excellent, and there is a good team spirit.

4. A recent public opinion poll showed that more than two-thirds of Canadians believe that most politicians are dishonest. Clearly, there is a crisis of confidence in Canadian politics.

5. As of 2009, 80% of Americans are graduates of high school or higher, compared with 25% in 1940 (U.S. Census Bureau, February 2012).

6. Laura gets pretty good grades, she is the best gymnast in the school, she has a lot of friends, and she organized the campaign last year that forced the school to start a recycling program. I think she will probably win the election for president of the Students' Council.

7. If he tells his teacher he cheated, he will be punished by the principal. But if he doesn't tell his teacher he cheated, he will be punished by his parents. Either way he is going to be punished.

8. Since angle CAB is 60 degrees, and angle ACB is 40 degrees, then angle ABC must be 80 degrees.

9. Any reporter who says that good reporters never slant their stories but simply report the objective facts must be either stupid or dishonest, since it is obvious that one cannot write anything without an element of interpretation creeping in....

10. ... and that reporter is obviously not stupid. He must be dishonest.

4.8 ANOTHER WARNING

People talk about all sorts of things for all sorts of reasons. Sometimes we can be fooled into interpreting something as an argument when it really isn't. Sometimes people use language that makes it appear that they are presenting an argument when they are really just expressing a strongly held opinion and not attempting to defend it with reasons. For example:

> *The press in this country seems quite uninterested in serious political discussion. Whenever an important political issue arises, such as the war in Iraq or free trade, the press seems interested only in personalities and whether the issue will hinder this party's chances of re-election, or improve that leader's public image. I think the press should take a good hard look at itself and ask whether a truly responsible press would conduct political discussions at such a juvenile level.*

Is this an argument? To answer this question we should ask whether we can, without doing violence to the author's apparent intentions, interpret it as presenting a conclusion accompanied by one or more supporting premises. Clearly, the author wants us to agree with his or her view that the press is irresponsible in its approach to serious political discussion. But it is probably unfair to the author to insist that any of the statements should be regarded as presenting a reason for this view. In fact, what is interesting about this passage is the absence of any real supporting evidence. All we are offered is the suggestion that the press ignores serious political discussion and deals only with peripheral matters, and if we regard this as a premise, it is an extremely weak one. It is much better to interpret this passage as an expression of an opinion. The principle of charity supports this interpretation, since otherwise we would have to regard the argument as a very weak one.

However, since we are sometimes entitled to supply missing premises and missing conclusions, we may be tempted to turn a non-argument into an argument by reading a great deal more into a passage than is really there. When dealing with a doubtful passage we should therefore be careful not to assume that it must be an argument, or we may find ourselves reconstructing an argument that the author never intended.

There is no simple way of determining when we are dealing with an argument and when we are not. We should remember that people do many things besides argue: they complain, express opinions, make observations, make accusations, tell stories, give illustrations, bestow praise, and so on. The principle of charity dictates caution. Common sense usually suggests the most plausible interpretation.

4.9 QUESTIONS FOR DISCUSSION

Read carefully each of the following passages, and, if you decide it is an argument, work out the best reconstruction.

1. (Background: A father is talking to his 16-year-old son.)

   It wouldn't matter if everybody in the school was going to the rock concert. The point is that you know that you shouldn't go. You promised me that if we didn't give you a curfew any more, you would ensure that every school assignment would be submitted on time. And there is no way you can finish your history essay if you go to that concert.

2. (Background: A student who has missed a mid-term approaches the instructor to ask for a make-up test.)

   I'm sorry I missed the test, but it really wasn't my fault. I went home on the weekend, and didn't get back until midnight. I studied until four in the morning, and as a result I didn't hear my alarm and missed the test. It would be really unfair if I were to be punished for something that is not my fault.

3. (Background: A letter to the editor commenting upon a recent court ruling that teaching scientific creationism in science courses in public schools is unconstitutional. Scientific creationism holds that the biblical account of creation is a legitimate scientific theory that should be taught in science courses along with the theory of evolution.)

   Your recent report on scientific creationism was very interesting and I don't disagree with anything it said, but it failed to point out the true nature of these so-called "scientific" creationists. The fact is that they are a bunch of intellectual misfits and misguided crackpots who wouldn't recognize a truly scientific theory if you hit them over the head with it. They are either lamentably ignorant, or bigots, or both.

4. (Background: Several students are discussing the US war on Iraq. One, who supported the war, is responding to the objection that the US has no right to act as a world policeman.)

But of course the US has the right to police the world. The US is one of the most powerful nations in the world; surely you don't deny that. Well, that's one of the things world powers can do. If a world power decides to act as a world cop, then it has that right.

5. (Background: A lawyer is attempting to persuade a client not to sue his doctor for malpractice.)

I understand why you feel a sense of grievance, but I don't think it is a good idea. First, you have to prove that the doctor was negligent, i.e., that he failed to provide medical care that is up to the accepted standard. And given what you've told me, I don't think we would prove that at all. After all, he did explicitly warn you that there was only a 70-per-cent chance of success. Second, a trial will be extremely stressful for your wife, since she will have to answer a lot of intimate personal questions that I'm sure she would prefer to avoid.

6. (Background: From a talk on student stress given by an educational psychologist to a group of high-school teachers.)

Finally, we come to the type of stress that is induced by the learning process itself, for example, stress that results from getting low grades, from not understanding the material, from being late with assignments, or from asking dumb questions in class. Unlike other types of stress, this type is caused by you as teachers. If you want to reduce this type of stress the solution is in your hands: develop better methods of presenting material and motivating the students to master it, make sure students don't get into courses they cannot handle, be more reasonable about accepting late assignments, and be polite to students who ask dumb questions.

7. (Background: A university student is talking to a friend about smoking marijuana.)

My mom and dad, and my older sister too, used to warn me about the evils of taking drugs. I remember the first time I went to a party where people were smoking pot; I mean, I thought I was in a den of iniquity and I left as soon as I could. But after a while you realize that there are all sorts of perfectly ordinary people walking around who smoke a bit of pot now and again. So I figure there can't be anything really wrong with it.

8. (Background: From an article entitled "Technology: Boon or Doom?")

These astonishing achievements—achievements that earlier generations could only dream of—have produced in many a faith in the limitless capacity of technology to benefit mankind. During the past two decades, however, there has been increasing evidence that this faith is unreasonable. The space shuttle disaster, the Chernobyl and Three Mile Island nuclear accidents, acid rain, and a host of other technological misfortunes have each in their own way shown that there are significant limitations to what technology can do.

9. (Background: Gord has gone to seek counsel for work and family trouble from a psychic.)

As your regular psychic, I understand exactly why you have been having a rough time lately, Gord. Your sign is Cancer, and for the last three weeks your moon has been in the house of Scorpio. Because of the tension between your sign, which is ruled by the moon, and Scorpio, which is ruled by Mars and Pluto, your entire universe is in disarray. Hence, all the trouble you're having at work and with your family is entirely predictable.

Part Three

ASSESSING ARGUMENTS

5. STRATEGIES FOR ASSESSING ARGUMENTS

We now come to the assessment of arguments. Before we consider the details of how this should be done, we need to say something about the nature of the task. Every argument, as we saw in section 1.1, supports its conclusion by making a double claim: (a) that its premises are true, and (b) that its premises support its conclusion. Whenever we assess an argument, we are really only asking whether these claims are true. An argument makes a kind of promise; assessing an argument is asking whether it can make good on its promise. A good argument is one that does what it claims to do, and a bad argument is one that fails to do what it claims to do. But how are we to tell whether an argument has made good on its promise?

Philosophers have developed two approaches for assessing arguments. The first and more traditional is the *FALLACIES APPROACH*, in which we identify all the specific fallacies (or mistakes) that an argument can make and then ask whether a given argument commits any of these fallacies. If it commits none of them, it will be a good argument, and if it commits one or more of them, it will be a bad argument. The second is the *CRITERIAL APPROACH*, in which we appeal to the criteria, or standards, that a good argument must satisfy and ask whether a given argument meets these criteria. If it meets them all, it will be a good argument, and if it fails to meet one or more of them, it will be a bad argument.

The fundamental approach of this text is criterial. It has several very important advantages over the fallacies approach, which will be noted below. Nevertheless, the fallacies approach is sometimes useful because it identifies certain common mistakes. In the following chapters we adopt the criterial approach but will introduce specific fallacies when they can help put us on our guard against certain mistakes. But first we need to discuss the two approaches in more detail.

5.1 THE FALLACIES APPROACH

The concept of a fallacy presents several theoretical difficulties for logicians that need not detain us here. For our purposes we can define a *FALLACY* as any error or weakness that detracts from the soundness of an argument yet somehow manages to disguise itself so as to give the argument the appearance of being better than it really is. For example, one traditional fallacy is the appeal to pity, as in:

Jane is a widow with three teenage children living in a two-bedroom basement apartment.
Therefore, her employer should promote her to supervisor.

Whether Jane should be promoted depends upon whether she has the qualifications and experience to be a good supervisor. The fact that she is a widow with three teenage children living in a two-bedroom basement apartment says nothing about her qualifications as a supervisor. But if someone can arouse our sympathies for Jane, we may want her to be promoted for reasons that have nothing to do with the qualifications necessary for the job. Since the pity we naturally feel is irrelevant to the question of whether she should be promoted, the appeal to pity is fallacious.

Logicians have long been fascinated by fallacies and have devoted much time and energy to identifying and explaining specific fallacy types. Aristotle listed 13 types, but modern logicians have identified approximately 150 different types. This proliferation of fallacies suggests a misleading picture of a logician as a kind of microbiologist of the intellect searching for new logical viruses.

One problem with the fallacies approach is that there is no limit to the number of ways in which an argument can be weak. The only way to limit the list of fallacies is to restrict ourselves to those errors that occur frequently. However, we still will never have a complete list of fallacy types, for there is no simple way to determine what counts as a "frequently" occurring error. Another problem is that as more and more fallacy types are identified, it has become increasingly difficult to use them effectively as the basis for assessing arguments. Not only do we have to memorize a very long list of fallacies, but we often find arguments that clearly contain a weakness but where we have difficulty in deciding which particular fallacy has been committed.

The underlying problem with the fallacies approach is that it is negative in nature. This is an especially serious problem when we are trying to develop good arguments for ourselves, rather than merely criticizing other people's arguments. Rather than telling us what we want to see in a good argument, it tells us only what we should try to avoid.

5.2 THE CRITERIAL APPROACH

The criterial approach, unlike the fallacies approach, is positive in nature. It begins by establishing the *CRITERIA* that a good argument must satisfy and then uses these criteria as the basis for assessing particular arguments. The English words *criterion* (singular) and *criteria* (plural) derive from the ancient Greek noun *kriterion*, which is a "means for judging" or a "standard of assessment." The Greek verb form with the same root is *kritikein*, which means *to judge* or *to assess*. All of these Greek words are, as you may have guessed, related to the English words *critic* and *critical*, which mean something more precise in connection to critical thinking than they do in ordinary contexts. Ordinarily, people think of a critic as a complainer, and being critical is fault-finding. However, in the context of argumentation, critical thinking has to do with being consciously aware of the general qualities that make an argument good, and assessing particular arguments on the basis of these standards, i.e., the criteria of a good argument. Criteria are like measuring sticks against which we can measure exact lengths. If we have a yardstick we can use it to measure the length of any piece of lumber. Similarly, if we know the criteria for a good argument, we can assess any argument.

The criteria we develop in this chapter refine the concept of a sound argument introduced in Chapter 1. In section 1.1 we defined a logically strong argument as one whose premises, if true, support its conclusion, and a sound argument as a logically strong argument whose premises are true. It is now time to expand on these concepts to establish the criteria for a sound argument. There are three criteria.

5.2.1 The Three Criteria of a Sound Argument

The requirement that a sound argument must have true premises is the basis for our first criterion for a sound argument. Obviously, since premises are offered as support for a conclusion, if a premise is false, then no matter how good the argument is in other respects, the premise provides no support for the conclusion.

But there is a problem here. Often we are not able to *prove* that a particular premise is true: most of us cannot actually prove, for example, that cigarette smoking is a health hazard. However, in most contexts there are reasons that justify the acceptance of such a claim, even though we cannot prove it is true. The fact that our government requires all cigarette packages to include the claim as a warning, for example, makes it reasonable for us to accept it, even though such a reason is clearly not a proof. We must therefore expand our first criterion to take account of those contexts where all that we can reasonably demand is that there be good reasons for accepting the premises. Naturally, if the truth of a premise is directly evident, then that is good for an argument. But if the truth of a premise is not directly evident, it need not be dismissed as false and we need not reject it. It may satisfy a wider standard than truth: *ACCEPTABILITY.* Our first criterion, therefore, is that the premises must be *ACCEPTABLE*. Of course, in some contexts, such as assessing mathematical proofs, the only good reason for accepting the premises will be that they can actually be proven.

Logical strength, the second requirement for a sound argument, gives rise to our second and third criteria. The second is that the premises must be relevant to the conclusion; in this case, we assess the *RELEVANCE* of each premise. We noticed in section 1.2 that an argument may have premises that are known to be true but that nevertheless fail to provide any support for its conclusion. This is what happens when the premises are not relevant to the conclusion. Clearly, if the premises of an argument are to support its conclusion, they must supply us with information that is relevant to the question, whether or not the conclusion is true. Precisely what information is relevant to the truth of a particular conclusion may sometimes be difficult to determine, but it is clear that what we are looking for is relevant information. Our second criterion, therefore, is that each individual premise should be relevant to the conclusion.

The logical strength requirement also gives rise to our third criterion, namely, that the premises must be adequate to support the conclusion. A premise may be both true and relevant to the conclusion, but it may nevertheless not be adequate to support the conclusion. *ADEQUACY* is usually (but not always, as we shall see later) a matter of degree. In most cases a true, relevant premise can provide support that ranges from very little to a great deal. Consider the following:

> *My neighbor, my wife, and all the people I work with, all of whom voted Republican in the last election, have decided to vote Democrat in the next election. Therefore, the Democrats will probably win the next election.*

The premise of this argument is obviously relevant to the conclusion, and it does provide some, albeit minimal, support for the conclusion. It is, we might say, a straw in the wind. We would be foolish to bet on the outcome of the election on the basis of this evidence. By itself, therefore, this premise is not adequate. If, however, we keep asking friends and neighbors, or better yet undertake a proper public opinion survey, we may accumulate more information that shows that large numbers of voters are switching from Republican to Democrat. If this extra information is included as additional premises, then the support provided for the conclusion is much more adequate. The third criterion, therefore, is that the premises, considered collectively, must provide adequate support for the conclusion.

Thus there are three different criteria that a sound argument must meet:

(1) The premises must be acceptable.
(2) The premises must be relevant.
(3) The premises must be adequate.

Notice how in moving from (1) to (2) to (3) the criteria become more complex. Accept-ability concerns the assessment of each premise considered on its own. The other two cri-teria ask us to assess the inference from the premise(s) to the conclusion of an argument. Relevance concerns the relationship between each individual premise, considered on its own, and the rest of the argument. And adequacy concerns the relationship between all the premises considered collectively and the conclusion. We are not entitled to pass final judgment on any argument until we have assessed it against each of these criteria. If it meets all three criteria, we should conclude that it is a sound argument. If it fails to meet any one criterion, we should regard it as a weak or defective argument.

5.3 SEVEN RULES FOR ASSESSING ARGUMENTS

At this point it will be useful to present a set of rules that should be followed when-ever an argument is being assessed. The brief comments included here are intended only to highlight points that are made elsewhere.

5.3.1 Rule 1. Identify the Main Conclusion

You may have noticed that none of the three criteria listed above asks us to assess the conclusion of an argument directly. When assessing an argument on the basis of these three criteria, we assess the conclusion indirectly by considering the evidence offered in support of it—that is, the acceptability, relevance, and adequacy of the premises. Still, even though we don't assess the conclusion directly, we must begin our assessment by identifying the conclusion. This is especially important when assessing the argument for relevance and adequacy.

The way to identify the main conclusion should be familiar by now: (1) Look for the main point of the passage, by asking, *What is the author driving at?* (2) Look for inference indicators, such as *therefore, hence, so, consequently,* and so on. (3) Pay attention to the context and background for clues as to what the argument is all about. (4) Bear in mind the principle of charity when interpreting an ambiguous conclusion or when supplying a missing conclusion. If the conclusion is difficult to elicit, it may be because we are not dealing with an argument at all. We have already come across several passages that look like arguments but should not be regarded as genuine arguments. Reports of arguments (see section 4.4.1) and forceful assertions can be especially troublesome. Remember that every argument presents a claim *and* a reason to support that claim.

5.3.2 Rule 2. Identify the Premises

The next step is to identify the premises. If the conclusion has been correctly identi-fied, the rest of the argument will include the premises. But it may also include other material, such as illustrations and examples. It may also include alternative versions of what is really a single premise. The question we should ask here is, *What information or reasons does the author provide to support the conclusion?* As always, it is important to pay attention to the context and the principle of charity when identifying the premises and when supplying missing premises.

5.3.3 Rule 3. Identify the Structure of the Argument

Once the conclusion and the premises have been identified, the structure of the argument must be identified. If the argument has a simple structure (see section 4.6.1), we can pass straight on to the critical assessment. In all other cases care should be taken to ensure that the structure of the argument has been correctly identified, if necessary by drawing a tree diagram (see section 4.6).

5.3.4 Rule 4. Check the Acceptability of the Premises

In Chapter 6 we will consider how truth-claims should be approached. Two warnings should be mentioned here. First, if the argument is intended to be a counterfactual argument (see section 1.3), it is irrelevant to ask whether the premises are true, since the author is not claiming that they are true. Second, we need to note that a false premise does not always deprive the conclusion of all support. If an argument has two independent premises, as in a V argument, the fact that one of them is false has no bearing on whether the other premise is true, and if the other premise is true, then the conclusion may still have some support.

5.3.5 Rule 5. Check the Relevance of the Premises

In Chapter 7 we will examine some common ways in which premises can seem relevant when in fact they are not. It should be stressed that the premises must be considered in context, for a premise that is irrelevant when considered by itself may have its relevance established by other premises in the argument.

5.3.6 Rule 6. Check the Adequacy of the Premises

In Chapter 8 we will examine the common ways in which premises can fail to provide adequate support for the conclusion. When assessing adequacy it is important to notice the degree of support that the argument claims is provided by the premises.

5.3.7 Rule 7. Look for Counter-Arguments

Finally, we should look for counter-arguments. Are there any reasons we can think of that would support a conclusion that is inconsistent with the conclusion of the argument being assessed? Strictly speaking, this goes beyond the assessment of a given argument, but if there is a sound counter-argument we know that the given argument must be deficient. Otherwise, we would have two sound arguments with inconsistent conclusions, which is impossible. We will discuss the role of counter-arguments in Chapter 11, Arguing Back.

6.   ASSESSING TRUTH-CLAIMS

6.1 THEORIES OF TRUTH

Pontius Pilate, before sentencing Christ to death, asked, *What is truth?* But, being a practical man, he did not stay around to debate the question. In its most general sense, the question is deeply troubling, for no one has yet been able to provide an entirely satisfactory answer. Philosophers have made numerous attempts to develop theories of truth, but all are open to plausible objections. However, our interest in truth, like Pilate's, is more practical than theoretical, so we need not delay too long over purely theoretical issues. Nevertheless, we should note the three main theories of truth, for they provide a useful background to our discussion of how truth-claims are to be assessed.

6.1.1 The Correspondence Theory

What makes a statement or belief true? (We can speak interchangeably here of beliefs or statements.) The most obvious answer is that a statement or belief is true when it corresponds to the facts. The statement *My birthday is October 22* is true if, and only if, it is a fact that I was born on October 22. The fact that I was born on October 22 is a necessary and sufficient condition for the truth of the statement *My birthday is October 22.* Anyone who is not sure whether this statement is true need only check my birth certificate. It seems reasonable, therefore, to hold that truth consists of a correspondence between a statement and a fact: that when the correspondence holds, the statement is true; and when it does not hold, the statement is false. This is the *CORRESPONDENCE THEORY OF TRUTH.*

There are a number of objections to this account of truth. The most obvious is that there are many statements that we believe to be true for which there seem to be no corresponding facts. But according to the correspondence theory, if there are no corresponding facts then we would have to conclude that these statements are false. Consider the following statements: what facts would we check to determine whether they are true?

> *There is no greatest prime number.*
> *You should keep your promises.*

God created the universe.

Bach was the greatest composer of the eighteenth century.

If Hitler had died in 1918, World War II would not have occurred.

Supporters of the correspondence theory have developed some ingenious strategies to overcome this objection. Some have held that there really are facts that correspond to these statements. They claim that there are mathematical facts, moral facts, etc. But these are not ordinary facts since they are not accessible to us in the way that facts about my birthday are, so the introduction of these special kinds of facts solves nothing. (There are, however, many philosophers who accept the existence of evaluative facts, but we need not pause over this interesting theoretical controversy.) Others have argued that some or all of these statements are not really true or false at all. They hold that when we say that you ought to keep your promises, we are expressing an attitude and that it is a mistake to regard our statement as making a truth-claim.

Despite this difficulty, the correspondence theory is a powerful account of one kind of truth. Sometimes the truth of a statement or belief does consist of a correspondence between the statement and certain facts. Whenever a statement makes a factual assertion, then, as long as there are facts that could be checked to determine whether they are as the statement claims they are, we can use the correspondence between the statement and the facts as our criterion of truth. But when a statement makes a non-factual assertion, or asserts a fact that is non-checkable, we cannot use correspondence as a criterion of truth.

The notion of checkable facts is important and needs some elucidation. We can only check facts, either directly or indirectly, by making observations. This is another way of saying that the fact must be empirical. An *EMPIRICAL FACT* is a fact that is observable in principle, that is, it could be observed if we could get ourselves into the right place at the right time. The notion of an empirical fact allows us to define an *EMPIRICAL STATEMENT* as a statement that asserts an empirical fact (or set of empirical facts). The correspondence theory of truth, therefore, provides an appropriate criterion of truth for empirical statements. And since the world around us consists, by and large, of empirical facts, the correspondence theory is an appropriate criterion for our knowledge of the external, observable world.

6.1.2 The Coherence Theory

But the critics have a second objection to the correspondence theory. Besides claiming that it is inadequate as a criterion for non-empirical statements, they also object that it is inadequate even for empirical statements. They point out that the theory presents us with two distinct and separate worlds: the world of facts and the world of statements and beliefs. Its claim that truth consists of a correspondence between empirical facts and statements or beliefs requires that the world of facts must be *brute* facts, or facts that are independent of our beliefs about them. Otherwise, we could not compare the facts with our beliefs about them in order to see whether they correspond. But, the critics ask, how can we know anything at all about the world of facts, since as soon as we turn to the facts the only thing we can obtain is yet another belief about the facts? We can never, it seems, have any knowledge of such brute facts, for we can never get beyond our *beliefs* about them. Brute facts presumably exist, but we can never know them directly. The very act of recognizing or knowing that something is a fact necessarily involves an element of selection and interpretation. Facts, as many philosophers of science claim, are never brute but are always constituted by a presupposed theory of what exists and what we should focus on when making observations. The empirical facts upon which correspondence theorists rely, therefore, presuppose that some theory or interpretation is already true, which means that the correspondence theory not only fails to provide a criterion of truth but presupposes some other criterion of truth.

This objection has led the critics to propose the *COHERENCE THEORY OF TRUTH*, according to which truth is defined by reference to the reasons we have for believing something to be true. When we consider whether any particular belief is true, we appeal to reasons, but these reasons are themselves beliefs. The only things available to us as justifications for believing something to be true are other beliefs. A particular belief, therefore, may be regarded as true when it is part of a coherent set of mutually supported beliefs. To show that any belief is true we appeal to our other beliefs: if it can be supported by some of them and is not inconsistent with the rest, we are entitled to regard it as true. But if it is inconsistent with one or more of our other beliefs, then one of the inconsistent beliefs has to be rejected, since we cannot simultaneously hold two inconsistent beliefs. In short, according to the coherence theory of truth, a belief or statement is true if, and only if, it coheres with a system of beliefs or statements.

Where do the beliefs that make up this system come from? They come from our experience. Some beliefs impress themselves upon us very strongly (for example, that you are now reading a book) while others seem less secure (for example, that you spent New Year's Eve, 2004, with your cousin). But the question whether any of these beliefs is true is not to be answered by looking at their source; this is the error made by correspondence theorists. Rather it is to be answered by appeal to other beliefs. Ultimately, the only test of truth lies in the appeal to the coherence of our beliefs.

The issue between correspondence and coherence theorists is quite theoretical and abstract, and we will not attempt to resolve it here. Since our interest is essentially practical, however, we should note that the coherence theory is strongest precisely where the correspondence theory is weakest—when dealing with non-empirical statements. Consider again the examples of non-empirical statements given in section 6.1.1. It seems obvious to some philosophers that we can deal with the question of their truth or falsity only in the way the coherence theory suggests. The coherence theory, therefore, seems to be an appropriate criterion of truth only for non-empirical sentences.

6.1.3 The Pragmatic Theory

Some philosophers reject both these theories on the ground that they ignore the problem-solving function of human beliefs. They argue that all human activity, including thinking and using language, arises from our need to solve problems. This is true at the level of the human species: humans would never have learned to notice colors if, for example, colors were not helpful in deciding when fruit is ripe enough to eat. It is also true at the individual level: we learn the multiplication table because it is useful in figuring out how much wallpaper to buy to paper a room. Since thought and language are essentially problem-solving tools, they argue, truth should be thought of as a property of beliefs or statements that can actually solve problems. A true statement or belief is one that is useful in solving a problem.

Not all the problems we face are practical problems, but the pragmatic theory is not limited to practical problems. Any real problem can give rise to a true solution. To understand what a real problem is, we have to ask the following sorts of questions. Why do we want to know whether World War II would not have occurred had Hitler died in 1918? What difference would it make if this claim were true rather than false? What would we do differently if we knew it were true? Such questions force us to reflect upon what the solution is needed for. For pragmatic theorists a problem is a real problem only if we have to solve it in order to go on to do something else. Otherwise it is only a pseudo-problem, one that makes no difference to anything. Thus, for the *PRAGMATIC THEORY OF TRUTH* a statement or belief is true if, and only if, it leads to the successful solution of a real problem.

One basic objection raised against the pragmatic theory is that many beliefs that we are quite certain of cannot be regarded as solutions to problems. Mathematicians are quite certain that there is no greatest prime number because they are certain that they have a valid proof, although they would be hard pressed to say what the real problem is to which their belief is a solution. We can be reasonably sure that

Caesar crossed the Rubicon in 49 BCE, even though this is unlikely to help in the solution of any real problem. At a more mundane level, it can be proven that when people hiccup, air travels through their windpipes at speeds of up to 97 miles per hour, but for what conceivable problem could this be a solution?

A rather different objection arises when we look at other types of problems. What problem is the belief in God's existence intended to solve? Suppose we say that the problem is how to find solace in a vast universe that seems to have no purpose? If, as is usually the case, belief in God does provide this kind of comfort, then we would have to conclude that a belief in God is true. But this puts the cart before the horse. Doesn't the belief in God have to exist *before* it can provide solace? Would the argument that belief in God provides spiritual solace to believers prove to an atheist that God actually exists? Surely not.

Critics of the pragmatic theory argue that while there is a connection between truth and problem solving, it cannot be as close as the pragmatic theory claims. It is true that when we act on the basis of true beliefs, our actions are much more likely to be successful than when we act on the basis of false beliefs. But it is a mistake to conclude that every belief that leads to a successful action must therefore be true. Consider the following situation:

> *I believe (a) that there is only enough gas in my car to drive 300 kilometers, and (b) that it is 250 kilometers from Guelph to Parry Sound. On this basis I conclude that I can drive to Parry Sound without refueling.*

Clearly if both (a) and (b) are true, I will be able to drive to Parry Sound without refueling. But (a) or (b), or both, may be false, and yet I may still get to Parry Sound without refueling. Suppose that (a) is false because there is really enough gas in my car to drive 400 kilometers; in this case if (b) is true, I will still be able to drive to Parry Sound without refueling. Or suppose that (b) is false because it is really 285 kilometers to Parry Sound; in this case if (a) is true, I will still get to Parry Sound without refueling. Or suppose both (a) and (b) are false, because I really have only enough gas to drive 250 kilometers, and because it is really only 225 kilometers to Parry Sound; in this case I will still get to Parry Sound without refueling. So false beliefs do not necessarily lead to unsuccessful actions.

It is also a mistake to hold that every belief that leads to unsuccessful actions must therefore be false. Many medical researchers have dedicated years to searching for the causes of cancer, although as yet none has been entirely successful. They all believe that cancer does have causes, that is, that it is not a purely spontaneous or uncaused phenomenon. This belief is one of the factors that has led them to conduct their unsuccessful research. Does this mean that their belief is false? Surely not.

The weakness of the pragmatic theory can also be seen when we consider what we have to do in order to tell whether a problem has actually been solved. To know whether we have solved a problem, we have to appeal either to empirical facts (as the correspondence theory tells us to do) or to reasons (as the coherence theory tells us to do). The empirical facts tell me whether or not I drove to Parry Sound without refueling, and reasons tell me whether I have really solved a mathematical equation. So, far from being a theory of truth, the pragmatic theory actually presupposes the two other theories of truth.

6.2 TYPES OF TRUTH-CLAIMS

Every statement can be regarded as making a claim to be true or, in other words, as making a truth-claim. The process of determining whether or not a truth-claim is true is called *VERIFICATION*. If we can show that a truth-claim is true, it has been verified; if we can show that it is false, it has been *FALSIFIED*. (Sometimes, of course, we can do neither, so the truth of the claim remains *UNDETERMINED*.) The method of verification we use depends upon the type of truth-claim being made. There are two main types of truth-claims, the empirical and the non-empirical. The first step in verifying any truth-claim should always be to decide which of these two types of claim we are dealing with. The simplest procedure is to begin with the question, *Is this an empirical claim?*

6.2.1 Empirical Truth-Claims

In section 6.1.1 we defined an empirical fact as a fact that could be checked, i.e., a fact that is observable in principle. Thus, when we want to verify an empirical truth-claim, we must be prepared to do the appropriate checking. Consider the following:

> *My car won't start.*
> *Jim has shaved off his moustache.*
> *The library owns a first edition of Fielding's* Tom Jones.

These are empirical statements because we can attempt to verify them by checking the relevant facts. If you doubt my claim that my car won't start, you can check it by trying to start the car yourself; if you cannot start it, then you will agree with my claim, and if you can, then you will have proven that my claim was false. If you doubt the claim that Jim has shaved off his moustache, all you need to do is look at him and you will know whether it is true or false. Finally, let us use the last example to make one further point. For you can check whether the library owns a first edition of Fielding's *Tom Jones* by (a) looking on the appropriate shelf or (b) consulting the catalogue; in the case of (a) the fact is directly verified, and in the case of (b) it is indirectly verified. Indirect verification is strong evidence in favor of the statement, whereas direct verification is conclusive.

However, not all empirical claims can be verified as easily as these: some are more difficult to deal with. Statements about the past or about the future rest only indirectly on the empirical facts that support them. For example:

> *Caesar crossed the Rubicon in 49 BCE.*
> *Sebastian first ran a four-minute mile five years ago when he was still in high school.*
> *Audrey will win the gold medal in physics next year.*
> *It will rain tomorrow.*

It is obvious that the empirical facts that would directly verify or falsify these statements are not available to us. For statements about the past, we have to rely on records and memories. For statements about the future, we have to use empirical evidence about the past and present that makes the predicted event likely to occur. Of course, we could wait and see whether the predicted event actually occurs, in which case we would have direct empirical support.

Our examples so far have been of particular empirical statements, that is, statements about particular empirical facts. Sometimes, however, we have to deal with statements about *classes* of objects or events. These are called *GENERAL EMPIRICAL STATEMENTS* and have to be approached somewhat differently because they usually make a claim that goes beyond the available empirical evidence. There are two types of general empirical statements. The first are *STATISTICAL EMPIRICAL STATEMENTS*, which make claims about some, or a certain proportion, of a class of objects or events. For example:

> *A majority of Canadians support the use of capital punishment.*
> *Ninety per cent of snapping turtles do not survive the first three months of life.*

These claims would be impossible to check if we had to do a survey of the entire population of Canada and every snapping turtle in the world. However, there is a procedure—called inductive generalization—that can provide us with an empirical basis for statistical statements. It allows us to use a representative sample of a class as an empirical basis for making statements about the entire class. Public opinion polls, for example, work on this basis. We will examine this procedure in detail in section 10.2.

The second type of general empirical statement consists of *UNIVERSAL EMPIR-ICAL STATEMENTS*, or statements about *every* member of some class. These are even more difficult to check. Consider the following:

All swans are white.

This is a statement about all swans, and, like statistical empirical statements, it too makes a claim that goes far beyond any available empirical evidence. But there is an important difference between statistical and universal empirical statements that allows us to approach universal statements differently: universal empirical statements can be refuted by a single exception. If we can find one swan that is not white, the universal statement must be false. In other words, even though we cannot verify the statement, we can falsify it on the basis of empirical evidence. This suggests a procedure for dealing with universal empirical statements that gives them a secure empirical basis. If we make a systematic attempt to find exceptions to some universal empirical statement and nevertheless fail to find any, we are entitled to assert that it is true. But since this procedure does not rest upon direct empirical evidence, we must always regard universal empirical statements as tentative. They are tentative because we will never be in a position to rule out the possibility of finding an exception. In principle, they can never be verified as conclusively as particular empirical claims in the present tense, but can only be imperfectly verified (though they can be conclusively falsified).

When gathering empirical evidence, we must be careful not to misinterpret it. Since empirical evidence rests upon observation, it can sometimes be misinterpreted in ways we are unaware of. An object that looks blue under artificial light may look green in natural light. Railway tracks really do look as if they come together in the distance. Sometimes we misinterpret our observations because we have not observed carefully enough. We think the bowl contains sugar because it looks like sugar, but had we tasted it, we would have realized it is salt. We will later look at certain ways in which empirical facts can be misinterpreted, but in general there are no rules that will prevent us from misinterpreting empirical evidence except for the injunction to be careful.

All the various types of empirical statements rest, one way or another, on empirical facts. To decide whether a statement is an empirical statement, we must ask whether there could be empirical evidence that would verify or falsify it. If there could be such empirical evidence, then it is an empirical statement, and all that remains is for us to do our best to obtain this empirical evidence. On the other hand, a statement that could never be verified or falsified by empirical evidence must be non-empirical.

6.2.2 Non-Empirical Truth-Claims

We now turn to non-empirical statements. Non-empirical statements are identified by the fact that empirical evidence would not be sufficient to verify or falsify them. Consider:

The government should provide free day-care programs.

What empirical facts could possibly show that this statement is true or false? It is an empirical fact that many people believe that the government should provide free day-care programs, but this clearly doesn't show that the statement is true. Nor does the fact that many people believe that the government should not provide free day-care programs show that the statement is false. It might be an empirical fact that an enlightened government promised it would provide free day-care programs, but by itself this doesn't show that the statement is true; to do so it would have to be assumed that governments should keep their promises, and *this* is not an empirical fact. It is impossible to specify any empirical evidence that would be sufficient to show the statement to be true or false, so we must conclude that it is a non-empirical statement.

How then are we to assess whether non-empirical statements are true or false? According to the coherence theory of truth we have to look not to the empirical facts but to other beliefs we have that are secure enough to serve as justifying reasons. What these justifying reasons will be depends upon the nature of the non-empirical statement we want to verify. If we want to verify the mathematical statement that the square of the hypotenuse of a right-angle triangle is equal to the sum of the squares of the other two sides, we have to work out the mathematical proof. It is not sufficient to draw several right-angled triangles and then measure their sides: mathematics teachers won't let us get away with this maneuver since it uses empirical evidence where a proof is required. If we wish to verify a moral statement like the one in the preceding paragraph, we must appeal to some general moral principle that is secure enough to justify it. We might, for example, appeal to the principle that governments ought to respond to the wishes of the majority of the voters, and this, along with the empirical claim that a majority of voters wants free day-care programs, would be sufficient to justify the moral claim. In short, to the extent that non-empirical statements can be assessed, they are verified or falsified by appealing to other non-empirical statements (sometimes in combination with empirical statements) that can serve as justifying reasons.

There are several different types of non-empirical statements. Analytic and contradictory statements (see section 3.4) are clearly non-empirical: once we know what they mean, we can determine their truth or falsity without reference to any empirical facts. Ethical statements, like the example above, are non-empirical. So too are aesthetic statements. For example:

J.S. Bach is the greatest composer of the eighteenth century.

Any empirical evidence about Bach's music and the music of his contemporaries is not going to be sufficient to show whether this claim is true or false.

Most religious statements are non-empirical as well. For example:

God is eternal and unchanging.

It is clear that there could not be any empirical evidence that we can appeal to that would be sufficient to determine whether this claim is true or false. It is, most theologians believe, something that must be accepted on faith, although some would regard it as analytic. For all such statements, determining whether they are true or false depends not on empirical evidence but on the strength of the justifying reasons we can provide.

Not every statement in an ethical, aesthetic, or religious work is non-empirical, for sometimes these works make claims that can be supported by empirical evidence. For example:

People who are treated unjustly feel entitled to compensation or retaliation.
Of all Dickens's novels, Pickwick Papers *relies most extensively on the use of caricatures.*
Jesus Christ was crucified by Roman soldiers.

Each of these statements is empirical, because empirical facts are sufficient to determine their truth or falsity. Sometimes, however, it is difficult to tell whether statements are empirical or non-empirical. For example:

In democratic countries, citizens have a duty to vote.
All music must have a recognizable rhythm.
God created the world.

These are difficult statements to deal with precisely because it is difficult to know how to determine whether they are true or false. If we regard them as empirical, we need to look for the appropriate empirical evidence; if we regard them as non-empirical, we need to look for non-empirical justifying reasons. Each of these statements can plausibly be interpreted in both ways, so whether we should regard them as empirical or non-empirical will depend upon what we think is the most reasonable interpretation of them. Ultimately, it is up to anyone who makes such claims to interpret them in one way or the other. It is, after all, the speaker who should be the final arbiter of what he or she means.

Finally, we should mention an important class of non-empirical statements consisting of what might be called *FOUNDATIONAL PRINCIPLES*. These are principles that lie at the basis of all knowledge claims, including empirical claims. Consider what is sometimes called the Law of Causality:

> *Every event must have a cause.*

Unlike most scientific laws, the Law of Causality is not an empirical law. It is a presupposition that underlies all science and all common sense as well. How we are to show that the Law of Causality is true is a difficult philosophical question about which there are different and conflicting theories.

Many foundational principles are not as secure as the Law of Causality. We saw in section 6.1 that there are at least three plausible theories of truth. These theories express alternative foundational principles about the nature of truth, all of which are non-empirical in nature. Most foundational principles are like this: there is agreement that some foundational principle is needed but disagreement on precisely what it is. Some foundational principles are subject to even deeper disagreement. The statement that God exists is a foundational principle for those who believe in God but is a principle that atheists reject altogether.

6.3 ACCEPTABILITY

In section 5.2 we noted that it is not always appropriate to demand that truth-claims be *proven*. Conclusive proofs are often hard to come by, and if we were not entitled to make assertions unless we could prove them, we would have a great deal less to say. Fortunately, we do not need to insist on a proof for every truth-claim we make. The first question we need to ask about a truth-claim is not *Can it be proven?* but *Are we justified in accepting it?* Sometimes, indeed, we do need a proof in order to be justified in accepting a truth-claim, but usually proofs are not needed. In fact, there are varying standards of acceptability, depending upon the nature of the statement and the context in which it is made.

The most stringent standard of acceptability is that of a *STRICT PROOF*. There are in fact two types of strict proofs, depending upon whether the statement is empirical or non-empirical. In section 6.2 we saw how empirical statements rest on empirical evidence in various ways. An empirical proof is one in which the empirical evidence is subjected to scrutiny designed to eliminate as far as possible any error. The evidence is, as it were, cross-examined. Is the evidence available to any normal observer? Does it avoid questionable interpretations? Have alternative explanations been refuted? Only when these questions have been answered satisfactorily are we entitled to regard empirical evidence as constituting a proof.

Non-empirical statements, we saw, rest on justifying reasons rather than on empirical evidence. A non-empirical proof, therefore, is an argument in which the premises are shown to be true and whose conclusion follows necessarily from them. Of course, showing that the premises of the proof are true requires another proof of the same sort, which in turn requires yet another proof. If we are to avoid an infinite regress we must ultimately reach premises that we are entitled to assert in the absence of proof. In other words, the premises from which a non-empirical proof is derived must ultimately be statements whose truth we can be quite certain of without proof. There are profound philosophical difficulties about the notion of statements whose truth is certain but not provable, which need not detain us here. It is sufficient for our purposes that there are premises that seem certain to us even though we cannot prove them. The best examples of non-empirical proofs are found in mathematics, for in mathematics we typically begin from premises that are known to be true and deduce conclusions that follow necessarily from them.

Strict proofs, of either the empirical or non-empirical sort, are only rarely called for. In most contexts it is irrelevant and a waste of time to demand, or to attempt to provide, a strict proof for every truth-claim. In other words, it is often reasonable to demand or provide less stringent support for our claims. When is it appropriate to look for strict proofs, and when is it not? The answer depends upon the context in which the claim is made. Suppose someone claims that a low-cholesterol diet reduces the chances of a heart attack. What can we demand of the speaker in order to show that the claim is acceptable? If it is made in the context of a discussion among people who are only interested in a healthy diet for themselves and their families, it would be sufficient to defend the claim by referring to what doctors and nutritionists commonly say or are reported as saying in magazine articles. But if the claim is made by a professor who is giving a university course on nutrition, we should demand better evidence. If the professor defends the claim by saying,

> *Well, a lot of nutritionists say that a low-cholesterol diet reduces the chance of heart attack, and besides there was an article in a recent issue of* Reader's Digest *that says so,*

we would suspect the competence of the professor. The claim ought to be defended by citing research that has been generally accepted by qualified nutritionists. Finally, if the claim is made by the researcher who conducted the research, we should not allow that researcher simply to refer to his or her own published articles on the subject but should expect a defense of the research itself.

Deciding what kind of support is required by the context is largely a matter of common sense. Unfortunately, most of us have a tendency to accept or reject claims too readily because we fail to pay attention to the context. We should use our common sense to answer the question *What is the appropriate defense for this claim in this context?* but should be cautious about using our common sense to answer the question *Is this claim true?* In the latter case we have a tendency to make one of two errors. If we want to believe something, we tend to ignore the context if it requires a stronger defense than we can easily provide. On the other hand, if we want to reject something, we tend to ignore the context and demand a strict proof where such a demand is not warranted.

In some contexts there are statements that are a matter of common knowledge and for which it is quite unnecessary to require a defense. Consider the following:

> *The US has 50 states.*
> *Christmas day is December 25.*
> *Snow melts when the temperature is above freezing.*
> *Shakespeare wrote* Hamlet.

In most contexts such statements will be common knowledge among all those involved in a discussion, and any demand that they be defended will be inappropriate. When used as premises in arguments, they will be acceptable, even though we might find it difficult to defend them. If we are challenged to defend them, we should first attempt to discover the reason for the challenge, for this will tell us what kind of defense is needed. It may be sufficient merely to check an encyclopedia, if, for example, the challenger is obviously ignorant of the common view. But it is possible that the challenger may require a more thorough defense. There are people who believe that many of the plays usually attributed to Shakespeare were in fact written by Francis Bacon; if this is the reason for the challenge, we should be prepared to admit that we may be wrong and that a great deal of careful analysis and argument would be needed to settle the issue. The idea of common knowledge is a relative term that depends upon the shared assumptions of a community or group. If some item of our common knowledge is challenged, we should be prepared either to defend it or to concede that there is a possibility that we are mistaken.

Let us consider some examples of statements where the kind of defense required depends upon the context and purpose of the argument:

> *Christ died on the cross for our sins.*

If said by a preacher in a sermon or by a theology student in a course on New Testament theology, this statement would be accepted because it has a biblical source. But if said in an ethics or philosophy course, it could not adequately be defended by appeal to the Bible.

> *The Republican Party lost the 2008 federal election because it ran on a platform of continuing the war in Iraq indefinitely.*

If said by a student in a history essay, this claim would be acceptable if it could be supported by the textbook for the course. If said by a historian, it should be supported by historical documents and analysis of the evidence.

> *Smith is guilty of first-degree murder.*

If said by a member of the jury while attempting to reach a verdict, this should be supported by a very careful assessment of the evidence presented in court. If said by someone after the trial, it should be supported by newspaper accounts of the verdict.

To decide whether or not a statement is acceptable, then, we should proceed as follows:

(1) If the statement is common knowledge, we should regard it as acceptable, unless the context requires a higher standard of proof.

(2) If the statement is not common knowledge, we should ask for, or be prepared to offer, the evidence upon which it is based, and accept it only if the evidence meets the appropriate standard, for example, personal experience, appeal to a recognized authority, or strict proof.

It is important to remember, however, that whenever we rely upon anything less than a strict proof, there is a possibility that a truth-claim may turn out to be false. All the weaker standards of acceptability presuppose that a strict proof could be found if we were to take the trouble to look for it or to work one out for ourselves, and this is a presupposition that may turn out to be false. History is littered with discarded "truths" that were once believed to be true in the absence of a strict proof. We should not forget this lesson.

6.4 SELF-TEST NO. 11
Which of the following are empirical claims?

1. The Democrats won the last election for Governor of Massachusetts.

2. My children are hoping for a white Christmas this year.

3. St. Paul's Cathedral in London is one of the great architectural achievements of Western civilization.

4. Human beings will not survive the destruction of the ozone layer.

5. The sum of the interior angles of a triangle is 180 degrees.

6. If the Toronto Maple Leafs win the Stanley Cup this year, I'll eat my hat.

7. If the US government ever succeeds in eliminating the federal debt, there will be a substantial reduction in taxes.

8. Paula won the prize last year for the best student in the school.

9. It is a sad reflection upon our society that suicide rates are highest around Christmas.

10. The illegal killing of elephants in Africa has been significantly reduced by the international ban on the sale of ivory.

11. Three out of four people make up 75 per cent of the population.

12. According to the American Academy of Motion Picture Arts and Sciences, *Titanic* was the best picture of 1997.

6.5 QUESTIONS FOR DISCUSSION
The following statements require some analysis and interpretation in order to determine whether they are empirical claims. Several contain both empirical and non-empirical claims that must be carefully distinguished.

1. Christians believe that the Bible is the word of God.

2. The human race was not created by God, but evolved from lower forms of life.

3. Everyone has a conscience, even those who deny it.

4. You should apologize to Miss Rothwell as soon as possible.

5. Every society has the values that are most appropriate for that society.

6. I know that President Gorbachev was very unpopular in the former Soviet Union, but you really have to admire him for bringing about the end of communism in what was one of the largest countries in the world.

7. I absolutely adore Toni Morrison's novels.

8. Science explains why things happen.

9. People who believe in God generally lead happier lives than atheists.

10. The fact that suicide rates are highest around Christmas is a sad reflection upon the failure of our society to deal with the breakdown of the family structure.

11. The game would have gone into overtime, if LeBron James hadn't scored on a three-point shot at the final buzzer.

6.6 ASSESSING THE ACCEPTABILITY OF PREMISES

Clearly, an argument with one or more unacceptable premises suffers from a major defect. Since the function of premises in an argument is to provide support for the conclusion, if the premises are unacceptable, then the argument provides no support for its conclusion. Such an argument fails to meet the first of our three criteria for a sound argument. Whenever we have reason to think that a premise lacks appropriate support, we can charge the argument with failing to meet the first criterion. To back up the charge, however, we must be able to state our reasons for claiming that it lacks the appropriate support.

In section 6.3 we examined what we need to do to determine whether a statement is acceptable. When a statement functions as a premise in an argument, we should approach the question of its acceptability in the same manner. Sometimes we know that a premise is false and can easily refute it. But often we are skeptical of the truth of an opponent's premise without being able to refute it. For example:

> P1. Potential murderers would be less likely to commit murder if they knew they would be executed if they were caught.
> P2. We should do whatever will reduce the number of murders.
> C. Therefore, we should support the retention of the death penalty.

In this example, P1 cannot be defended on the ground that it is common knowledge. Anyone who has followed the debate on capital punishment will be aware that many people who have examined the statistical evidence believe that it shows that P1 is false. Even if we are not familiar with this evidence ourselves, we should at least ask the speaker to produce the evidence he or she believes supports P1. In this case the evidence will be empirical and will consist of facts about the frequency of murders in countries where murderers are normally executed as compared to the frequency of murders in countries where murderers are not executed. If the evidence produced does not seem to be solid and accurate, we should charge the argument with violating our first criterion. Any good reason for thinking that a premise is unacceptable entitles us to raise this objection.

So the application of the first criterion for a sound argument is simply a matter of asking whether each of the premises is acceptable, and we do this using the approach outlined in section 6.3. We should always begin by deciding which of the various standards of acceptability we should use, and this, as we saw, should be decided on the basis of the context. In fact, the argument itself provides important information about the context that is usually helpful in deciding which standard of acceptability we should use.

6.7 SOME PARTICULAR FALLACIES

We now turn to four particular fallacies that describe special kinds of unacceptable premises. The first two—begging the question and inconsistency—are important because they identify arguments where it is unnecessary even to ask whether their premises are acceptable. The other two—equivocation and false dichotomy—are easy to commit and often difficult to spot if we are not on our guard, and deserve special mention for this reason.

6.7.1 Begging the Question

An argument *BEGS THE QUESTION* when its premises presuppose, directly or indirectly, the truth of its conclusion. An argument of this sort obviously fails to support its conclusion, since any reason we might have for doubting the conclusion will obviously also lead us to doubt any premises that presuppose it. The function of the premises of an argument is to support the conclusion, and if we have to accept the truth of the conclusion in order to accept the premises, then obviously the premises have failed to do their job. The argument actually presupposes what it is supposed to prove. Begging the question is sometimes referred to by its Latin name: *petitio principii*. Many people nowadays use the phrase *beg the question* to mean *raise the question.* This was originally a mistake, but by now it has achieved such wide currency as to be found acceptable by many authorities. But careful language users (and logicians) stick to the original meaning of the phrase.

Begging the question typically arises when we want to defend some claim, yet have difficulty in finding reasons that will persuade others of its truth. For example:

> *We can be certain that [C] Lance never cheated to win a race in his entire career, because [P] he never once circumvented rules designed to ensure fair play by all the competitors.*

The conclusion of this argument may be true, but the evidence offered by the argument does not support it because P presupposes that he never cheated. Only someone who already accepts the conclusion would be able to accept that premise. It takes a minute to detect the fallacy, because the wording is different in the premise and the conclusion; however, in most contexts, "cheating" may be defined as "circumventing rules designed to ensure fair play by all the competitors." We are especially prone to beg the question when we want to defend a conviction that we hold strongly but for which we have trouble finding reasons. For example:

> *Morality is very important, because without it people would not behave according to moral principles.*

We are even more likely to beg the question when we are challenged by a skeptical opponent to defend an important claim. For example:

> North: *I believe I was justified in lying to Congress because I was doing so in order to protect the national interest.*
> South: *How can you defend such a position?*
> North: *Because a good citizen should always protect the national interest even if they have to tell lies to do so.*

Notice that North's second statement (the premise) is roughly equivalent to the first statement (the conclusion). Anyone who is unwilling to accept North's conclusion will obviously be equally unwilling to accept North's premise. Perhaps telling lies to protect the national interest is justified, but the argument fails to show this because it begs the question.

A somewhat more complex way of begging the question is when we use premises that are clearly different from the conclusion and thus do not beg the question directly, but that are themselves defended by other premises that presuppose the truth of the original conclusion. For example:

> East: *I deserve a larger salary than you because as sales manager my job is more important to the company.*
> West: *I dispute that. As production supervisor my job is just as important as yours.*
> East: *No it isn't. My job is more important because I get paid more than you.*

East is arguing in a circle: *A therefore B, and B therefore A*. Notice that neither of East's two arguments begs the question when considered in isolation from the other. It is only when they are taken together that they beg the question.

6.7.2 Inconsistency

The fallacy of *INCONSISTENCY* arises when an argument contains, implicitly or explicitly, a contradiction, usually between two premises. In section 3.4 we defined a contradictory statement as one that is false by definition. The kind of contradiction we are now referring to is that where two statements, neither of which is contradictory on its own, create a contradiction when they are asserted together. For example, consider the following statements:

> *Mary is older than Gord.*
> *Gord is older than Mary.*

Neither statement by itself is a contradiction, but asserting them together amounts to saying,

> *Mary is older than Gord and Gord is older than Mary.*

Since this is a contradiction, we know that it must be false without having to check the facts. We may not know which of the contradiction's components is false, but we know that one of them must be. Clearly, any argument that includes a contradiction must fail to provide support for its conclusion.

Arguing from a blatant inconsistency is not common, doubtless because even the most irrational person can see that an argument with contradictory premises is not going to succeed. We sometimes get carried away and contradict ourselves when under pressure, but usually the contradiction is implicit. Some parents will recognize the following:

Son: *Dad, I'm going over to the park for my football practice.*
Father: *Son, you missed school today and were excused from raking leaves for being sick.*
Son: *Oh, I can play football. I feel better now.*
Father: *Well, then you must rake the leaves and catch up on your missed school work first.*
Son: *But, dad, you know I can't do anything strenuous when I'm sick.*

The son argues (a) that he feels well enough for football practice, and (b) that he is not feeling well enough to do chores or school work. Assuming that football is more strenuous than leaf raking and homework, (a) and (b) are inconsistent. It's easy to imagine the son making the last remark as a joke, and in fact inconsistency is often used in humor. Consider this old joke about a couple on an all-inclusive vacation cruise:

Wife: *The food they serve on this ship is so awful it's inedible.*
Husband: *I agree entirely. And the portions are too small.*

Recognizing the husband's inconsistency is essential for catching the humor here: on the one hand, the husband agrees that the food is inedible, but on the other hand, he wants to eat more of it. If we read "inedible" literally, it's humorous because it's fallacious.

In serious contexts, however, the fallacy of inconsistency usually arises when the contradiction is implicit rather than explicit. In these cases we need to make the contradiction explicit by showing how it arises. For example:

There are three reasons why the free trade agreement with the US is bad for Canada. First, open competition has created a significant increase in unemployment and will eventually produce a drastic reduction in the GNP as more and more branch plants are closed by their American owners and Canadian industries are driven into bankruptcy. Second, we are under continual pressure to dismantle social programs such as medicare and family allowances, which the Americans regard as "unfair" subsidies to industry. Third, all the new wealth that is being created in Canada is concentrated in the hands of a prosperous middle class while the workers become poorer.

Now, it certainly seems that the first and third reasons are inconsistent with each other. The first predicts *a drastic reduction in the GNP* while the third admits that *new wealth is being created*. Are these two claims really inconsistent? The principle of charity would require us to give the speaker a chance to explain, or explain away, the apparent inconsistency, but in the absence of a convincing explanation, we can charge the argument with committing the fallacy of inconsistency because it relies on inconsistent premises.

A more common type of inconsistency in argument is between what someone says in the course of an argument and other relevant things they have said on other occasions. For example:

> Jock: *The city cannot afford a performing arts center. Taxes are already too high and cause hardship for many ordinary people.*
> Art: *Wait a minute. Last year you made a presentation to City Council in support of a proposal to build another hockey arena, and that would have cost even more than a performing arts center. Fortunately, the Council turned down that proposal.*

Art's charge is that Jock has presented two arguments dealing with the same subject (i.e., city taxes) that contain inconsistent premises. In the argument above, Jock has used the premise that taxes are too high, while in his earlier argument he used the premise (or perhaps presupposed as a missing premise) that taxes are not too high. But this by itself does not entitle Art to charge Jock with the fallacy of inconsistency. Because the inconsistency arises between two arguments presented at different times, Art must allow for the possibility that Jock has changed his mind. Jock might respond to the charge by saying that since last year he has reconsidered his position and now thinks that his earlier argument was unsound because it used a premise he now believes is false. If Jock takes this line, then Art's charge of inconsistency will fail. Of course, Jock may be only pretending to have changed his mind in order to avoid having to respond to Art's charge. In this case Jock will have avoided the charge of inconsistency at the price of being a hypocrite.

There is another type of hypocrisy, however, that can give rise to the charge of inconsistency. This is where the inconsistency is between what someone says and what he or she does, that is, between words and actions. For example:

> Mary: *I'm just appalled at my sister-in-law. She had an affair and then when my brother found out, she expected him to forgive her. That sort of thing is unforgivable, and I think he should leave her. It would be good riddance to bad rubbish.*
> Francine: *Cool it, Mary. I know about the little extramarital fling you had a couple of years ago, and when your husband found out, you were grateful when he forgave you.*

Francine's accusation of hypocrisy is probably justified, assuming she has her facts right. Mary's premise is that an extramarital affair should not be forgiven by a spouse. But, as Francine points out, Mary not only had an affair herself but wanted her husband to forgive her. Clearly, Mary's premise is inconsistent with her earlier actions, and her conclusion—that her brother should not forgive, and should leave, her sister-in-law—lacks real support. Francine should, however, give Mary a chance to explain her apparent hypocrisy. Perhaps her affair took place during a period when her husband was also having an affair, and this might allow her to argue that the two situations are not parallel. But in the absence of some such explanation, Francine is justified in refusing to accept Mary's premise and charging her with the fallacy of inconsistency.

6.7.3 Equivocation

In Chapter 3 we examined various ways in which language can be ambiguous, and we indicated the importance of ensuring that the meaning of what we say is clear and unambiguous. We now consider some ways in which ambiguities can destroy or weaken an argument. The fallacy of *EQUIVOCATION* arises when a term is used with more than one meaning within a single argument. Usually, what happens is that one meaning is acceptable in one part of the argument and another meaning is acceptable in another part of the argument. Because the term is repeated, it looks as if the argument follows a single thread throughout; however, if we notice the shift in meaning, the line of reasoning is broken.

Here is a silly example that clearly illustrates the nature of this mistake:

> *Noisy children are a real headache.*
> *An aspirin will make a headache go away.*
> *Therefore, an aspirin will make noisy children go away.*

There is a sense in which noisy children are a headache, but it is only a metaphorical sense. When taken literally, as the second premise uses the term *headache*, the claim is false. The conclusion of this argument, however, follows only if the first premise is literally true. The argument, therefore, commits the fallacy of equivocation.

Usually, the equivocation arises in more subtle ways. For example:

> *There's a lot of talk these days about how we shouldn't discriminate. Well, I don't agree at all. Everybody discriminates all the time. It is unavoidable. We discriminate when selecting a wine or buying a car or choosing new wallpaper. We discriminate when deciding which friends to invite to a party or which candidate to vote for. We discriminate when we hire someone, or admit someone to a college. We always make such decisions on the basis of the qualities we admire: i.e., we discriminate. So there is nothing wrong with discrimination.*

The equivocation here is with the term *discrimination*. In the premises the speaker uses the term to mean *making decisions on the basis of relevant qualities*. This is an accepted sense of the term, which is reflected in sentences like *He is very discriminating in his choice of clothes*. But the conclusion uses the term to mean *making decisions on the basis of irrelevant qualities such as race, religion, or gender*. This is the sense of the term that is obviously used by those who believe we should not discriminate. The sense in which the premises are true is not the sense required by the conclusion, so the argument commits the fallacy of equivocation.

Any of the types of ambiguity we discussed in Chapter 3 can give rise to the fallacy of equivocation. Sometimes it may rest on a failure to recognize linguistic ambiguities, for example, the ambiguity between the collective and distributive use of a term. Or it may arise through the failure to distinguish between the analytic and synthetic interpretations of a statement, between the descriptive and evaluative meanings of a term, or between necessary and sufficient conditions.

Here are three more examples of arguments that commit the fallacy of equivocation:

> *If you don't like organized political parties, then vote for your local Anarchist Party candidate. Its membership is so dysfunctional no one could ever call it an organized political party.*

> *National Savings and Trust. A name you can trust with your money.*

> *According to Judge Wapner's ruling, the Country Club cannot build an indoor swimming pool unless the membership agrees. Well, I am a member, and I most certainly do not agree. Therefore, the Club cannot build its new pool.*

6.7.4 False Dichotomy

We often have to deal with alternatives. Sometimes there are only two alternatives: either we are pregnant or we are not. But frequently, when we are offered two alternatives, there are really more than two: we may be neither rich nor poor, neither young nor old, neither hairy nor bald. In addition, some alternatives do not exclude each other. When we are offered a choice of cake or pie for dessert, we may, if we are lucky, be able to choose both. With any range of alternatives we can ask whether they are exhaustive and whether they are exclusive. Alternatives are *EXHAUSTIVE* when they cover all the possibilities. *Being pregnant* and *not being pregnant* are exhaustive alternatives, for there is no other possibility. *Being young* and *being old* are not exhaustive alternatives, for there is a third possibility: *being middle-aged*. Alternatives are *EXCLUSIVE* when the choice of one rules out the other(s). For example, the designations *a.m.* and *p.m.* are exclusive, at least when applied to a time on a particular place on earth. *Being a faculty member* and *being a student* are not exclusive, since some faculty are also students.

Thus, every set of alternatives will be either exhaustive or non-exhaustive *and* either exclusive or non-exclusive. The famous choice between liberty and death (*Give me liberty or give me death*) is exclusive but not exhaustive. It is exclusive because one cannot choose both liberty and death, but it is not exhaustive because one could choose neither liberty nor death but slavery. The bumper sticker *America: Love It Or Leave It* presents a choice that is neither exhaustive nor exclusive. It is not exhaustive because it is possible to neither love it nor leave it: for example, to be indifferent to it but stay. It is not exclusive because it is possible to love it and to leave it.

The fallacy of *FALSE DICHOTOMY* arises when the premise of an argument presents us with a choice between two alternatives and assumes that they are exhaustive or exclusive or both when in fact they are not. Most commonly it arises when the alternatives are presented as if they were exhaustive when in fact they are not. For example:

> David: *Let me get this straight, Paul. You mean that you have been going out with your girlfriend for almost a year, and she never told you she has a three-year-old daughter by a previous marriage?*
> Paul: *That's right. And I only found out by accident last week.*
> David: *Well, whatever you do, Paul, don't marry her. She is a liar.*

David is assuming that telling the truth and telling lies are exhaustive alternatives, when in fact not telling the truth is not the same as telling a lie. We can fail to tell the truth by not saying anything, which is what Paul's girlfriend did, and this is quite different from telling a lie. Here are three more examples of the fallacy of false dichotomy:

> *I'm against giving aid to countries in which people are starving. We will never be able to eradicate starvation completely, so it is a waste of time even trying.*

> *Good students will study and learn if there are no examinations, and bad students won't study and will learn nothing even when there are examinations. So exams are useless.*

> *These days students have to choose whether they want to get good grades or whether they want to have fun. Well, Tamsen has decided she wants to have fun at college, so I guess she's not going to get good grades.*

6.8 SELF-TEST NO. 12

Identify any weaknesses in the following arguments due to unacceptable premises, after making sure you have correctly identified the conclusion. Note in particular any fallacies of acceptability.

1. If we want economic prosperity, we should be looking for even more wars to get involved in. Every nation that has fought a major war in the last century emerged from the war economically stronger than it was before. It seems to be the one sure path to economic prosperity.

2. In our democratic system, government is supposed to be based on the consent of the governed. Well, I am one of the governed, and I certainly do not consent to public school taxes for families with no children. So the government has no right to force me and others who think the way I do to pay this iniquitous tax.

3. The outboard motor I bought last year turned out to be a real lemon. As soon as the warranty expired everything started going wrong; it has cost me over $600 in repairs so far this year. The trouble is there's nothing I can do about it. I thought about suing the manufacturer, but the lawyer's fee would cost more than I could ever hope to win.

4. History shows that only in democracies does the human spirit flourish. And the reason is clear: undemocratic societies deny to most of their members any opportunity to take part in the political life of the community, and without such participation the human spirit withers and dies.

5. Members of the jury, there are two compelling reasons why you should find my client not guilty. First, the prosecution has failed to prove beyond a reasonable doubt that he was anywhere near the warehouse on the night the theft occurred. And second, even if he was there, I have presented evidence to show that he was acting under threats from his companions. In either case he should be found not guilty.

6. Most people are much more interested in local issues—such as property taxes, garbage collection, their children's education, and zoning by-laws—than they are in state and national political issues. This is shown by the fact that a much higher percentage of the electorate votes in municipal elections than in state or federal elections.

7. It never ceases to amaze me that so many scientists deny that the miracles reported in the Bible actually took place. After all, science itself has

presented us with many miracles, such as lasers, antibiotics, computers, and space flight. Since scientists accept that these modern miracles actually exist, they should accept that biblical miracles also actually occurred.

8. The choice confronting us is clear. Do we want a defense policy that relies upon the threat of nuclear annihilation to deter aggression, or do we want a non-aligned foreign policy that is aimed at reducing international tensions? It is obvious that we should reject the first alternative since it embodies a dangerous and outmoded cold war mentality, and that we should therefore adopt a non-aligned foreign policy.

9. Last year I took a great course in history of science that was developed and team-taught by Professors Smith, Jones, and Brown. They were excellent teachers; in fact they received an award for teaching excellence for the course. So I am going to register next term for a new course being offered by Professor Smith. I am sure it will be a great course, too.

10. There are 13 chapters in this book, and I am now almost finished Chapter 6. Therefore, I am almost halfway through the book.

6.9 QUESTIONS FOR DISCUSSION

Each of the following arguments involves a weakness, although it may take careful analysis to identify the precise nature of the weakness.

1. There is no such thing as an unselfish act. If you examine any so-called unselfish act, such as donating money to charity, you will always find that there is a selfish motive. There has to be, for nobody can do anything unless they think it will give them some kind of satisfaction. Seeking self-satisfaction is the only reason why anybody does anything. So every act is selfish.

2. Individuals are born, struggle through childhood, grow to maturity, and after a few years decline and finally die. So we should expect all societies, which are mere aggregations of individuals, to do the same.

3. I have attended several operas, and I always come away with the same reaction, which is that opera is a vastly over-rated art form. The plots could never be described as great literature, and some are as bad as any TV melodrama. Even when performed superbly, the music itself is always a mixture of good and mediocre, usually more mediocre than good. The costumes and the staging are often well done, but the whole experience

is always destroyed for me by the atrocious acting. Why can singers never learn to act? The fact that opera lovers always seem to be unaware of these drawbacks is a great mystery to me.

4. The great experiment in communism that began in Russia in 1917 with such high hopes finally came to an inglorious end in 1991, and all that is left is to diagnose the fatal flaw that destroyed the noble dream. The view one hears most frequently is that it was the failure of the communist system to provide its citizens with material goods that brought it down. But this view ignores the role of the denial of freedom that has characterized the Soviet Union since its inception. If the history of the Soviet Union proves anything, it is that the human spirit needs freedom not merely to flourish but to survive. People will tolerate the denial of their freedom for a time in order to achieve security, but eventually the demand for freedom will burst forth, destroying everything that stands in its way. The death of communism can only be explained by its denial of freedom, not by its admitted failure to give its citizens material prosperity.

5. In his book *Utilitarianism*, John Stuart Mill defends the view that the ultimate test of right and wrong is the greatest-happiness principle. The principle states that we should always seek to promote the general happiness, which he defines as the greatest happiness of the greatest number of people. To show that the principle is true, Mill argues as follows: Each person's happiness is a good to that person. Therefore, the general happiness is a good to the aggregate of all persons.

6. Every voluntary act performed by a human being originates from that person's own conception of what is good. Since selfishness consists in acting to further one's own good, every voluntary action is selfish.

7. ASSESSING RELEVANCE

7.1 THE CRITERION OF RELEVANCE

Our second criterion for a sound argument is that the premises must be relevant to the conclusion. An argument whose premises are irrelevant to its conclusion obviously suffers from a major weakness. But what precisely is relevance? What are we looking for in an argument when we ask whether its premises are relevant? What we need from our premises, if they are to be relevant to the truth of the conclusion, is that they should make it more likely that the conclusion will be true. We cannot expect that the truth of a premise will always guarantee the truth of the conclusion, but we can demand that it make the conclusion more likely to be true than it would be if the premise were false. In brief, a premise is relevant when it helps to make it reasonable to accept the conclusion.

The idea of relevance is easier to grasp if we compare some examples of arguments with relevant premises and arguments with irrelevant premises:

> *You should vote for Johnson because she is honest and is well informed about the issues.*
> *You should vote for Johnson because her mother used to be my kindergarten teacher.*

The first of these arguments supplies two reasons for voting for Johnson, both of which are clearly relevant. Anyone who thinks they are irrelevant would have to hold that it is a matter of indifference whether a politician is honest or well informed about the issues and would see no reason to vote against a politician who was dishonest or poorly informed about the issues. Such a view is unacceptable to most of us because we are convinced that being honest and well informed are desirable qualities in a politician. If pressed, we could defend this view by pointing to the disastrous social and political consequences of having dishonest or poorly informed politicians. The second of the above arguments supplies an irrelevant reason for voting for Johnson. It is difficult to imagine why anyone would seriously think that the fact that the candidate's mother was a kindergarten teacher is a good reason to vote for that candidate. If pressed to justify our view that this is an irrelevant premise, we could argue that there is no evidence that the children of kindergarten teachers make better politicians than anyone else.

Thus, for any premise we can always ask whether it has any relevance to the acceptability of the conclusion. Usually it is quite clear whether a premise is relevant, but where it is not clear, we can address the question directly by trying to find an argument that will determine the question one way or the other. This is not always a straightforward matter. Consider the following:

You should vote for Johnson because she is the only female candidate.

Is the fact that Johnson is a woman a relevant reason to vote for her? This is a debatable question. Many people believe that there should be more women elected to public office, and they defend this view by arguing that women bring a different and better perspective to politics, that women are more likely than men to address women's issues seriously, that women are still handicapped in politics by their gender, and so on. On the other hand, many people reject this view on the ground that we should vote only for candidates whose policies we agree with, and that not all women candidates support the policies we may agree with. It is not obvious whether a candidate's gender is relevant; to decide whether it is, we have to grapple with the issue on its own terms.

There is one complicating feature of questions of relevance we must note. Sometimes the question whether a premise is relevant depends upon the standard of acceptability that is appropriate in the context. In section 6.3 we discussed the different standards of acceptability that we can use when determining whether statements are acceptable. These varying standards also have a bearing on whether premises are relevant. If we want to show that a high-cholesterol diet increases the chances of a heart attack, the context will determine which premises are relevant and which are not. Appealing to an article in *Reader's Digest* will be relevant in a casual conversation with friends about diet, but irrelevant in a discussion by nutritionists about recent research. Again, measuring the interior angles of a triangle with a protractor to show that they add up to 180 degrees may be relevant in some contexts but irrelevant when a mathematical proof is called for. Generally, when the standard of acceptability is very demanding, premises that may be relevant with a lower standard of acceptability will become irrelevant. Whenever we raise the question of relevance about a premise, we should always take account of the standard of acceptability that is appropriate in the context.

7.2 RECOGNIZING IRRELEVANT PREMISES

The traditional term used to describe arguments with irrelevant premises is *NON SEQUITUR*, which means, literally, *it does not follow*. It is an unfortunate human tendency to believe that much more follows from premises than really does. We are too willing to appeal to premises that may be irrelevant on the off chance that they might convince others or even ourselves. Fortunately, it is usually easy to decide whether a premise is relevant if we can remember to ask ourselves whether the premise, if accepted for the sake of the argument, makes the conclusion more likely to be true. Simply raising the question often suggests a plausible argument that shows whether the premise is relevant. The kind of argument we need is not usually a lengthy one, but it should be clear and specific. For example:

I washed my car this morning. So we can be certain that it's going to rain later today.

We can show the irrelevance of the premise of this argument by noting that there is no reason to believe that washing a car has any role to play in the weather. If someone were to say this while laughing and rolling their eyes, the principle of charity would oblige us to interpret this claim as a joke. But if it is asserted seriously, the conclusion simply does not follow. Many superstitions exhibit *non sequitur*s of this sort.

Here are two more arguments with irrelevant premises:

I am opposed to the proposed anti-smoking by-law and will vote against it at the Council meeting. Such a by-law is inappropriate in a city in which the Imperial Tobacco Company is one of the largest employers.

The movie of Anna Karenina was pretty boring; it is really nothing more than a soap opera set in Imperial Russia. I'd always thought it was supposed to be a great novel. I guess I was wrong.

The irrelevance of the premise of the first argument can be shown by arguing that the fact that the Imperial Tobacco Company is one of the city's largest employers has no bearing on whether the citizens want or are entitled to an anti-smoking by-law. Would anyone argue that Windsor should get rid of its No Parking zones merely because Ford is one of its largest employers? In the second case, a comparison of even a few great novels with films that have been based on them is sufficient to show that the quality of the film usually has very little to do with the quality of the novel.

There is no limit to the kinds of irrelevant premises people can appeal to except for the limits of their imagination. Certain types of irrelevant appeals, however, occur so frequently that they have been given particular labels. These labels are useful because they remind us of the common kinds of irrelevancies we should be on the lookout for and because they help us to explain why the premises are irrelevant.

The *APPEAL TO PITY* that we mentioned in section 5.1 is one such. Here is another example of an appeal to pity:

> *The judge was very unfair. He shouldn't have found Evelyn guilty. She is a single parent with three small children and an ex-husband who refuses to make his support payments, and I'm sure she would not have started shoplifting if she weren't really hard-pressed for money.*

Evelyn certainly deserves our pity (or sympathy), but this has no bearing on whether or not she is guilty of shoplifting. If there is strong evidence that she shoplifted, then the judge has no option but to find her guilty. There are situations, however, where the appeal to pity is relevant. If the conclusion of the above argument were

> *The judge shouldn't have given Evelyn a jail sentence,*

then the appeal to pity would be relevant, since we could argue that single parents with small children should not be jailed for non-violent criminal offences.

Another type of irrelevant appeal is the *APPEAL TO FORCE*. It arises when the premise of an argument threatens the use of force (either physical force or other kinds of pressure, such as economic pressure or emotional blackmail) as a reason for accepting the conclusion. Obviously, an appeal to force normally provides no reason for accepting the truth of a claim, although it might well provide a good reason for pretending to accept it. For example:

> *Listen, I'm telling you that my son did not cheat on his exam: if you don't agree, we'll step outside and settle the matter man to man.*

Clearly, the son's innocence cannot be established by his father beating up his teacher, although the son might nevertheless be innocent. And even if the teacher agrees with the father out of fear, the son has obviously not been shown to be innocent.

An appeal to force may be relevant when it is used in an attempt to get someone to do something, rather than to accept a truth-claim. However, in order to decide whether we are justified in using threats of force to get people to do something, we must establish a moral or political principle to serve as an additional premise. The criminal law, for example, works on the basis of the principle that society is entitled to use the threat of punishment to secure obedience to the law. If we accept this principle, then it is relevant to argue that people should not commit murder because otherwise they will be punished.

Another type of irrelevant appeal worth mentioning is the *APPEAL TO POPULAR-ITY*. It arises when an argument uses the popularity of a belief as a reason for holding that the belief is true, when its popularity is irrelevant to its truth or falsity. Obviously, the mere fact that a belief is popular is usually no guarantee that it is true. History provides many examples of discarded beliefs that were once widely held to be true. Typically, the popularity of a belief is not a good reason for accepting it. For example:

> *Well, obviously capitalism is the most efficient economic system ever devised by humankind. Everybody knows that.*
> *Phrenology is unscientific nonsense. Nobody believes it any longer.*

Clearly, the popularity of capitalism does nothing to show that it is the most efficient economic system, nor does the unpopularity of phrenology do anything to show that it is false. It is also easy to recognize the cases where the appeal to popularity is relevant, that is, cases where the conclusion makes a claim that depends upon the popularity (rather than the truth) of some belief. If we are trying to predict who will win an election, or the future sales of a product, or the size of an audience for a concert, we will obviously need to use the appeal to popularity.

There are, however, harder cases where the relevance of the appeal to popularity is unclear. For example:

> *According to a recent poll 64 per cent of citizens are in favor of the death penalty for a person convicted of murder. This is supposed to be a democratic country, so the government ought to keep capital punishment legally permissible.*

Is this a sound argument? It does not attempt to show that capital punishment is justified in itself, but only claims that it ought to continue to be legally permissible because the majority support it. It thus relies upon a missing premise: the political principle that government policy ought to reflect the will of the majority. It is on the acceptability of this principle that the strength of the argument depends. If it is acceptable, then the argument is strong. If it is not acceptable, then the argument is weak, for it appeals to an irrelevant premise.

7.3 APPEALS TO AUTHORITY (1)

Often in discussion we make numerous claims that we do not attempt to defend. When we are challenged to do so, a common response is to cite an authority, in other words, we present an argument of the form:

> *So-and-so says X.*
> *Therefore, X is true (or probably true).*

The authorities we appeal to in order to defend a claim are many and varied: the President, the family doctor, Uncle Fred, the weatherman, mom, the encyclopedia, a physics professor, the media, LeBron James. In each case, the argument is in effect claiming that the mere fact that so-and-so says something is a good reason for us to accept it as true.

It is obvious that sometimes such appeals are quite irrelevant and give rise to very weak arguments. When Uncle Fred tells me that the Detroit Lions are the best team in the NFL, it is unreasonable for me to agree with his view merely because he holds it. He is an enthusiastic fan, but he knows very little about football. What he says is irrelevant to the issue of whether or not the Detroit Lions are the best team in the NFL. But not all appeals to authority are as obviously weak as the appeal to Uncle Fred. Consider the following examples:

> *Albert Einstein, even after all his research into the nature of the universe, still believed in God. He once wrote, "I do not believe that the universe was the result of blind chance." If belief in God made sense to Einstein, then it makes sense to me.*

> *I've decided not to take any more philosophy electives. Some philosophy is kind of interesting, but the problem is that it consists merely of opinions and not knowledge. At least that's what my psychology professor says.*

These arguments may seem plausible, but they appeal to irrelevant authorities. It is (or should be) evident that the fact that a famous physicist believed in God is not a good reason for believing in God. And the fact that a psychology professor thinks that philosophy consists merely of opinion and not knowledge is not a good reason for accepting his or her claim.

However, not all *APPEALS TO AUTHORITY* are irrelevant. In fact, our lives would be intolerable if we were never to rely upon authorities. The reason we consult lawyers, doctors, architects, and engineers is that we have to rely upon their advice on matters about which we lack knowledge. In general, an appeal to authority is relevant whenever the following two conditions are met: (1) we lack information or experience that is needed to make a reasonable decision, and it is difficult or impossible on the matter in question to obtain it directly for ourselves; and (2) the authority appealed to is entitled to authoritative status. The first condition recognizes that if we could get the needed information and experience directly and without appealing to some authority, we ought to do so. For example, we should not rely upon someone else's view that a book is offensive if we could easily read it and decide for ourselves. Similarly, we shouldn't accept the view that euthanasia is right merely because some person we admire for their general good judgment holds that it is. The appeal to authority, even when it is legitimate, should always be regarded as second best; if we are in a position to learn about the matter and decide for ourselves, we should do so. Only in situations where we lack the expertise needed to make some decision or judgment are we entitled to turn to an authority, such as a doctor, lawyer, or engineer. But when we do so, we must bear in mind the second condition and make sure we are relying upon the judgment of someone who really is entitled to be treated as authoritative on the matter in question. There should be good reasons to believe that what the authority says really is likely to be true. How much reliance we should place on authorities will be discussed in section 8.2.

7.4 SOME PARTICULAR FALLACIES

The particular fallacies described in this section all involve an irrelevant appeal of some sort. They deserve a more extended discussion because they are so common and because recognizing them requires sensitivity to their complexities. They figure prominently in arguments about virtually every controversial issue and account for much of the frustration we typically experience when we are drawn into such debates. Understanding them will not only help us to avoid them but also show us how to respond when our opponents use them against us.

7.4.1 Ad Hominem

The *AD HOMINEM* fallacy is committed when an argument substitutes irrelevant personal or circumstantial information discrediting the author of a statement for genuine evidence that the statement is false. Loosely speaking, the ad hominem fallacy involves a personal attack upon someone in an attempt to discredit what that person says, when such an attack is irrelevant to the issue. The traditional name for this fallacy is *argumentum ad hominem*, which literally means *argument against the man*. Some contemporary logicians call this fallacy *abusing the person*, or *attack on the person*, but the Latin name is still widely used in ordinary speech, and we shall follow this usage here.

Let us look at some examples of arguments that commit the ad hominem fallacy:

According to the supporters of capital punishment, the death penalty is an effective deterrent against murder. This is nonsense. These people are not interested in deterrence at all. They want vengeance pure and simple. They suffer from a kind of blood-lust; they are the people who flock to see Dirty Harry *movies. They get turned on by the thought of shooting up the bad guys.*

What makes this an ad hominem is that the facts (or alleged facts) cited about the personal qualities of supporters of capital punishment are completely irrelevant to the question of whether or not the death penalty is an effective deterrent against murder.

The ad hominem is usually easy to detect as long as we can remember to separate our views about the personal qualities of people whose opinions we do not share from our views about their opinions. We may not like to admit it, but nasty people sometimes say what is true and sometimes argue impeccably. The ease with which so many people commit the ad hominem fallacy doubtless derives from the fact that it is psychologically satisfying to attack nasty people. This also explains why an ad hominem can be so successful in public debates and discussion: audiences enjoy seeing nasty people under attack and often feel that such attacks actually refute their opinions and arguments. It is important, therefore, not to allow ourselves to be taken in by such attacks when they constitute an ad hominem, especially in situations where we feel very strongly that someone's opinion is not only false but deeply immoral as well. These are the types of situations where we may commit an ad hominem without realizing it. We should strive to develop the intellectual self-discipline to separate our views about our opponents from our views about the truth or falsity of what they say.

Not every attack upon a person's personal qualities, however, constitutes a fallacy. It is only when such attacks are irrelevant to the point at issue that the fallacy arises. Sometimes the personal qualities of someone are central. When we are looking for a baby-sitter, or considering asking someone out on a date, our decisions should be based upon a judgment about personal qualities. In such cases the personal qualities of the person are not used as a basis for rejecting what the person says, and for this reason no ad hominem fallacy is committed.

There are two types of arguments that seem to, but do not actually, commit the ad hominem fallacy. First, in some situations it is appropriate to argue that a person's opinions should not be relied upon because he or she is untrustworthy. When we are trying to assess the reliability of someone's testimony about an event, it is relevant to point to facts about the person's character. If you tell me that you have no idea how my bicycle came to be in your garage, the fact that you were convicted for bicycle theft last year is relevant to the question of whether I should accept your claim of innocence. This does not, of course, prove that you stole my bicycle, but it is relevant to the question of whether or not it is reasonable to believe you. Or, if I tell you that you will get better grades in school if you buy a particular encyclopedia, the fact that I get a 10 per cent commission is relevant to the question of whether you should accept my claim.

Second, sometimes it is appropriate to argue that a person's opinions should not be taken into account because of a conflict of interest. When a body such as a city council or school board makes decisions that might affect the financial interests of its members, it is an accepted principle that any member whose financial interests might be affected should not participate in such decisions. Here we do not dispute what a person says, but rather whether that person's views ought to be taken into account in the decision-making process. An argument that someone ought to abstain from voting on an issue because of a conflict of interest does not commit the ad hominem fallacy.

7.4.2 Tu Quoque

The *TU QUOQUE* fallacy is a special case of the ad hominem. Like the ad hominem, it typically arises in an argumentative context when someone attempts to refute or rebut something said by another person. The tu quoque fallacy is committed when the conclusion of an argument claims that an accusation is unwarranted and supports it by claiming that the accuser is also open to a similar accusation. This fallacy is sometimes called the *Two Wrongs* fallacy, but we shall use the traditional Latin name (pronounced tew-kwoh-kway), which means *you too*.

It is clear that a tu quoque response to an accusation can never refute the accusation. Consider the following:

Wilma: *You cheated on your income tax. Don't you realize that's wrong?*
Walter: *Hey, wait a minute. You cheated on your income tax last year. Or have you forgotten about that?*

Walter may be correct in his counter-accusation, but that does not show that Wilma's accusation against him is false. Wilma's guilt can in no way reduce or eliminate Walter's guilt.

It is easy to understand why tu quoque arguments are so popular. After all, what better way to avoid an accusation than to hurl the same accusation back at our accusers. Many important public issues suffer from an abundance of tu quoques. For example:

I don't see why our company should be singled out by the city just because of some leakage problems at our chemical storage facility. The city should pay more attention to the more serious pollution that is occurring at its landfill site.

Your party is in no position to attack the current administration for not reducing spending as a measure for deficit reduction. When your party formed the government a few years ago, you created a massive deficit that we are still coping with.

7.4.3 Straw Man

This, too, is a very common fallacy. It usually arises in debates over controversial issues when one side is attempting to avoid or deflect criticisms presented by the other side. The *STRAW MAN* fallacy is committed when someone attacks a position that appears similar to, but is actually different from, an opponent's position, and concludes that the opponent's real position has thereby been refuted. The opponent being attacked, however, is not the real opponent but an unreal opponent, a *straw man* who has been constructed by the attacker solely for the purpose of destruction. To recognize this fallacy we must, of course, know what the opponent's real position is in order to see that it is different from the position being attacked. The question we need to ask when a position is under attack is, *Is the position being attacked really held by those under attack, or is it a false interpretation of their position?*

Examples of the straw man fallacy abound. When the issue is controversial, the straw man fallacy is often committed by both sides. Consider the following arguments:

What I object to most about those people who oppose capital punishment is that they believe that the lives of convicted murderers are more important than the lives of the police officers and prison guards who protect us.

Those who want the death penalty restored have not really thought their position through. They hold that every murderer would have been deterred from committing murder had the death penalty been in force, and this is absurd. Otherwise, countries with the death penalty would have no murders, which is obviously false.

With regard to the first argument, there is no evidence that anyone who is against the death penalty has ever believed that the lives of murderers are more important than anyone else's lives. With regard to the second argument, there is no evidence that anyone who supports the death penalty has ever seriously argued that the death penalty would deter all potential murderers. In both cases, the accusers have attacked an unreal position and have thus committed the straw man fallacy.

Clearly, the principle of charity is being ignored in these cases. We have no difficulty recognizing when our opponents have committed a straw man fallacy by attacking a travesty of our position. We know that they have violated the principle of charity. It is more difficult for us, however, to avoid stooping to the same level as our opponents. We need to remind ourselves that committing the straw man fallacy accomplishes nothing other than perhaps making us feel better for the moment. Our opponents are certainly not persuaded by such arguments; neither should anyone else be persuaded, since the position our opponents really hold has not been attacked at all and survives unscathed. Even worse, people who are not yet committed to either side of the issue may well conclude that our position must be very weak indeed if our straw man attack is the best that can be said against the other side.

Here are some other examples of straw man arguments:

> *If the Green Party ever forms the government in the United States the economy would be crippled. After all, they have repeatedly made it clear the economy is not at all important to them.*

> *The government's immigration policy denies political asylum to women who want to come to the US to flee government sanctioned rape. This is an indefensible policy. What we want are enlightened laws that broadly interpret political persecution.*

> *The demands made by native Americans are totally unacceptable. They claim that the whole country was stolen from them without their consent and are demanding compensation for their loss. This is crazy. There isn't enough money in the world, let alone in the US, to pay compensation for the whole country.*

7.5 SELF-TEST NO. 13

Explain the weaknesses due to irrelevance, if any, in the following arguments. Note in particular any fallacies of relevance.

1. I wouldn't take his word for anything, if I were you. His father has been convicted for fraud, and you know what they say: Like father, like son.

2. *NCIS* is the best show on television. It must be the best because it gets higher ratings than any other show.

3. Many mathematicians used to believe that formal logic could provide a foundation for the whole of mathematics. But they were wrong. Their view was decisively refuted by Kurt Gödel in his famous paper published in 1931.

4. How can anyone seriously believe in evolution? I certainly don't. How can you take seriously a theory that claims that humans are just monkeys with less hair and that our ancestors were apes?

5. I'm fed up with the feminist movement. I used to think they had some valid concerns, but they are just another special-interest group who are upset because they aren't getting all the good jobs. They talk a lot about justice but it all comes down to selfishness.

6. Throughout recorded history, the family unit has always had a single head, usually the father, but sometimes the mother or a grandparent. But in recent years this tradition has been challenged by those who think that the mother and father can be equal partners. Do these people really think that their limited perspective is better than the wisdom of history? The idea is preposterous.

7. I hate flying, and I don't see why everyone thinks I'm just being silly. Look at Janine. She hates flying as much as I do.

8. My son wants to be an opera singer, but he'll have to do it without any support from me. I've tried to persuade him to go into something useful, like business or law, but he insists on being a singer. He seems to think that everybody should be free to do whatever they want in life. Well, where would we be if everybody did whatever they wanted? That's what I said to him when he told me he wanted to study music at university. And his only response was to walk out of the room.

9. (Background: Two neighbors are talking to each other over the back fence in a suburban neighborhood.)

Ed: Your party last night was very loud and kept us awake until 2 a.m. Really, you must be more considerate towards the people around you, especially late at night when your noise is so unpleasant.

Ralph: Don't be so self-righteous, Ed. I can't count the number of times I've heard your dog barking late at night.

10. For years Spanish-speaking workers have had to put up with an economy that was dominated by Anglophones (English speakers). Often they could not get equal pay for the same jobs, and usually could never get a promotion, unless they spoke good English. Now that in some cities more people speak Spanish than English we should make Spanish the official language. Let the English speakers suffer for a change.

11. (Background: A schoolteacher resigned his position, charging that the principal persistently treated him in an unfair and arbitrary manner. A school board official gave the following response.)

We conducted a thorough investigation to determine whether or not there is any validity to the charge, and we have concluded that there is not. The teacher in question seems to have embarked upon a campaign to undermine the authority of the principal. It is not clear whether his reasons for doing so were ideological or personal, but in either case he seems to have been a troublemaker.

12. (Background: A Senator responding to complaints that the stimulus package has done little to cut the rate of job loss.)

Naturally, I would expect this member of the opposing party to complain about these things. She objected to the program when it was first proposed, argued against it both on the floor of the Senate, and in the media, and voted against it when it was passed in the legislature. She just won't accept that this is a valuable thing.

13. The President promised that infrastructure development would reduce unemployment, stimulate the economy, and improve the standard of living for the poor. This is a ridiculous, simple-minded policy, for it doesn't address the need to develop international trade, reduce taxes, or reduce the national debt.

7.6 QUESTIONS FOR DISCUSSION

Each of the following arguments relies upon a premise that might be regarded as irrelevant. Identify the offending premise and suggest an argument that shows it is irrelevant.

1. There are no absolute values, i.e., no values that are valid for all times and all places. To see this you only have to look at the wide variety of values that have been held by other societies and at earlier times in our history. Pick any value you like: there will be some society somewhere that has rejected it. You simply cannot find a value that has been valid at all times and all places.

2. Although there are no strict proofs that God exists, it is still rational to believe that He does exist. Suppose God does exist: in this case heaven and hell exist and God will send unbelievers to hell for eternity, while believers stand a good chance of going to heaven. Obviously it is rational to do

whatever is necessary to avoid hell and to get to heaven, so it is rational to believe in God if He actually exists. On the other hand, suppose God doesn't exist: in this case there is no heaven or hell, so even if we believe He exists, we run no risk of being punished for having a false belief. It is rational, therefore, to believe in God even if He does not exist. So it is rational to believe God exists, whether He exists or not.

3. The Israeli government should accept the right of Palestinians to a national homeland, because otherwise the Palestinians will continue their campaign of terrorism indefinitely. Israel will never have peace until it recognizes this right.

4. Recently, a number of manufacturers have begun marketing so-called green products, i.e., products that are supposed to be environmentally friendly. The supermarket shelves are now full of them, everything from detergent to peanut butter. These companies seem to think that these products will show their concern for the environment. This is absurd. They have developed these products not because they care about the environment but because they think they can make more money. Sadly, they probably will make more money because the public wants to help preserve the environment and thinks that buying green products will make a difference. But don't be fooled into thinking that these manufacturers care about the environment. It is profit, pure and simple, that motivates them.

5. There are a few people who believe that prostitution is morally acceptable, but in fact it is immoral behavior. It is contrary to the accepted standards of our community as reflected in public opinion and in the legal system. The vast majority of Americans strongly believe that prostitution is immoral and therefore quite properly reject any proposal to legalize prostitution.

6. Why does the public get so upset when people refuse to render assistance to someone in need? That incident last month where a woman was beaten in a park by her boyfriend while several hundred people looked on and did nothing produced a great outpouring of righteous indignation. But I can't for the life of me see why everyone gets so upset at the bystanders. According to the law, these people did nothing illegal, since the law imposes no duty on ordinary citizens to go to the aid of someone who is in distress. That's what the law says, so I don't see that the bystanders did anything wrong at all.

8. ASSESSING ADEQUACY

8.1 THE CRITERION OF ADEQUACY

Our third criterion of a sound argument is that its premises should be adequate to support its conclusion. We need this criterion because even if an argument satisfies the first two criteria (i.e., each premise is acceptable and relevant to the conclusion), the set of premises may nevertheless be inadequate to support the conclusion. Clearly, an argument with premises that are inadequate to support its conclusion suffers from a major weakness. Relying on premises that are inadequate to support a conclusion is sometimes called jumping to conclusions, or reaching a hasty conclusion.

We saw in section 5.2.1 that adequacy is a matter of degree. In this respect the criterion of adequacy differs from the first two criteria. If the premises of an argument are unacceptable, then they give us no reason to think that its conclusion is true. Again, if the premises are irrelevant, then they give us no reason to think that the conclusion is true. But if the premises are inadequate, they may still provide some support for the conclusion, although this support may be too weak or inadequate to make the conclusion acceptable. The fact that premises may be partly but not entirely adequate to support a conclusion is often reflected in the tentative way we assert the conclusion. For example:

> *Look at those dark clouds on the horizon. We might be in for some rain, so maybe we should head back to the car.*

Notice the tentative nature of the inference. By using the words *might* and *maybe*, the speaker is acknowledging that the evidence is not conclusive. Suppose, however, the argument had been:

> *Look at those dark clouds on the horizon. It's going to rain, and if we don't head back to the car right away, we're going to get soaked.*

Here, the inference is not tentative at all. The speaker is arguing that the dark clouds mean that it will rain, and since, as we all know, the presence of dark clouds on the horizon does not always mean that it will rain, the argument violates the criterion of adequacy.

When assessing the adequacy of the premises of any argument, therefore, we always need to look for the degree of strength that the argument claims to have. If it claims to *establish* or *prove* its conclusion, it is more likely that it may violate the criterion of adequacy. If its conclusion is presented tentatively, it is less likely to violate the criterion. It is important to interpret an argument with this question in mind before asking whether it violates the criterion of adequacy. Frequently, it is unclear what degree of strength a speaker is claiming for an argument, and we have to rely upon the contextual clues and the principle of charity when interpreting the argument.

However, we also need to make a judgment regarding the degree of support the premises actually provide for the conclusion, as opposed to the degree of support that is claimed by the speaker. This degree of support can range from none to a great deal and may fall anywhere in between. When an argument violates the criterion of adequacy, it may be because the premises provide no support for the conclusion, or it may be because the premises provide some, although not enough, support to justify accepting the conclusion. Thus, many arguments that violate the criterion of adequacy can easily be amended to meet the criterion by changing the wording of the conclusion to reflect the degree of support actually provided by the premises. This is what we did in the above example. To determine the degree of support provided by a set of premises, we need to examine the full context and use whatever relevant background knowledge we possess in order to make the best judgment we can.

Once we have decided, however, that an argument violates the criterion of adequacy, we must be prepared to say why the premises are inadequate to support the conclusion. The reasons we offer will depend upon the content of the argument. In the above example, we pointed out that a few dark clouds on the horizon do not always mean that it is going to rain. In other cases we will explain the inadequacy of the premises by pointing out other relevant factors. For example:

> *Steve always got As in high school, so we expect him to get high marks in university.*

> *All Margot's classmates think that Mr. Braithwaite is a great teacher, so I'm sure she does too.*

The fact that Steve always got As in high school provides some support for concluding that he will get high marks in university, but, as many of us know to our sorrow, it is no guarantee. And that Margot's classmates think Mr. Braithwaite is a great teacher is no guarantee that she agrees with them. We would have to know more about both Margot and Mr. Braithwaite to know how much support this argument provides for its conclusion.

When assessing the adequacy of an argument, it is sometimes important to take account of what the consequences would be if the conclusion turns out to be false or unacceptable. If we are considering major surgery, the consequences could be very serious if the operation fails; in a matter as important as this, we should normally demand a very high standard of adequacy, and it would therefore be reasonable to seek a second medical opinion. But when an auto mechanic recommends that we use higher octane gasoline, the relative unimportance of the consequences, if it turns out to be bad advice, means that it would normally be inappropriate to demand a second opinion.

Our inclination to jump to conclusions, and thus violate the criterion of adequacy, is the product of a very widespread human tendency. We have a small amount of relevant evidence and cannot resist claiming that we have a good argument, or even a proof. We all know of cases like the following:

Classical music is terrible; I sang in the school choir for a year, and we had to do some really boring classical music.

Sure, I believe in astrology. The day I broke my leg my horoscope said I should avoid risky situations, but I went skiing anyway. After that, I started taking it seriously.

Additionally, there are practical reasons why we might act on a conclusion that is not adequately supported by the evidence at hand; in such cases, we might be aware that the available evidence is weak, but the consequences of acting or not acting are such that we accept the inference. For example, if someone tells you they once read that eating potatoes with green patches under the skin can cause cancer, then you might accept the conclusion even though this is very weak evidence. It is easy to avoid eating these potatoes, and the consequences of not accepting the conclusion, if it is true, are very serious. We can say in this case that the cost of a false negative is low, and the danger of a true positive is high; therefore, the conclusion is accepted for practical reasons. Also, anyone who comes to the hospital complaining of chest pains is treated as if they are having a heart attack, even though chest pains alone are weak evidence of a heart attack. There is no real harm in being cautious with every complaint of chest pain, but there may be a serious, preventable harm if an actual heart condition is left untreated while they wait for more conclusive evidence of a heart attack. Again, the cost of a false negative is low, and the danger of a true positive is sufficiently high that the conclusion is accepted for practical reasons.

There seems to be no limit to the different ways in which we can violate the criterion of adequacy, but it is possible to identify two generic criteria of adequacy. The first and most stringent generic criterion is deductive validity, which is explained in Chapter 9. The second generic criterion, inductive strength, is explained in Chapter 10. For the rest of this chapter, however, we will concentrate on a few familiar types of argument where determining the adequacy of the premises raises special difficulties.

8.2 APPEALS TO AUTHORITY (2)

In section 7.3 we saw that appeals to authority are relevant in circumstances where we lack information or experience that is needed for some decision and which we are unable to obtain for ourselves directly. But not all appeals to authority are equally strong. The adequacy of any appeal to authority depends upon a number of factors, all of which must be taken into account. There are five criteria we should use when determining the adequacy of any appeal to authority.

1. THE AUTHORITY MUST BE IDENTIFIED.

The reason for insisting that an authority must be identified is obvious: if we don't know who the authority is, we cannot determine whether he or she is reliable. Using an anonymous authority undermines the very purpose of citing an authority at all. An expert's acknowledged good judgment in previous situations gives us reason to be confident in their judgment in the situation at hand. We must be aware of unnamed authorities because we have no way of knowing the track record that justifies the appeal in the first place.

2. THE AUTHORITY MUST BE GENERALLY RECOGNIZED BY THE EXPERTS IN THE FIELD.

The characteristics someone must have to be an authority depend upon the particular field in question. In some fields there are licensing requirements that are intended to ensure an appropriate level of expertise, as in medicine, dentistry, and many other professions. In fields where there are no licensing requirements, there are often generally accepted standards of expertise, such as a Ph.D. or a diploma in auto mechanics. Meeting licensing requirements or accepted standards, however, does not by itself guarantee that what an expert says is true. There are "qualified" crackpots in every field. The best general test is whether the expert is generally recognized as an expert by other experts in the field. Beware of authorities who lack the support of their fellow-experts.

3. THE PARTICULAR MATTER IN SUPPORT OF WHICH AN AUTHORITY IS CITED MUST LIE WITHIN HIS OR HER FIELD OF EXPERTISE.

No one is an expert on everything, and the authority that experts can legitimately claim is limited to their field of expertise. Bank presidents are presumably experts on banking, but when they make pronouncements on what is a fair tax system they probably lack the relevant kind of expertise. Beware of authorities who make claims beyond their area of expertise.

4. THE FIELD MUST BE ONE IN WHICH THERE IS GENUINE KNOWLEDGE.

In certain fields individuals may have a great deal of experience, but this experience does not produce genuine knowledge. By genuine knowledge we mean a systematically ordered body of facts and principles that are objective in nature. In this sense, an experienced novelist may not have any knowledge of how to write a good novel and may be an abysmal teacher. In some fields there is no expertise: experience may produce familiarity but no genuine knowledge and hence no expertise. Experience is sometimes not merely the best but the only teacher. Beware of authorities who pretend to have expertise in a field in which there is no genuine knowledge.

5. THERE SHOULD BE A CONSENSUS AMONG THE EXPERTS IN THE FIELD REGARDING THE PARTICULAR MATTER IN SUPPORT OF WHICH THE AUTHORITY IS CITED.

In virtually every field of knowledge there are some controversial issues. This is true in mathematics, law, medicine, economics, accountancy, and molecular biology, as well as in plumbing, wine-making, and coaching athletes. Such controversies mean that on that particular issue there is no knowledge, even though the field in general may have a secure knowledge base. Always be cautious when authorities disagree among themselves.

When deciding whether an appeal to an authority is adequate, we should always apply these criteria as best we can. In practice, it is sometimes difficult to gather the information that would show they have all been satisfied, but at the very least we should always look for evidence that one or more criteria is not met. To the extent that the criteria are not satisfied by some authority, we should reduce our reliance upon that authority, especially when there is something important at stake. We can be forgiven if we accept the authority of our grandmother that chewing a garlic bud will stave off a cold, but it would be foolish in the extreme to accept our horoscope as an authority on whether to undergo surgery.

8.3 APPEALS TO ANECDOTAL EVIDENCE

Anecdotes are a common source of hasty conclusions. On the basis of a colorful story or experience, a person might leap to a claim that is much broader and stated more strongly than the story really suggests. Suppose some friends of ours vacation at a resort in Belize. Suppose also that the beach at their resort was polluted, and that the hotel was an overpriced dump with poorly trained staff. Suppose also that they were robbed and suffered from food poisoning during their stay. It would be inappropriate to conclude on the basis of this single tale of woe that "Belize is a terrible place to visit." Their experiences are not adequate to draw conclusions about the entire country or the Belize tourist industry. Perhaps the resort they stayed at is the worst-run place in the entire country, that the food poisoning was due to unsanitary conditions that are unique to its kitchen, and that our friends were simply unfortunate to be robbed on top of all their other difficulties. As long as we have no reason to rule out these and other possibilities, our friends' experiences at this single resort do not furnish enough evidence to draw a broad conclusion, nor do we have reason to believe that this resort is representative within the class of Belize tourist destinations. The anecdote is not adequate to draw a strong conclusion about what other travelers can expect.

Because anecdotes are concrete and memorable, an appeal to anecdotal evidence can have a disproportionate influence on the conclusions we draw. We are especially prone to such appeals when an anecdote confirms a prejudice. Anecdotes can disguise the irrational source of a prejudice because they give the impression that such opinions can be traced to objective facts. Many bigots can relate at least one story to support broad claims about people of a specific group. Indeed, the factual basis of an anecdote such as the story of our friends in Belize may be undeniable. But one story is rarely adequate to support broad conclusions, and general conclusions about an entire class cannot be supported without good evidence, preferably evidence that is gathered methodically and analyzed systematically. Anecdotes may be useful to illustrate a general claim that is supported by other evidence, but in itself an anecdote is weak evidence. For this reason we must distinguish between using an anecdote for expository purposes, as an example that clarifies a general claim, and using one as evidence to support a general claim. The expository value may be quite great, but anecdotes have very limited probative value.

If we accept an anecdote, then we may be permitted to draw *some* conclusion from it. However, we must be careful to formulate our conclusions within the limits of what the evidence allows. This is not an easy task, but it's not an impossible one. Our friends' disastrous vacation may spur us to look for further evidence before we travel to Belize ourselves. In this case, we may draw several conclusions, among them the following:

> *Our friends should request a refund from the resort company.*
> *Someone planning a trip to Belize should investigate this resort before staying there.*
> *Someone planning a trip to Belize should consider staying at other resorts.*

We may draw the first conclusion, and pass on this advice. Suppose, now, that we have already booked non-refundable flights to Belize before learning about our friends' misfortunes. In this case, we may want to draw the second conclusion, and the story seems to warrant the move. If several guide books and independent travel-advisory websites voice complaints about the resort that are similar to that of our friends, then we may then draw the third conclusion. If, however, other sources are inconsistent with our friends' experience, then we must consider how all this information fits together. Perhaps the anecdote is exceptional, or perhaps other sources are out of date and our friends' experiences are indicative of a recent change in the quality of the resort. In any case, only further evidence can justify which potential conclusions we may draw, not anything in the anecdote itself. On its own, the anecdote is of limited value as evidence, and any argument that depends exclusively on it to draw a broad and strong conclusion will be inadequate.

Here are two more problematic uses of anecdotal evidence:

> *Don't buy a Ford. My parents drove a Ford. They had nothing but trouble with that rust-bucket for years, and it cost them a bundle in repair bills in the first four years. First it was the transmission, then the suspension, then the brakes, then the engine.*

> *Our company will never hire another graduate from one of the MIT engineering programs. Three years ago we hired two electrical engineering graduates from MIT and they were impossible to work with. They strutted around as if they were hot-shots, completed sub-standard work, one of them was always calling in sick, and they both quit after eight months. So we don't even consider applicants with an MIT background anymore.*

Still, there is one use of anecdotal evidence that may generate an adequate conclusion. When cited as counter-evidence to a universal claim, such as "all swans are white," a single anecdote is logically adequate to draw a strong, negative conclusion. Europeans believed all species of swan to be white on the basis of centuries of experience. That is all anyone had ever seen or reported seeing. However, those who first traveled to Australia returned with reports of black swans. In every other respect these birds resembled swans as Europeans knew them, but they were black. One genuine story of a black swan sighting was sufficient to falsify the universal claim, "all swans are white." (Equally, it may be adequate to conclude that "some swans are not white.") The converse case is also instructive. For approximately 50 years it was believed that the ivory-billed woodpecker was extinct. Then in 2004 a kayaker told a story of seeing a bird fly over him in an Arkansas swamp that matched the woodpecker's description. This single incident is enough to conclude that "the ivory-billed woodpecker may not be extinct." Seven further sightings (although with no good photographic evidence) have made this conclusion stronger, enough so that some ornithologists have drawn the further conclusion that "the ivory-billed woodpecker is not extinct." In both cases, the evidence about non-white swans and living woodpeckers is anecdotal, but the unrestricted nature of the claims they falsify make them adequate to support properly formulated conclusions.

8.4 APPEALS TO IGNORANCE

Sometimes people defend a claim by appealing to the fact that there is no evidence that it is false. By itself this is a completely inadequate reason, for it assumes that in some mysterious way the absence of evidence that something is false supports the claim that it is true. For example:

> I believe in astrology and always read my horoscope in the paper every day. I can't actually prove that it is true, but nobody can disprove it.

In fact, the absence of evidence against something is by itself never a good reason for believing it. Otherwise, we would have a good reason to believe all sorts of silly things. For example:

> The world will come to an end at exactly 12:00 noon EST on a Saturday.

> There are seven invisible leprechauns living in my garden.

> Bill Clinton was never the president of the United States. The real Bill Clinton died in his sleep in 1991, but his body was taken over by creatures from outer space.

None of these statements can be disproved, even though there is no evidence that they are true.

In certain contexts, however, the absence of contrary evidence can be a good supporting reason for a conclusion. If we have some evidence that supports a claim, then the absence of contrary evidence does add some additional support. This additional support is even stronger if we have actually looked for contrary evidence and failed to find any. This is what medical doctors sometimes do when faced with a condition that is difficult to diagnose. The symptoms suggest the patient has a certain disease; a test is performed that could prove that the patient does not have that disease, but the test result is negative. The absence of this piece of contrary evidence is then used as additional support for the initial diagnosis. The legitimacy of the appeal to the absence of contrary evidence in such cases, however, usually requires that there be some direct supporting evidence. And even then, the additional support it provides is usually only of secondary importance. Thus, the tree diagram for an argument with an appeal to the absence of contrary evidence as a premise would have to be a T-argument structure, since it only provides support when joined to other premises. Even in cases where such an appeal is relevant, however, its adequacy as a supporting premise should be assessed by appeal to the criterion of adequacy in the usual way.

8.5 THE SLIPPERY SLOPE FALLACY

We often want to assess a proposal to take some action or adopt a new policy. One important and legitimate way of doing so is to examine the consequences that would result if the action were taken or the policy adopted. If the action or policy is likely to lead to undesirable consequences, then we have a good reason to reject it, and if it is likely to lead to desirable consequences, then we have a good reason to support it. This method of assessment involves making predictions about the future, and it is important to realize that such predictions are always somewhat tentative. Even when there is a wealth of empirical support for predictions, we know how easily they can be wrong: think of weather forecasts and stock market predictions. There is one important aspect of predictions that needs to be noted. When we chain predictions together in the following way:

A will probably lead to B; B will probably lead to C; C will probably lead to D; D will probably lead to E, and E will probably lead to F;

we are not entitled to conclude that A will probably lead to F. This is because when we multiply probabilities, the resulting probability is always reduced. There may be a 50 per cent chance that the next person to walk around the corner will be a woman, and a 50 per cent chance that the woman will be married, but that means that there is only a 25 per cent chance that the next person to walk around the corner will be a married woman. So if each of the probabilities between A and F is 80 per cent, the probability that A will lead to F is only 33 per cent. Clearly, to conclude that A will probably lead to F would be a mistake. Such arguments commit the *SLIPPERY SLOPE* fallacy. The premises of a slippery slope argument present a chain of predictions, each of which may be very strong, but the chain as a whole is weak. The conclusion of such an argument is not adequately supported.

Usually, however, when we make a chain of predictions we cannot, or do not bother to, assign numerical probabilities to each step in the chain. But it is clear that even a chain of "pretty likely" predictions will become weaker as it becomes longer. And if, as often happens, one step in the chain violates the criterion of acceptability, then the prediction of the final outcome will be very weak indeed. For example:

> *If abortion on demand were to become legal, there would be a great increase in abortions. And once abortion became commonplace, there would be a weakening of respect for human life in general. Once the respect for human life was weakened, we would see an increase in euthanasia of all kinds: the elderly, the mentally handicapped, and the physically disabled. Before long we would be getting rid of anyone who is unproductive. In short, it would threaten our civilization. Therefore, we should oppose any move to broaden the grounds for legal abortions.*

This is a clear example of a slippery slope fallacy. Which step is the weakest in the chain is debatable, for none of them is very strong. But the second step—that if abortions become commonplace, there would be a weakening of respect for human life in general—seems especially weak. It might be true that there would be a weakening of respect for human life in general, but there is very little evidence to support this claim.

This example shows another common characteristic of slippery slope arguments: they often omit some of the steps in the chain. It is possible that if society began to get rid of anyone who is unproductive, our civilization would be threatened, but clearly there must be a number of intermediate steps, which the argument omits. There are missing premises that would have to be supplied in order to undertake a complete assessment of the argument.

Sometimes slippery slope arguments omit all the intermediate steps in the chain. For example:

*You should never drink during the day. Once you start doing that, you will end up
as a skid-row bum.*

The only charitable interpretation of this argument is to regard it as having a series of
missing premises that would provide the intermediate steps in the chain. Of course, it is
difficult to assess a series of missing premises of this sort. All we can do is use our own
knowledge to decide whether the chain would be a strong one if it were spelled out in
detail. (And there are some cases in which the slope genuinely is slippery. Alcoholics who
stop drinking are aware that one drink really can lead to disaster, because they find it so
difficult to stop after the first one.)

Slippery slope arguments are superficially similar to another kind of argument
that is not open to the same kind of objection. Sometimes we explore the consequences of a policy by predicting the different consequences that would arise if we
were to adopt the policy. Here our reasoning is as follows:

*A (the policy) will probably lead to B; A will probably lead to C; A will probably
lead to D; A will probably lead to E, and A will probably lead to F.*

If these consequences are bad we will reject the policy, and if they are good we will
accept the policy. But we need to note that each of these predicted consequences is
independent of the others, and thus they do not constitute a *chain* of predictions.
Chained predictions can be diagramed as follows:

We are now considering a series of independent predictions that are diagramed
as follows:

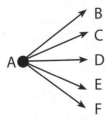

It is important to understand the crucial difference between the two types of reasoning. In slippery slope arguments, our interest is in the last item in the chain, and
it, as we have seen, is vulnerable to the weakness that results from the cumulative

effect of each step being only probable. But when we work out a series of independent predictions, our interest is in all the predictions taken together. Any weaknesses in our predictions are therefore not cumulative. In slippery slope arguments, a single false prediction breaks the chain, whereas a single false prediction in a series of independent predictions leaves the others intact. An argument whose conclusion rests on a series of independent predictions thus is not a slippery slope argument.

Sometimes an argument that commits the slippery slope fallacy will not at first appear to be a slippery slope argument because the author uses another metaphor. In particular, arguments that invoke a domino effect, or arguments claiming that one action is the thin edge of the wedge, have the same logical structure of slippery slope arguments. Because they have this structure, they commit the slippery slope fallacy. Here are two more slippery slope arguments. Note that the first is part of a reductio ad absurdum argument:

> *The IRS's recent decision that many of the perks employers give their employees are taxable benefits is a silly and dangerous precedent. It is one thing to tax food and lodging when it is routinely provided by employers. But now they are going after things like free parking. Next will be the pencils and paper clips we all take home from work. Then it will be office Christmas parties: there will be auditors hovering, clipboards in hand, keeping track of how many free drinks and peanuts we have consumed. And when they realize that for many of us the greatest perk is being able to daydream on the job, they will even begin to tax our dreams.*

> *Everyone accepts the general principle that lying is immoral. Many people also believe that some exceptions to the rule are permitted. This, of course, raises the question of what these exceptions should be. People always start with the easy ones: we should be prepared to lie, they say, if it is the only way of preventing the death of an innocent person, and they point to examples such as lying to the Gestapo to protect Jews. But then, they argue, since lying in these cases is justified, surely it is justified to tell lies to protect your country in wartime; for example, when captured by the enemy. And then, of course, lying would be justified to protect your country in peacetime, and so also must lying to protect your government. It is then but a very short step to lying to protect your reputation if you happen to be a government official. Once you allow that any lie is capable of being justified, you are inexorably led to telling lies whenever you feel like it.*

8.6 CAUSAL FALLACIES

We now come to a group of fallacies that often arise when reasoning about causes. But first we need to say something about the concept of causation. The idea of a cause is an extremely elusive concept, and a great deal of philosophical and scientific energy has been devoted to giving an adequate account of it. Scientists often avoid the term altogether and refer instead to correlations between variables. It is clear, however, that these correlations are intended to reveal causal factors (see section 11.1). These causal factors can best be expressed as statements of necessary and sufficient causal conditions in the way described in section 3.8.

It is misleading to speak of an event as having a single cause, for there are always a large number of causal conditions involved in any event. When we ask, *What caused the explosion at the mill?*, we are not usually looking for a complete causal explanation of the explosion. We don't want to know about the various necessary conditions (the presence of oxygen, the presence of a combustible gas, etc.). We are usually looking for the one condition that, along with these necessary conditions, is sufficient to cause the explosion. In explaining the *CAUSAL FALLACIES*, we shall simplify the causal picture by assuming that events have only a single cause. It is possible to explain these fallacies without this simplifying assumption, but the explanations would be extremely cumbersome. The nature of the fallacies is the same in either case.

8.6.1 Post Hoc

If A causes B then A must occur in order for B to occur, and the cause usually precedes its effect in time as well as in the causal order of events. If watering and fertilizing a house plant cause it to bloom, then we have to water and fertilize it before we can expect it to bloom. But the fact that causes precede their effects in this way does not mean that everything that precedes some event must be its cause. It is a necessary, but not a sufficient, condition of a cause that it must precede its effect. If we forget this distinction, we can be led to commit the *POST HOC* fallacy. The name comes from the Latin phrase *post hoc ergo propter hoc*, which means *after this therefore because of this*. The fallacy of post hoc is committed when it is argued that something that occurs before some event must be its cause. For example:

> *The stove in your apartment was working perfectly until you moved in, but the next day the oven stopped working. It must be something you're doing that has caused the problem.*

This inference is obviously fallacious. It is possible that the landlord's conclusion is correct, but the argument provides very little support for it.

Here are some more examples of post hoc fallacies:

In the 1960s the trend towards married women working outside the home began to emerge. Within a few years we began to see a significant increase in the divorce rate, which has now reached alarming proportions. Obviously, if we value the family as an institution, we should try to prevent married women from working outside the home.

I tried some Russian caviar at Mattie's cocktail party last Saturday and was so sick when I got home that I got almost no sleep that night. There must have been something wrong with the caviar or else I'm allergic to the stuff.

In Aesop's fable, the rooster reasoned as follows: Every morning without fail, the sun rises just a few minutes after I start crowing. I must be the greatest creature in the world since I cause the sun to rise every day.

8.6.2 Confusing Cause and Effect

If A causes B, then whenever A is present (under the appropriate circumstances) we will find B as well. If inflation causes unemployment, then wherever we find inflation we should also find unemployment. This fact can sometimes make it difficult to know which is the cause and which is the effect. The fallacy of *CONFUSING CAUSE AND EFFECT* is committed when an effect is identified as a cause and the cause is identified as the effect. For example:

According to a recent Gallup poll, married couples with no children have approximately 20 per cent more disposable income than married couples with children. This shows that it is affluence that causes declining birth rates.

The conclusion of this argument is not as well supported by the premise as the conclusion that having children leads people to have less disposable income. It is, of course, *possible* that affluence causes declining birth rates, but not very likely.

Here are some more examples of arguments that commit (or seem to commit) the fallacy of confusing cause and effect:

As the population of dark spotted moths grew larger throughout the Industrial Revolution in nineteenth-century England, smog and air pollution in the country grew worse. Therefore, the increasing number of dark spotted moths was the source of the smog and air pollution.

Did you notice at the party last night that as soon as Kevin and Paula arrived, she told him not to drink too much, and then Kevin proceeded to get really drunk? That always seems to happen when they are at a party together: she always complains about his drinking, and he always gets drunk. If only she would shut up about it, he probably wouldn't get drunk at all.

Most people are afraid of hospitals. They have friends and relatives who have gone into hospital for routine surgery or for some tests and then either died or came down with some chronic debilitating illness. In fact, when you come to think of it, almost everyone who dies seems to die in a hospital. Hospitals really are dangerous places.

8.6.3 Common Cause

One reason why A and B may always occur together is that one of them causes the other (either A causes B or B causes A). But there may be another explanation: it may be that A and B are each caused by some third event, C. In these cases, if we ignore C, we can easily misinterpret the causal relationship. The *COMMON CAUSE* fallacy is committed when it is claimed that there is a causal relation between A and B when in fact both A and B are caused by a third factor, C. For example:

During the trial of a 17-year-old Toronto youth accused of raping and then murdering a 26-year-old suburban housewife, the prosecution presented evidence that the youth had a large collection of pornography downloaded on his laptop computer. He had over 50 video clips of what is normally classified as hard-core pornography, and over 4000 violent, pornographic images. Before passing sentence, the judge made the following observation: "If anyone still needs persuading that pornography causes violence against women, this case provides conclusive proof."

The relationship between pornography and violence is a complex one, and we cannot say that the judge's conclusion is false. But the evidence is quite weak in this instance, since it is anecdotal and the argument does not consider a range of cases in a systematic manner. The judge is overstating the degree of support a single example lends to the general claim. Anecdotes can exert a powerful influence on our general opinions if, as in this instance, we overestimate their probative value. A second point to note about this conclusion is that the judge fails to meet two of the criteria of a legitimate authority in this case: (1) questions about the causal relationship between pornography and human behavior do not fall within the realm of a judge's authority (criterion no. 3 in 8.2); and (2) there is little consensus among social scientists about the specific nature of this relationship (criterion no. 5 in 8.2). The evidence cited is probably better interpreted as showing that the youth's fascination with pornography and his crime were both caused by some underlying psychological factor.

Here are some more arguments that commit (or seem to commit) the fallacy of common cause:

Recent studies have shown that people who are commonly regarded as being successful have much larger vocabularies than average. This is no accident. Having an extensive vocabulary is an important factor in producing success.

The solution to the problem of poverty in is obvious. People who live below the poverty line normally have very little education: more than half have less than a grade eight education. Therefore, the way to overcome poverty is to provide incentives and encouragement for poor people to go back to school to complete their education.

The best way to clear up the sinus congestion that usually accompanies a sore throat is to get rid of the sore throat by taking some of those medicated throat lozenges you can get at the drug store. After all, it's the sore throat that causes the congestion: haven't you noticed that you always get a sore throat just before your head gets stuffed up?

8.7 SELF-TEST NO. 14

Explain any weaknesses in the following arguments:

1. They say there is no proof that living near nuclear power plants causes birth defects. Well, my sister-in-law, who lives only two miles from the Southport nuclear power plant, had a miscarriage last year, and they can't prove that it wasn't caused by the power plant.

2. A recent study showed that students who cram immediately before examinations usually get lower grades than those who do not. Well, I certainly won't make that mistake this term. I'm not even going to open a book during the exam period.

3. Our major objection to international trade agreements such as the North American Free Trade Agreement and the General Agreement on Tariffs and Trades is not with the short- and medium-term consequences, since it is likely that, on balance, the US will benefit economically. Our concern is

with the long term. Gradually, our government will lose the ability to use domestic regulations and foreign trade tariffs to keep jobs in the US when industries find cheaper labor markets in places such as Mexico and southeast Asia. Each time the government capitulates to pressure from international corporations, it is another nail in the coffin of American job security.

4. I was in good health until they started that darn fluoridation program. Within a few weeks I started getting an upset stomach every day or two, and within three months I was having really bad stomach cramps. I went to the doctor, who discovered that I had a duodenal ulcer. The doctor treated me, of course, but I knew what I needed to do—start drinking bottled water, which I do now. That was two years ago, and I've been fine ever since. But it just goes to show how dangerous fluoridation is.

5. The high-school drop-out rate in Saskatchewan has declined by more than 50 per cent since 1950. During the same period, there has been an increase of about 40 per cent in the rate of juvenile delinquency. I can't believe this is a mere coincidence. Clearly, we should have higher academic standards in school to force the weaker students out and into the real world where they will develop a sense of responsibility.

6. Pope Francis is one of the most open-minded pontiffs ever, and he has spent years thinking about what is best for the Roman Catholic Church. If he believes that it would be wrong to admit women into the priesthood, then we should accept his judgment.

7. (Comments by a city politician on a proposal that the city should fund a drop-in center for unemployed workers.)

   I would be prepared to support the proposal if I thought there was a need for it. But I really don't see that there is a need. I get phone calls from taxpayers about all sorts of things, but I cannot recall ever getting a phone call from anyone suggesting we need such a center.

8. All the public opinion polls for the last year have shown that the Obama government has an exceptionally low approval rating. So everyone obviously knows that incumbent Democrats are not going to be re-elected to Senate or Congress.

9. Last weekend there was a large demonstration by people protesting US involvement in the Middle East. There were so many people that they spilled out all over the northbound lanes of University Avenue, and the police had to

re-route traffic. Like many other innocent people, I was seriously inconvenienced by the inconsiderate behavior of the demonstrators. The incident has convinced me that the time has come to ban all demonstrations on public property.

10. If some of the poorest developing nations are released from their debts, then other poor, developing countries will also want their debts forgiven. And if all the national debts of these poor countries are forgiven, then they won't feel obliged to pay back loans in the future. After a while wealthy countries won't see the point of paying off their own debts, and all the lending institutions will be bled dry. So we can't release very poor countries from their debts without crippling the global economy.

11. Our family physician says that marijuana should not be decriminalized for medical use because it has no real value for treating any physical condition. According to him, people who want to decriminalize it just want to get high, not help people with medical problems. With 30 years of medical training and practice behind him, that's enough for me. We shouldn't trust these people who are lobbying to decriminalize marijuana.

12. "This bill and the foregoing remarks of the majority remind me of an old Arabian proverb: 'If the camel once gets his nose in the tent, his body will soon follow.' If adopted, the legislation will mark the inception of aid, supervision, and ultimately control of education in this country by the federal authorities." (US Senator Barry Goldwater)

8.8 QUESTIONS FOR DISCUSSION

Discuss the strengths and weaknesses of the following arguments:

1. Almost all military experts hold that we must have standing armies because of the continuing threat of war. The reality is quite different: the continuing threat of war is caused by the existence of standing armies.

2. There has been a great deal of criticism recently of the quality of high-school education in Alberta. People seem to think the quality is declining. But the statistics don't bear this out; in fact they show that quality is increasing. The average grades of high-school graduates have increased by at least 10 per cent since 1977.

3. People who believe they have a duty to help those who are less fortunate

than themselves almost always get pleasure from their unselfish actions. This just proves that it is the expectation of pleasure that causes people to act morally or to adopt their moral beliefs.

4. Athletes who earn multi-million-dollar salaries deserve them. Those who are so critical of these "astronomical" salaries conveniently overlook two reasons that make such salaries entirely justified. First, these athletes are supremely talented. They are able to perform better than almost everyone else, including most other athletes. Second, they have only a few short years to make their fortune, since in most cases they will have retired from professional sport by their mid-thirties. To compare their salaries with what most people earn you would have to spread athletes' million-dollar salaries out over 40 years to make the comparison fair.

5. Ken is the leading scorer on the university hockey team this year. He is averaging one goal per game this year, whereas last year he scored only three goals in the entire season. He claims that what made the difference is that he found God last summer; before each game he prays to God to give him the strength and concentration to score at least one goal. Well, maybe he's right, and we should try to get the rest of the team to get religion. If it works for Ken, who is to say it won't work for the other players.

6. Same sex marriage was legalized in Canada on July 20, 2005, after much debate among politicians and the public. The following letter responds to the debate:

If we allow people to marry without regard to their sex, who is to say that we can't discriminate on the basis of number? It is a small step then to legalizing polygamy.

Once we open up marriage beyond the boundary of one man and one woman only, there will be no difference based on the Charter of Rights and Freedoms between gay marriage and polygamous marriage. (Letter to the editor, *Globe and Mail*, June 19, 2003.)

9. DEDUCTIVE REASONING

In this and the next chapter we consider two types of reasoning, each of which has distinctive features and therefore requires special treatment. Both of these types still rely upon the three criteria of a sound argument for assessment, but the application of the criteria requires a detailed understanding of how these arguments work.

9.1 THE NATURE OF DEDUCTIVE REASONING

In section 1.2, we defined logical strength as the property of an argument whose premises, if true, support its conclusion. We also pointed out that logical strength is a matter of degree, and we distinguished deductive and inductive arguments on that basis: deductive arguments are those whose premises guarantee the truth of the conclusion, and inductive arguments are those whose premises make it reasonable to accept the conclusion but do not absolutely guarantee its truth. To understand the nature of deductive reasoning, it is essential to understand the fundamental difference between the two types of reasoning.

Most of the logically strong arguments we have considered so far in this book have been inductive arguments, i.e., arguments that do not provide absolute guarantees. This is not necessarily a weakness, for in many cases the most we can expect of an argument is a degree of strength that falls somewhat short of constituting an absolute guarantee. Consider the following inductive argument:

The Gordon Street bridge is regularly inspected by qualified engineers.
Vehicles have been driving over it for years.
Therefore, it will be safe to drive over it tomorrow.

This is a logically strong argument, but it does not provide an absolute guarantee that it will be safe to drive over the bridge tomorrow. There is a remote possibility that it will collapse at the very moment I cross it. If the premises are true, then the conclusion will very likely, or probably, or almost certainly be true; but the truth of the premises cannot absolutely rule out the possibility that the conclusion will be false. In other words, the conclusion might turn out to be false even though the premises are true.

But deductive arguments are not like this. The conclusion of a logically strong deductive argument cannot possibly be false if its premises are true. Consider the following argument:

> *If you are under the age of 18, then you are legally a minor.*
> *If you are legally a minor, then you cannot be sued.*
> *Therefore, if you are under the age of 18, then you cannot be sued.*

Unlike the argument about the Gordon Street bridge, it is impossible for the conclusion of this argument to be false unless at least one of the premises is also false. If its premises are true, the truth of the conclusion is guaranteed.

Logically strong deductive arguments are able to guarantee, or conclusively establish, their conclusions because the logical strength of deductive arguments does not depend upon their specific content, but on their form or structure. Consider another example of a deductive argument:

> *If Sadie lost her purse, then she lost her student ID card.*
> *If she lost her student ID card, then she won't be allowed to write her exams.*
> *Therefore, if Sadie lost her purse, then she won't be allowed to write her exams.*

This argument has the same logical form or structure as the previous example. This form can be expressed as follows:

> If p then q.
> If q then r.
> Therefore, if p then r.

What is significant about these arguments is not merely that they have the same form but that their logical strength is derived from their form. If we ask why the premises provide strong support for the conclusion, we can ignore the particular content of the arguments because the facts about being under 18 or losing ID cards have no bearing on the logical strength of the argument. It is the form of the argument (i.e., the form or structure of the premises and conclusion and the formal relationships among them) that makes these arguments strong. They are strong arguments *because* of their form. This means that *every* argument with this form will be a logically strong argument. It is their form that determines their strength.

9.2 TRUTH-FUNCTIONAL STATEMENTS

Deductive reasoning relies upon what are called *TRUTH-FUNCTIONAL STATE-MENTS*: every deductive argument includes at least one truth-functional statement. In order to understand deductive reasoning, therefore, it is necessary to understand what a truth-functional statement is. All statements can be divided into two classes: simple and complex. A *SIMPLE STATEMENT* is one that does not contain any other statement as a part, and a *COMPLEX STATEMENT* is one that contains another statement as a component part. Here are some simple statements:

Virginia got a job with HSBC in 1973.

I lost the keys.

Mark has had a great deal of experience dealing with emotionally disturbed children.

Shirley loves him.

Here are some complex statements with the component statements underlined:

Virginia got a job with HSBC in 1973, and she became a vice-president after 22 years.

Either I lost the keys, or they have been stolen.

It is false that Mark has had a great deal of experience dealing with emotionally disturbed children.

Tom believes that Shirley loves him.

Truth-functional statements are a sub-class of complex statements that are distinguished by the way their truth is determined. Ordinarily, when we want to determine whether a statement is true, we look directly for facts or reasons to tell us whether what the statement says is true. With truth-functional statements, however, the procedure is a little different. We have to proceed indirectly, for the truth of truth-functional statements is determined not by directly seeing whether what *it* says is true but by seeing whether *its components* are true. The truth of truth-functional statements is thus a function of the truth values of its component statements.

Consider the first example given above. It is a truth-function because in order to determine whether it is true, we must separately determine the truth or falsity of its two component statements. If they are both true, then the complex statement will also be true. But if either component is false—either because Virginia did not get a job with HSBC in 1973, or because she did not become a vice-president after 22 years—then the statement as a whole will be false. The second example is also a truth-function. Unlike the first example, however, it asserts an *either/or* relationship between its two components. In order for the statement as a whole to be true, only one of the component statements needs to be true. The third example is also a truth function. It is true only when its component statement is false.

The fourth example, however, is not a truth-function even though it is a complex statement, because its truth is not a function of the truth value of its component statement. Tom might believe that Shirley loves him even when she does not, in which case the statement *Tom believes that Shirley loves him* will be true even though the statement *Shirley loves him* is false. Or, Tom might not believe that Shirley loves him even when she does, in which case the statement as a whole will be false even though the component statement is true.

Each of the truth-functional statements includes what is called a *LOGICAL OPERATOR*: *and, either/or,* and *it is false that.* The presence of the logical operator is crucial, since it tells us precisely how the truth of the statement as a whole is determined by the truth values of its component statements. The logical operators define the different kinds of truth-functional statements. There are four kinds of truth-functions that are important for understanding deductive reasoning. We shall follow the standard convention in logic and use the letters p, q, r, and so forth, to stand for the component statements, which may be either simple or complex statements.

1. *NEGATION*: The statement *p is false* is a negation. (Sometimes, negations are written as *not-p*.) A negation is true when its component statement is false, and false when its component statement is true. Thus, the statement *p is false* is true when *p* is false, and false when *p* is true. For example:

It is false that falcons mate while flying.

This statement is true if the statement *falcons mate while flying* is false. If falcons do mate while flying, then the statement is false.

2. *CONJUNCTION*: The statement *p and q* is a conjunction. It is true only when *p* is true and *q* is true; it is false when *p* is false, or when *q* is false, or when both *p* and *q* are false. For example:

Ted and Alice have been married for six years, and they have no children.

This statement is true only if both its component statements, or *CONJUNCTS*, are true. If either conjunct is false, then the conjunction as a whole is false. If Ted and Alice have been married for only five years, then the statement is false even though it may be true that they have no children. If they have a child, then the statement is false, even though it may be true that they have been married for six years.

3. *DISJUNCTION*: The statement *p or q* is a disjunction. It is true when *p* is true, or when *q* is true, or when *p and q* are both true; it is false when both *p and q* are false. For example:

Either Mac did it or Bud did it.

This statement is true if either or both of its component statements, or *DISJUNCTS*, is true. If both disjuncts are false, then the disjunction as a whole is false. If Mac did it, then the statement is true. If Bud did it, then the statement is true. If they both did it, then the statement is true. If neither of them did it, however, the statement is false.

It is important to note that in a disjunctive truth-function the two disjuncts are exhaustive but not exclusive. (Recall the discussion of false dichotomy in section 6.7.4.) This means that the disjuncts cannot both be false, since they are exhaustive, but both may be true, because they are not exclusive. In other words, a sentence such as

Stephen will drive his car or Karen will drive her car

will be true if Stephen drives his car and Karen does not, or if Karen drives her car and Stephen does not, or if both drive their cars; it's false only when neither one drives their own car. This is not how most of us understand disjunctions, however. Ordinarily, we think it is false if both disjuncts are true. But logicians use *or* in a way that suits truth-functional logic but is counterintuitive to most people. The technical reasons behind this special interpretation of *or* need not detain us, but we need to be aware that this is how truth-functional disjunctions operate.

4. *IMPLICATION*: The statement *if p then q* is an implication. The two component sentences in an implication have different names since, unlike conjuncts and disjuncts, each plays a different role: the first is called the *ANTECEDENT*, and the second is called the *CONSEQUENT*. An implication such as *if p then q* is false only when *p* is true and *q* is false; in all other cases (i.e., when *p* is false, or when *q* is true), it is true. For example:

> *If Moe studies hard, then he will get an A average.*

This statement is true if both the antecedent and the consequent are true, that is, if Moe studies hard and also gets an A average. And it is clearly false if the antecedent is true while the consequent is false: if Moe studies hard and does not get an A average. But what about the other two possibilities? If both the antecedent and consequent are false—if Moe doesn't study hard and fails to get an A average—logicians regard the original implication as still being true. And if the antecedent is false while the consequent is true—if Moe doesn't study hard and yet does get an A average—logicians also regard the original implication as true. These last two cases are somewhat counterintuitive. What we want to say is that the original implication *could* still be true in these cases, but not that it *is* true. Logicians admit the oddity but defend it by pointing out that it results from treating implication as a truth-function, and that the power of deductive reasoning is greatly enhanced when implication is given a truth-functional interpretation.

Truth-functional statements are expressed in a variety of ways in English, but it is usually easy to recognize that they are truth-functions. Here are some alternative ways of expressing negations:

> *It is not true that organized crime is controlled exclusively by the Mafia.*

> *John did not win the Alexander Prize for Physics.*

> *His claim that he was at a concert when the break-in occurred isn't true.*

It is easy to see how these statements can be rewritten in the standard *p is false* form.

Here are some truth-functional conjunctions that do not use the word *and* but rely on an equivalent word or phrase:

> *Sarah always worries about getting poor grades, even though she has never had a grade of less than B+.*

The rent on my apartment has increased by 40 per cent in the last 10 years, but my income has only increased by 35 per cent during the same period.

Our conference lost more money this year despite the fact that twice as many people attended as last year.

All these statements express truth-functional conjunctions, since each asserts that both its component statements are true.

Here are some disjunctions that are expressed in variant terms:

You should either fix his lawnmower or buy him a new one.

He must have been extremely upset to have trashed his bicycle like that, or maybe he was just drunk.

There are just two possibilities: raising taxes or reducing expenditures.

Each of these statements is clearly equivalent to a disjunction expressed in the standard *p or q* form.

Implications may be expressed in a wide variety of different sentences. For example:

Once your lease has expired, the landlord is free to raise the rent up to the limit set by the Rent Review Board.

Being a teenager these days means that you have to face a tremendous amount of peer pressure.

Anyone who takes horoscopes seriously must be very gullible.

The theory of evolution implies that God did not create human beings in the way described in the Bible.

Whenever the pressure reaches 300 psi, the release valve automatically opens and reduces the pressure to a safe level.

Being wealthy entails having obligations to those who are less fortunate.

If we rewrite these statements in the appropriate *if p then q* form, we can see that their meaning remains the same:

> *If your lease has expired, then the landlord is free to raise the rent up to the limit set by the Rent Review Board.*

> *If you are a teenager these days, then you have to face a tremendous amount of peer pressure.*

> *If someone takes horoscopes seriously, then that person must be very gullible.*

> *If the theory of evolution is true, then God did not create human beings in the way described in the Bible.*

> *If the pressure reaches 300 psi, then the release valve automatically opens and reduces the pressure to a safe level.*

> *If you are wealthy, then you have obligations to those who are less fortunate.*

9.3 FORMAL VALIDITY AND SOUNDNESS

The concept of logical strength is central in our approach to the assessment of arguments, since, as we saw in section 5.2.1, it provides the basis for the second and third criteria of a sound argument—relevance, and adequacy. When applied to deductive arguments, however, the concept of logical strength has a narrower meaning than it does when applied to non-deductive arguments. Logical strength is the property of an argument whose premises, if true, provide support for its conclusion. But the support claimed by a deductive argument amounts to a guarantee of the truth of its conclusion. The term *FORMAL VALIDITY* is used to describe this special kind of logical strength; a formally valid argument is defined as an argument such that, if its premises are true, then its conclusion must also be true. The phrase *must be* in this definition is to be interpreted strictly. Since it expresses the idea of a guarantee, it does not mean *is very probably*, but *is necessarily*.

The concept of validity or formal validity has a corollary that it is useful to note. It follows from the definition of formal validity that a valid argument cannot have true premises and a false conclusion, and this means that if we know that the conclusion of a valid argument is false, then we know that at least one of the premises must be false. Otherwise, the argument would violate the definition of a valid argument.

Notice that the definition of validity does not claim that the premises of a valid argument *are* true, but only that *if* the premises are true then the conclusion must also be true. Conversely, an argument can be valid even if its premises are false, since validity is entirely a structural feature. Saying that an argument is valid thus does not mean that it satisfies the first criterion of a sound argument—that is, that it must have acceptable premises. On the other hand, all valid arguments satisfy the second and third criteria—that is, relevance and adequacy. This is the great strength of deductive reasoning: once we know that a deductive argument is valid, we know that it completely satisfies both the second and third criteria, and we know this simply because the form or structure of the argument constitutes a valid argument form. A valid argument form thus guarantees both that the premises of the argument are relevant to the conclusion and that they are adequate to prove the truth of the conclusion. Let us now identify some of these valid argument forms.

9.4 VALID ARGUMENT FORMS

A valid argument form is any set of statements such that every argument with that form is a valid argument. In other words, if an argument has a valid argument form, then if its premises are true, its conclusion must also be true. To show that an argument is valid, therefore, we need only to show that it has a valid argument form. There are a great many valid argument forms, but we shall consider only four basic forms from truth-functional logic. They are basic in the sense that they frequently occur in everyday use, and that many other valid argument forms can be derived from these four forms.

1. AFFIRMING THE ANTECEDENT

If p then q.
p.
Therefore, q.

2. DENYING THE CONSEQUENT

If p then q.
Not-q.
Therefore, not-p.

3. CHAIN ARGUMENT

If p then q.
If q then r.
Therefore, if p then r.

4. DISJUNCTIVE SYLLOGISM

Either p or q.
Not-p.
Therefore, q.

Whenever we find an argument whose form is identical to one of these valid argument forms, we know that it must be a valid argument. We identify the form of a deductive argument by reconstructing it. But when reconstructing deductive arguments, we proceed a little differently from the way described in Chapter 4. Consider the following argument:

> *If the police knew that Jones had a motive for the crime, then he would be a suspect. But he is not a suspect, so they obviously don't know that he hated the victim.*

To reconstruct this argument we first need to identify the truth-functional statements and their logical operators. This would give us:

> *If the police knew that Jones had a motive for the crime, **then** Jones would be a suspect.*
> *Jones is not a suspect.*
> *Therefore, the police do not know that Jones had a motive.*

(We'll explain why we changed the way the conclusion is formulated in a moment.)

But now, instead of numbering the premises and drawing a standard tree diagram, we symbolize the statements to bring out their truth-functional relationships:

If p then q.
Not-q.
Therefore, not-p.

Now, we simply compare this form with the valid argument forms. If it matches one of them, then it is a valid deductive argument. Our example has the form of denying the consequent, so we know that it is a valid argument. Note that the tree diagram for each of these valid argument forms is always a T-argument structure, since clearly it is only if both premises are true that they provide support for the conclusion.

When reconstructing deductive arguments, there are two things we need to watch for. First, we must be careful to ensure that the meaning of the component statements is the same each time it appears in the argument. If a statement is used ambiguously in an argument, the argument will not be valid. In the above example, for example, we have changed the wording of the conclusion from *They obviously don't know that he hated the victim* to *The police do not know that Jones had a motive.* In the context of the argument, it is clear that these two statements have the same meaning, since hating the victim means that Jones had a motive.

Second, we must be consistent in symbolizing negative statements. A statement such as

Jones is not a suspect

can be symbolized either as *not-p* or as *p*. If the argument has the form of affirming the antecedent or of a chain argument, it is better to symbolize a negative statement simply as *p*. But in arguments whose form is denying the consequent or disjunctive syllogism, the negative statements play a special role, and if a negative statement appears in the first premise it should always be symbolized simply as *p*. For example:

If he has an alibi, then he is not a suspect.
But he is a suspect.
Therefore, he does not have an alibi.

The first premise should be symbolized as *if p then q*. And this means we must symbolize the second premise as *not-q* since it is the negation of the consequent of the first premise. Since the conclusion must be symbolized as *not-p*, it is now easy to see that the argument has the form of denying the consequent.

As long as we have correctly identified the form of an argument as valid, then, to repeat the point made earlier, we will know that if its premises are true, its conclusion must also be true. Of course, when a valid argument has false premises, the guarantee is voided: the conclusion may be true or it may be false, for we have lost our guarantee.

These valid argument forms underlie many arguments we encounter in a variety of contexts. Often they are combined together in the same argument, and sometimes they produce quite complex logical structures. Consider the following argument:

> If we want a healthy economy, then we must have a balanced budget, and if we are to have a balanced budget, then government funding for social programs will have to be cut back drastically. But if government funding for social programs is cut, then the private sector will have to do more to support education, health care, and private welfare organizations. So, if we are to have a healthy economy, then the private sector must provide much more support for social programs. The question is whether the private sector is willing to provide this support. There is little doubt that a healthy economy should be our top priority. Therefore, the private sector must be willing to do much more to support social programs.

When we reconstruct this argument we have the following:

> (1) If we want a healthy economy, then we must have a balanced budget. (if p then q)
> (2) If we are to have a balanced budget, then government funding for social programs will have to be cut back drastically. (if q then r)
> (3) If government funding for social programs is cut, then the private sector will have to do more to support education, health care, and private welfare organizations. (if r then s)
> (4) Therefore, if we are to have a healthy economy, then the private sector must provide much more support for social programs. (if p then s)
> (5) There is little doubt that a healthy economy should be our top priority. (p)
> (6) Therefore, the private sector must be willing to do much more to support social programs. (s)

Is this a valid argument? If the premises are true, must the conclusion be true as well? Even though some of the premises may be false or unacceptable (for example, 2 and 5), this is a valid argument. To show that it is valid, however, requires us to show that it uses only valid argument forms. To do this, we first write down the forms of the statements that constitute the argument:

> (1) If p then q.
> (2) If q then r.

(3) If r then s.
(4) If p then s.
(5) p.
(6) s.

To show the validity of this argument we reason as follows:

    (a) 1 and 2 are the premises of a chain argument whose conclusion is *if p then r*.

    (b) This conclusion (i.e., *if p then r*) and 3 are the premises of another chain argument whose conclusion is 4. (This means that 4 is validly derived from 1, 2, and 3.)

    (c) 4 and 5 are the premises of an argument affirming the antecedent whose conclusion is 6.

    (d) Therefore, 6 has been validly derived from the given premises.

In other words, if 1, 2, 3, and 5 are true (these are the premises whose truth we are being asked to accept), then we can derive 4 and 6. Therefore, the argument is a valid one. If we believe that the premises are true, then we must accept the conclusion. On the other hand, if we believe that the conclusion is false, we will have to reject one of the premises.

9.5 FORMAL INVALIDITY

Just as there are certain arguments whose strength depends solely upon their form, there are certain arguments whose weakness depends solely upon their form. Such arguments are called formally invalid. A formally invalid argument is one that lacks formal validity; if its premises are true, its conclusion may nevertheless turn out to be false. *FORMAL INVALIDITY* is not always a crushing verdict on an argument, for many strong arguments (including most strong inductive arguments) lack formal validity. Arguments can be strong even when they are formally invalid, for all strong inductive arguments lack formal validity. The strength of such arguments depends upon their particular content; the premises do provide support for the conclusion, but the support does not derive from the logical form of the argument.

However, there are two types of fallacies involving formal invalidity that are worth considering. Both occur frequently in real life, and sometimes it is difficult to recognize them because of their similarity to the valid argument forms of affirming the antecedent and denying the consequent.

1. Fallacy of *DENYING THE ANTECEDENT*

> If p then q.
> Not-p.
> Therefore, not-q.

For example:

> *If the police knew that Jones had a motive for the crime, then he would be a suspect. But the police do not know that Jones had a motive. Therefore, he is not a suspect.*

The form of this argument shows that it commits the fallacy of denying the antecedent. We can see why this is a fallacious argument by noting that there are other reasons for regarding someone as a suspect besides knowing that the person had a motive. For example, those who had the opportunity to commit a crime are usually treated as suspects. So the fact that the police do not know that Jones had a motive does not rule out the possibility that he may still be a suspect. Thus, the truth of the premises of this argument would be consistent with the falsity of the conclusion, which of course means that the argument must be invalid.

2. Fallacy of *AFFIRMING THE CONSEQUENT*

> If p then q.
> q.
> Therefore, p.

For example:

> *If the police knew that Jones had a motive for the crime, then he would be a suspect. And he is a suspect. Therefore, the police must know that he has a motive for the crime.*

The form of this argument shows that it commits the fallacy of affirming the consequent. We can see why this is a fallacious argument by noting that there are other reasons the police might have for regarding Jones as a suspect. They may, for example, have an eyewitness who claims to have seen Jones at the scene of the crime. In this case, the fact that Jones is a suspect might not rest on the police claim that he has a motive but on the testimony of the eyewitness. Thus, the truth of the premises of this argument would be consistent with the falsity of the conclusion, which means that the argument must be invalid.

9.6 SELF-TEST NO. 15

Reconstruct the following deductive arguments and determine whether they are formally valid, and, if they are not, whether they are formally invalid.

1. Look, if you buy a new coat, you won't be able to buy your textbooks for next term. And if you don't have the textbooks, your grades will suffer. So if you get a new coat, your grades are going to suffer.

2. I'm sure it wasn't Ellen who violated the confidentiality of the committee by revealing what took place at the meeting. If she had done that, then she would have harmed herself more than anyone else. And you know what Ellen is like: she would never do anything that was not in her self-interest.

3. I have an appointment to see my doctor this afternoon. He called yesterday to tell me that after consulting several specialists he has decided that surgery would be useless, but he wants to see me today. In general, as I understand it, there are only two treatments for my condition that are likely to do any good: either surgery or a long program of physiotherapy. So I suppose he wants to see me to set up a physiotherapy program.

4. The coach is worried that the football team will lose if it rains during the game next Saturday: he thinks the team doesn't play very well when the field is muddy. But the weather forecast is for sunny weather for the whole weekend. That's good news; it means we will win the game on Saturday.

5. If the Republicans had won more than 50 per cent of the popular vote in the 2008 election then they certainly would have gained a mandate from the voters to implement the Marriage Protection Act. But they did not win more than 50 per cent of the popular vote. So they certainly did not have a mandate to implement the Marriage Protection Act.

6. Chris has decided to run for president of the students' council. That's a pity because he is bound to lose. If Chris is going to win the election, he will have to be known to a lot of students. But hardly anyone knows Chris.

7. I told you Chris would lose the election. If he had been known to a lot of students, then he would have won. But hardly anyone knew who he was.

8. Left-wing radicals talk a great deal about their right to freedom of speech when they are under attack, but are strangely silent when it is the freedom of speech of conservatives that is under attack. If they were really committed to freedom of speech, then they would defend freedom of speech whenever and wherever it comes under attack. Their silence when conservatives like Rush Limbaugh are under attack shows that they are not really committed to freedom of speech at all.

9. If this is really question 5, then I must be losing my mind. But this is not question 5, so (thank heavens) I'm not losing my mind.

10. If I have not lost my mind, then this must be question 10. This is question 10. Therefore, I have not lost my mind.

9.7 QUESTIONS FOR DISCUSSION

The following deductive arguments may combine two or more argument forms, and may have missing premises. Supply the missing parts you think are intended, and test for validity.

1. Ken says that he does not have a logical mind: he complains that whenever he hears the word *validity*, he goes into a state of intellectual shock. Well, he is just being perverse. Anyone who can pass university-level courses must be able to think rationally, and anyone who can think rationally must have the capacity to reason logically. And Ken is obviously successful in passing his courses. So, he must have the capacity to reason logically.

2. *Jay*: There is a rumor going around that Fred is going to resign. This creates a really interesting situation. You see, if Fred resigns, then Grace will be promoted to Fred's position. And if Grace gets promoted, then Howard is going to be so upset that he will certainly quit. So, if Fred resigns then Howard will quit.

   Alf: But I happen to know that Fred is definitely not going to resign. Therefore, Howard will not quit.

3. If he tells his teacher he cheated, he will be punished by the principal. But if he doesn't tell his teacher he cheated, he will be punished by his parents. Either way he is going to be punished.

4. Despite the fact that the social sciences must, if they are to sustain their

status as sciences, claim to be able to make accurate predictions of human behavior, it is not surprising that the social sciences have such an abysmal record when it comes to making actual predictions. To predict anything, including human behavior, one must rely upon a deterministic theory about the causes of whatever behavior one is trying to predict, whether it is the movements of the planets, a rise in the inflation rate, or an increase in violent crime rates. Therefore, since the social sciences are committed to the claim that they can predict human behavior, they must rely upon a deterministic theory of human behavior. But these deterministic theories are false, as can be seen by the following argument. If some human behavior is genuinely free, then it is false that all human behavior is subject to deterministic laws. But we all know from our personal experience that some of our behavior is free: every time we deliberate about something, we are directly conscious that what we decide is not determined by anything, but is a decision freely arrived at. Otherwise, we would not waste our time thinking about the matter, and would just let deterministic fate decide for us. So, since we know that some human behavior is free, we know that deterministic theories must be false. This, of course, means that the social sciences cannot really predict human behavior, and their failure to do so should no longer surprise us.

5. In Dostoevsky's novel *The Brothers Karamazov*, Ivan tries to persuade his brothers that if God did not exist, then everything would be permitted. He means by this that if there is no God, then anything we do would be morally acceptable. One brother, Dmitri, happily accepts Ivan's claim, apparently because he reasons that since there is no God, then everything really is permitted. The other brother, Alyosha, is deeply troubled by Ivan's hypothesis and Dmitri's response. He believes that not everything is permitted, since he is convinced that the slaughter of innocent children is inherently wrong. He is willing to accept Ivan's claim about the moral implications if God does not exist. However, he does not share Dmitri's acceptance that Goes does not exist.

10. INDUCTIVE REASONING

10.1 THE NATURE OF INDUCTIVE REASONING

Inductive arguments are distinguished from deductive arguments by the fact that they don't guarantee their conclusions. (The ability to guarantee their conclusions, as we saw in Chapter 9, is a defining characteristic of valid deductive arguments.) It will help us to understand the nature of inductive reasoning if we explain this difference in more detail. The ability of valid deductive arguments to guarantee their conclusions derives from the fact that deductive reasoning merely draws out, or makes explicit, information that is already contained in the premises. Consider any formally valid argument, and it can be seen that the premises always implicitly contain the information that is stated in the conclusion. Often this is quite obvious, but sometimes it is not. When it is not obvious, however, seeing that the argument is formally valid is the same thing as seeing that the conclusion is implicit in the premises. But if the conclusion is implicitly contained in the premises, then to assert the premises *is* to assert the conclusion. Clearly, then, if the premises are true, then the conclusion must also be true. Stating that the conclusion is true is only making explicit what has already been stated in asserting that the premises are true.

But this characteristic reveals the major weakness in deductive reasoning, namely, that its usefulness is limited to exploring the implications of what we already know or assume to be true. Wherever there is an organized body of knowledge or truth-claims—as in science, law, theology, history, mathematics, indeed any academic discipline—deductive reasoning can generate knowledge that seems to be new, but this knowledge is actually implicit in our current knowledge. Genuinely new knowledge, however, cannot be derived from deductive reasoning alone. When we want to generate genuinely new knowledge, we must rely upon inductive reasoning. Almost every increase in scientific knowledge and most new common-sense knowledge is genuinely new and was not implicit in our previous knowledge. The knowledge of the causes of cancer or of how the stock market will behave if the price of oil drops suddenly cannot be discovered merely by drawing out the logical implications of our current knowledge. Our current knowledge is indeed necessary as a basis for such discoveries, but it is not sufficient. Genuinely new knowledge can arise only through the use of inductive forms of reasoning. Inductive reasoning is thus much more powerful than deductive reasoning. It can overcome ignorance in a way that deductive reasoning cannot.

But the power of inductive reasoning comes at a price. The absolute guarantee that valid deductive reasoning can provide for its conclusions is beyond the capacity of inductive reasoning: the conclusion of an inductive argument can never be more than probably true. This is because inductive reasoning *extrapolates* on what we know, using our current knowledge to arrive at conclusions that go beyond what is strictly, deductively implied by the available evidence. The probability that a conclusion reached through inductive reasoning is true may be very high and may even approach certainty. But certainty can never, in principle, be achieved. There is only one way of achieving certainty through reasoning, and that is by using a deductive argument. If we want to reach new knowledge that goes beyond what is implicit in our premises, we have to settle for something less than certainty.

The strength of inductive arguments depends not on their form but on their content. Only deductive arguments derive their logical strength from their form alone. This means that we cannot produce a catalogue of logically strong inductive argument forms as we could for valid deductive arguments. There are certain important inductive argument forms, but these forms by themselves tell us nothing about the logical strength of the arguments. To determine the strength of an inductive argument, we must always examine its content. For example, as we saw in section 8.2, in order to determine whether appeals to authority are legitimate, we have to examine the particular authority being appealed to and the particular claim involved. Indeed, most of the weaknesses described in Chapters 6, 7, and 8 rest upon an analysis of content.

There are, however, four types of inductive arguments that are widely used and that are strong arguments when certain conditions are met. It is useful to briefly examine these inductive argument forms, in order to learn what these conditions are and what weaknesses to look for. If any of these weaknesses is present, then the probability that the conclusion will be true is reduced. Each inductive argument form is prone to its own type of weaknesses, so it is important to be able to recognize the form of an inductive argument before assessing it. The four inductive argument forms we will examine all play a significant role in both the natural and social sciences, but they are also frequently and legitimately used outside the domain of science.

10.2 INDUCTIVE GENERALIZATION

The inductive generalizations we will look at have the following form:

> *Z per cent of observed Fs are G.*
> *It is probable, therefore, that Z per cent of all Fs are G.*

For example, suppose we want to know what percentage of students at a particular university believe in God. Clearly, it would be extremely difficult to ask every student at the university whether they believe in God. It is much easier to select a *sample* of students and determine their religious beliefs and then to generalize the results to the whole student body. *SAMPLING* involves observing a portion of a population in order to draw a conclusion about the entire population. This is a useful method for making justifiable claims about what trends can be found in a population without observing each and every member. Moreover, if the population size is large, it may be the only way to make such claims. Whenever we use a sample of some population as the evidence from which we draw a conclusion about the whole population, our reasoning will be in the form of an inductive generalization. Thus, our example would be written out as follows:

> *Sixty per cent of students at the University of X who were questioned believe in God.*
> *It is probable, therefore, that approximately 60 per cent of all students at the University of X believe in God.*

There are two possible weaknesses in inductive generalizations, both of which pertain to the nature of the sample. The first and most important is that the sample may not be representative of the population it is drawn from. If it is an *unrepresentative* or *biased* sample, the argument is significantly weakened. So when assessing any inductive generalization we should always ask:

(1) Is the sample representative?

In other words, is the sample of observed Fs referred to in the premise representative of the entire class of Fs referred to in the conclusion? Suppose we had questioned only science students. Would this weaken the argument? Unless we are sure that studying science (rather than economics or philosophy) has no bearing upon one's religious beliefs, we would have to conclude that the argument is weak, since the sample is unrepresentative or biased in a way that might affect the conclusion. In a similar way the sample would be biased if our sample included only graduate students, or only first-year students, or only students who were in the pub on Friday night. Ideally, the sample should reflect the same percentage distribution as the entire student body at the University of X as regards degree program, major, year, grade average, age, sex, place of birth, type of religious upbringing, drinking habits, and marital status, to name a few variables. The more closely the sample is representative of the entire student body, the stronger the argument.

The second weakness that can arise with inductive generalizations is that the sample may be too small, and thus there is a second question we should ask:

(2) Is the sample large enough?

Even if a sample is adequately representative, it may nevertheless be so small that an inductive generalization from it is weak. We might, for example, be fortunate and discover a sample of 20 students who are more or less representative of students at the University of X in general, but the argument clearly would be stronger with a sample of 40 students who were equally representative. In general, the larger the sample the stronger the argument. However, as the size of the sample is increased, the increase in strength becomes smaller with each additional increase in the size of the sample. For example, an increase from 20 to 40 students produces a much greater increase in strength than an increase from 220 to 240. In practice, therefore, we can often work with relatively small samples, especially if the population is homogeneous and we are careful to ensure that our sample is representative.

When an inductive generalization is weak for either of these two reasons it violates the criterion of adequacy. The premises of the above argument are presumably acceptable and are clearly relevant, but if the sample is unrepresentative or too small then the premises will be inadequate to support the conclusion.

10.3 STATISTICAL SYLLOGISM

All *STATISTICAL SYLLOGISMS* have the following form:

> Z per cent of all Fs are G.
> x is an F.
> There is a Z per cent probability, therefore, that x is G.

In this schema, *x* refers to a single individual. The phrase *There is a Z per cent probability* ... is the way statisticians normally express the precise probability that something will occur. It means the same as *There is a Z per cent chance that* ... some claim is true.

Statistical syllogisms always start from a generalization and use it as the basis for determining the likelihood that it will apply to a particular individual case. So we have seen two forms of induction: generalizations, which move from the particular to the general, and statistical syllogisms, which move from the general to the particular. For example, if we want to predict how likely it is that a particular student at the University of X believes in God, we would start with the conclusion of our previous inductive generalization and develop the following statistical syllogism:

> *Sixty per cent of students at the University of X believe in God.*
> *Fred is a student at the University of X.*
> *There is a 60 per cent probability, therefore, that Fred believes in God.*

To determine whether a statistical syllogism is weak, it is necessary to look beyond the premises for any other information that might be relevant. The question we need to ask is:

> *Is there additional relevant information available concerning x that has not been included in the premises?*

For example, if we know that Fred is a regular churchgoer, then it is likely that the chance that he believes in God is much higher than 60 per cent. Or if we know that Fred refuses to go to church even for family funerals or his friends' weddings, then it is likely that the chance that he believes in God is much less than 60 per cent. Or if we know that Fred is a history major *and* that only 40 per cent of history majors believe in God, then it is likely that the conclusion of our argument will be false. Whenever we use or assess a statistical syllogism, it is important to ensure that no relevant information has been overlooked.

When a statistical syllogism leaves out relevant information, we can usually charge it with violating the criterion of adequacy, since the missing information significantly weakens the argument. In some cases, however, leaving out relevant information will lead to the charge of violating the criterion of relevance. For example, if it is known that Fred has explicitly stated that he is a committed atheist, the appeal to the generalization about University of X students becomes quite irrelevant.

10.4 INDUCTION BY CONFIRMATION

Induction can be used to provide support for a hypothesis. A *HYPOTHESIS* is a principle or statement that, if true, would explain the event(s) or situation(s) to which it applies: for example, that Third World poverty is caused by international monetary policies, or that excessive exposure to sunlight causes skin cancer. To test the truth of a hypothesis we follow a two-stage procedure. First, we deduce from the hypothesis a number of *OBSERVATION STATEMENTS*. An observation statement is an empirical prediction, which states that under certain conditions a certain fact will be observed. By deducing observation statements from our hypothesis, we are claiming that if our hypothesis is true, then we would expect to find that these empirical predictions are true. We then proceed to the second stage and make observations to determine whether or not our empirical predictions turn out to be true. If our actual observations agree with the predicted observations, they inductively support the hypothesis from which the predictions were deduced. They provide *CONFIRMING INSTANCES* for the hypothesis.

The form of such arguments is:

If h then o.
o.
It is probable, therefore, that h.

In this schema, *h* stands for a hypothesis and *o* stands for an observation statement that is logically deducible from *h*. When, as is usual, we have several observation statements, the form would be:

If h then o1, o2, o3, and o4.
o1.
o2.
o3.
o4.
It is probable, therefore, that h.

INDUCTION BY CONFIRMATION is widely used in the sciences, especially in the physical and natural sciences. For example:

If the theory of general relativity is true, then it follows that light rays passing near the sun will be bent.
During the solar eclipse of 1919 it was observed that light rays passing near the sun were deflected.
It is probable, therefore, that the general theory of relativity is true.

Induction by Confirmation is also used in other contexts. It is often used for solving such mundane problems as discovering why a car won't start. It is used by doctors when diagnosing diseases. It is also used in criminal trials, where the evidence presented by the prosecution is intended to provide inductive support for the prosecutor's hypothesis that the accused is guilty. Consider these two examples:

> *If my car has failed to start because the battery is dead, then I should find that the radio and lights don't work.*
> *The radio and lights don't come on properly.*
> *It is probable, therefore, that the battery is dead.*

> *If the bookkeeper intended to embezzle money, she would have kept a second copy of the company's financial records and a secret bank account to store large sums of money.*
> *We have found a second copy of the company's financial records and a bank account in the bookkeeper's name with over $300,000 in it.*
> *It is probable, therefore, that she was embezzling money from the company.*

There are two possible weaknesses in inductive arguments by confirmation, and hence there are two questions that need to be asked. The first is:

(1) Is the number of confirming instances relatively high?

One swallow does not a summer make, and one confirming instance of a hypothesis usually does very little to show that the hypothesis is true. It is therefore important to gather a large number of confirming instances before asserting that the hypothesis is probably true. How large this number should be depends upon several factors: the range of different kinds of confirming instances, the scope of the hypothesis (i.e., does it apply to a large or small range of phenomena?), and whether the hypothesis is consistent with other well-established hypotheses. In general, the larger the number of confirming instances, the stronger the argument and the more likely it is that the hypothesis is true. This means that if the number of confirming instances for some hypothesis is relatively small, the argument could be charged with violating the criterion of adequacy.

The second question that needs to be asked is:

(2) Are there any disconfirming instances?

A *DISCONFIRMING INSTANCE* arises when an observation statement that is predicted by the hypothesis is found to be false. Unlike the first weakness, which is a matter of degree, the presence of any disconfirming instances does not merely weaken the hypothesis, it refutes it altogether. Any hypothesis will be refuted by a single disconfirming instance. There is an asymmetry between confirming and disconfirming instances in the way that they affect the hypothesis. Each confirming instance adds a little strength to the hypothesis, whereas a single disconfirming instance conclusively refutes the hypothesis.

This asymmetry is important. To understand the reasons for it, we need to recall two of the argument forms discussed in Chapter 9: the valid argument form of denying the consequent, and the formal fallacy of affirming the consequent. Since observation statements are logically deduced from the hypothesis, we have to treat *if h then o* as a truth-functional statement. A disconfirming instance, therefore, presents us with a formal argument of the form:

> If h then o.
> Not-o.
> Therefore, not-h.

This is a valid argument because it has the form of denying the consequent. Any disconfirming instance, therefore, entails that the hypothesis is false. On the other hand, a confirming instance presents us with a formal argument of the form:

> If h then o.
> o.
> Therefore, h.

This, however, has the form of affirming the consequent and thus is formally fallacious. Clearly, we cannot rely upon a single confirming instance to prove that a hypothesis is true. It is a mistake, however, to regard Induction by Confirmation as relying upon an invalid argument. Induction by Confirmation is genuinely inductive in nature, as is indicated by the fact that its conclusion is claimed only to be *probably* true. Each confirming instance does add support to the hypothesis by making it more probable that the hypothesis is true, unless, of course, we have one or more disconfirming instances, in which case we must conclude that the hypothesis is false.

In practice, however, scientists do not usually give up a hypothesis merely because of a single disconfirming instance. If the hypothesis is one that seems very promising and fruitful, it is reasonable to look for some other explanation for a disconfirming instance. Perhaps one of the test tubes was dirty, or there were impurities in the acid, or a piece of equipment malfunctioned, or a laboratory assistant was distracted when taking measurements, or any of a hundred other possibilities. If some such explanation seems likely, then it is reasonable not to reject the hypothesis. But if a plausible explanation is unavailable, the hypothesis should be rejected, since the argument in support of it actually refutes it. Scientists usually refer to disconfirming instances as *negative results*. Although it is disappointing to obtain negative results from one's research, it is important to report that fact to other scientists so that they will know that a particular hypothesis has been refuted.

Another way of saving a hypothesis for which there is a disconfirming instance is to revise the hypothesis. Often only a minor revision is needed to save a hypothesis. For example, a hypothesis put forward to explain how a particular disease is transmitted may be saved by adding the qualifications ... *at temperatures between 32 and 212 degrees Fahrenheit.* Strictly speaking, the *original* hypothesis has not been saved: the revised hypothesis is a different one, even though the difference is slight. Much scientific research consists of this kind of refinement in an attempt to discover hypotheses that can withstand testing, that is, for which there are a large number of confirming instances and no disconfirming instances.

Induction by Confirmation should not be regarded as a description of the temporal order of steps in which scientific research is conducted, but as an analysis of one kind of scientific reasoning. If it is regarded as a simple description of how scientists do research it is somewhat misleading. The method suggests that we must have a hypothesis *before* we can make the observations to test it. In fact, many scientists reverse this order. They gather data that they believe might be helpful in explaining some phenomenon, and then attempt to find the hypothesis that best explains the data. There is nothing wrong with proceeding in this way, although it needs to be noted that no scientist would ever set out to gather data without having at least a vague idea of the kind of hypothesis that would explain the data being gathered. Data by itself is scientifically meaningless; it explains nothing. Data becomes meaningful only when it is used to support or reject a hypothesis, and science can only explain phenomena when it can produce a hypothesis that is supported by the data. Thus, Induction by Confirmation, regarded as a method of reasoning, is still necessary to transform data into a scientific explanation.

Two more points must be made before we complete the account of Induction by Confirmation:

(1) While Induction by Confirmation is a common form of reasoning within the sciences, it is common in other contexts, too. In fact, it is one of the most common forms of reasoning we use every day. Here are some examples of Induction by Confirmation in non-scientific contexts:

Stephanie's family moved when she was six, and before her first day at a new school her parents told her that being pleasant and outgoing with strangers is a great way to meet people and make new friends. Her family moved seven more times by the time she finished high school, and she always made an effort to be pleasant and outgoing with her new classmates. In every new school she developed friends quickly, so there must be something correct about her parents' advice.

The defendant insists that he didn't intend to shoot his wife. But the only conclusion that fits the facts is that he did intend to kill her. If he intended to do it, then he would have purchased the gun ahead of time, which he did. He would have taken her to a secluded place, which he did. He would have arranged an alibi, which he did. He would have had a motive, which he does. All the evidence you have heard supports the conclusion that he intended to kill his wife, and you should therefore find him guilty of first-degree murder.

For several years Alfred had been bothered by insomnia. He had a hunch that it was caused by drinking coffee during the evening, so he began keeping a record of when he drank coffee in the evening and whether or not he suffered insomnia that night. After a month he analyzed his records and discovered that on 17 of the 18 nights when he suffered insomnia he had drunk coffee after 8 p.m. and on 11 of the 12 nights when he did not suffer insomnia he had drunk no coffee at all. He concluded that it was the coffee that caused his insomnia.

(2) Not only can we find Induction by Confirmation outside scientific contexts, but we also find other forms of reasoning within scientific contexts. So it is not *the* method of scientific reasoning; it is *one* method. In fact, entire books have been written about the repertoire of argument forms that have been used in science.

10.5 ANALOGICAL REASONING

REASONING BY ANALOGY is probably the most creative form of reasoning. Whenever we encounter something we do not understand, it is a natural reaction to try to understand it by reference to something that is familiar to us. When we see a man behaving erratically in a way that reminds us of Aunt Ethel, we conclude that he too is suffering from Alzheimer's disease. When a president is at an impasse with a Congress controlled by the other party, commentators look at past situations of this sort in order to understand the possibilities of the present situation. Sometimes scientists seeking an explanation for a new phenomenon begin by comparing it with other phenomena that have already been subsumed under familiar laws or principles. In all such cases the reasoning presupposes an analogy between two things (objects, classes of objects, situations, relationships), one of which is familiar and one unfamiliar.

Some analogies are better than others, and some are downright misleading. The quality of an analogy depends upon the purpose of drawing it. If the purpose is merely to clarify a difficult concept, any analogy will be a good one if it succeeds in clarifying the concept. For example:

> *According to quantum mechanics, particles move in accordance with wave-like principles. They are not physical waves, however, but probability waves. They are not like the waves on a lake but are more like a crime wave.*

The crime-wave analogy is helpful in grasping the concept of a probability wave, and for this purpose it is a good analogy. In general, any analogy that helps us to understand something is a good one.

Another purpose of analogical reasoning is to suggest possible explanations. Charles Darwin got the idea for the principle of natural selection, which is central to the theory of evolution, by reading a book on economics by Thomas Malthus. Some scientists have used the digital computer as a source of possible explanations for how the human mind works. In these cases, the analogy is used not to prove anything but merely to suggest a hypothesis that would have to be defended independently of the analogy.

Our concern, however, is with analogies that are used in arguments, that is, where the analogy is being used to provide support for a conclusion. Here we need to be careful in choosing our analogies, for a weak analogy will fail to provide the support our conclusion needs. Analogies by themselves are never sufficient to prove anything, and if an argument claims to prove its conclusion, any premise that introduces an analogy would be irrelevant. However, a strong analogy can provide an adequate reason for conclusions that are claimed to be only probably true. For example:

> *Last year I put some fertilizer on my strawberries in the fall and got about 20 per cent more strawberries. You should do the same with your strawberries, since you've got the same kind of soil. You'll probably get more strawberries too.*

Clearly, this conclusion is not derived with the certainty of a deductively sound argument, but the analogy between your soil and mine is strong enough to make it reasonable for us to accept it, at least tentatively. A weak analogy, on the other hand, is one that is used as a premise in an argument but fails to provide adequate support for the conclusion. For example:

> *Driving a car is basically just like riding a bicycle: it's all a matter of physical coordination and keeping an eye on where you are going. Well, I taught myself how to ride a bicycle, so I reckon I can teach myself how to drive a car.*

Clearly there are some similarities between riding a bicycle and driving a car, but the analogy is not strong enough to provide much support for the conclusion of this argument.

The usefulness of analogical arguments derives from the similarities between different things. If there are enough important similarities between the two things being compared in an analogy, we can draw conclusions about things we do not know based on evidence from comparable things that we know better. In the first example in the previous paragraph, for instance, similarities between the soil in the two gardens help predict how fertilizer will encourage the growth of strawberries in one garden based on how it affected another garden. We should say that the analogy compares two *cases*. The *SUBJECT CASE* is that about which we are trying to draw a conclusion in an analogical argument. The *ANALOGUE CASE* is that with which we are more familiar and that is used to draw the conclusion in an analogical argument. In this example, the speaker's garden is the analogue case and the garden of the person the speaker is addressing is the subject case. The speaker's garden is used as an analogue because the soil in that garden and the plants being grown in it are comparable to the soil and plants in the garden of the person being addressed. Since there is no direct evidence of the effect of fertilizer on the production of strawberries in the subject case, the analogy is used to provide indirect evidence, which is reasonable to use because of the similarities.

The easiest way to identify the subject case and the analogue case in any analogical argument is to find the conclusion. The conclusion will always be about the subject case. The conclusion will also indicate what the target feature of the analogy is. The *TARGET FEATURE* is that feature of the subject case about which the conclusion is being drawn. This is the focus of the comparison between the two cases. For example, the conclusion above is *You'll probably get more strawberries too*. The conclusion is not about every feature of the garden, but rather only about the production of strawberries in the garden. Similarly, the conclusion of the second passage is not about every aspect of driving a car, but only about the prospect of the speaker teaching himself how to do it.

There are two kinds of analogical argument, each with its own form. The first analogical argument is based on a comparison of the *properties* of the subject case and those of the analogue case, and the second is based on a comparison between *relations* that obtain in the subject case and those of the analogue case. The difference between a property and a relation is important and straightforward, although it is abstract and may require some practice to get used to. But because analogies by properties and analogies by relations are different in important respects, it will be helpful to make this clear before we look at the two analogical argument forms. A *PROPERTY* is a feature that is attributable to a thing considered on its own and as a single entity, whereas a *RELATION* is a feature that is attributable to the relationship between two or more things. So, for example, *red, juicy,* and *sweet* may be properties of an apple, whereas *inside, next to,* and *in front of* may describe the relations between the same apple and a bowl. Similarly, *exciting, realistic,* and *647 pages long* may be properties that are attributable to a novel, whereas the same novel may be related to other things in ways such as *shorter than* War and Peace, *written before the author won the Nobel prize,* or *not as good as the movie based on it.*

One special set of examples must be noted before we turn to the forms of analogical arguments based on properties and those based on relations. Sometimes we might describe a single thing by noting the *relations* between its *parts*. For example, we might say that "a clock's minute hand *moves faster than* its hour hand," or "Chapter 2 of this book is *longer than* Chapter 5." Even though both "a clock" and "this book" are single entities, the italicized phrase expresses a relation because the sentences are about the relations between parts of a clock or this book. These may look like exceptions to the distinction between properties and relations specified above, but they really are not, because the parts (the minute and hour hands of the clock, Chapter 2 and Chapter 5 of this book) are themselves treated as different things.

An *ANALOGICAL ARGUMENT BY PROPERTIES* has the form:

x has A, B, C.
y has A, B.
It is probable, therefore, that y has C.

In this schema, *x* refers to the analogue case, *y* refers to the subject case, and *A, B,* and *C* refer to properties. The first premise describes the analogue case (*x*) as having properties *A, B,* and *C,* and the second premise describes the subject case (*y*) as having properties *A* and *B*. The target feature is *C*, which is one of the properties of the analogue case. On the basis of the analogy between *x* and *y*, there are probable grounds to infer that *y* also has property *C*. Here are some examples of analogical arguments by properties:

> *Canada Geese are water birds that nest in Canada in the early spring and migrate south to a warmer climate for the winter months. Ducks are also water birds that nest in Canada in the early spring. Therefore, ducks probably migrate south for the winter, too.*

> *The Montreal Symphony Orchestra's last recording was of a Beethoven piano concerto, led by their current conductor, featuring Marc-André Hamelin as the soloist and on the CBC recording label. I loved it. The orchestra's next Beethoven recording will have the same conductor and the same pianist and is also recorded on the same label. I'm confident that I'll enjoy it as well.*

> *Running a university is like running a business: just as a business cannot function in the face of massive debts, so a university cannot function with a debt load; just as a business must make itself appealing to prospective customers, so a university must make itself appealing to prospective students; just as a business must meet the practical needs of its paying customers, so a university must meet the practical needs of its tuition-paying students. Therefore, each university must cover its own costs, just as each business should cover its own costs.*

An *ANALOGICAL ARGUMENT BY RELATIONS* has the following form:

> x is to y as a is to b.
> x is R to y.
> It is probable, therefore, that a is R to b.

In this schema, *x* and *y* are related in the analogue case, and *a* and *b* are related in the subject case. The target feature is specified as *R*, which is said to describe the relation between *x* and *y* in the analogue case. On the basis of the analogy, there are probable grounds to infer that *R* describes the relation in the subject case. Here are some more examples of analogical arguments by relations:

> *Just as Pavlov's dog salivated whenever it heard a bell ring, so can my kids get excited whenever they hear the theme song to The Simpsons. Pavlov's dog started*

salivating because it associated the sound of the bell with food. I suppose my kids associate The Simpsons *theme song with the fun of watching the show.*

Politicians are like doctors for the country. Like doctors, they are there to cure the ills of an economy. When you go to a doctor, you acknowledge that she knows more about good health than you do, and you happily follow her advice. There is no point in electing politicians if you aren't going to give them a free rein to act once they are in power. Criticizing politicians is defeating them and yourself, and it's just as silly as going to the doctor and then refusing to act on her advice.

The proposal to give clean needles to prison inmates to stop the spread of the AIDS virus from the use of dirty needles is ridiculous. It is like giving bank robbers normal bullets to stop them from using dum-dum bullets, which are much more damaging to the victim.

To determine the strength of an analogy, we examine the similarities and dissimilarities between the two cases. A strong analogy is one in which there is a large number of relevant similarities and a small number of relevant dissimilarities between the cases. A weak analogy is one in which there is a small number of relevant similarities and a large number of relevant dissimilarities between the cases. It is important that the similarities and dissimilarities are relevant. The fact that both riding a bicycle and driving a car are done in a sitting position is not a relevant similarity. The fact that I learned to ride a bicycle in June whereas I am proposing to teach myself to drive a car in September is not a relevant dissimilarity. On the other hand, the fact that both require good physical coordination is a relevant similarity. And the fact that cars are faster and more powerful than bicycles is a relevant dissimilarity. The relevance of a similarity or dissimilarity depends upon the target feature of the analogy and the conclusion being inferred. For each of the above similarities and dissimilarities, we would have to be prepared to say why we think it is or is not relevant, and to do this we would have to rely upon what we know about riding bicycles and driving cars, as well as what we know about learning to drive a car. Determining the strength of an analogy involves weighing the relevant similarities against the relevant dissimilarities. We have to make a judgment, in the light of the similarities and dissimilarities, as to whether the analogy is strong enough to support the conclusion. There are no hard and fast rules here: all we can do is to look for relevant similarities and dissimilarities and make our judgment on that basis.

10.6 SELF-TEST NO. 16

For the following passages, (1) indicate the type of inductive argument being used, and (2) identify the parts of the passage that correspond to elements of the schematic forms provided in this chapter. Then (3) assess the strength of the argument by identifying and describing any weaknesses.

1. In order to discover whether people were satisfied with the recreational facilities provided by the City, a questionnaire was included with the tax bills that were mailed out last spring. The results showed that almost 80 per cent were satisfied with the current recreational facilities.

2. Giving fathers a period of paid leave when their wives give birth would not be prohibitively expensive. In Sweden, where such a policy has been in effect for more than a decade, only 12 per cent of Swedish men take the leave.

3. The Washington State Department of Tourism responded yesterday to recent charges by some resort operators that the state of Washington provides inadequate facilities for tourists. He claimed that the tourists themselves—approximately 70 per cent of them—stated that they were satisfied with the facilities provided for tourists and cited a study conducted by the Department last summer, in which questionnaires were distributed to every car with out-of-state license plates leaving Washington and entering Canada. Approximately 18,000 questionnaires were returned. The results showed that 23 per cent were very satisfied and 46 per cent were satisfied with the facilities provided for tourists.

4. The Career Placement office predicts that 90 per cent of this year's graduates will find a job within three months of graduation. This is good news indeed for my roommate. He will be relieved to know that even though he will have only a general B.A. with a D average he still has a 90-per-cent chance of getting a job.

5. Almost everyone would throw a life preserver to a drowning person; indeed, someone who could easily do so but refused would be regarded by everyone as a sick or immoral person. The same thing applies to nations when a famine occurs in a Third World country. We should be prepared to throw them a life preserver in the form of emergency aid. Yet we continually hear complaints from those who are opposed to such aid. Surely we are entitled to regard them as sick or immoral people.

6. Recently the Philosophy Department surveyed all students registered in its introductory courses. One of the questions asked students whether they expected that a university education would improve their communication skills, and 88 per cent answered yes to this question. So it seems that 88 per cent of students at the university think that a university education will improve communication skills.

7. Many people support gun-control legislation because they think it will reduce the number of murders. They are making a serious mistake, however. Have they forgotten the failure of prohibition to reduce the amount of drunkenness?

8. I recently read about a survey which showed that 90 per cent of Americans knew less about the Canadian political system than the average Canadian ten-year-old. Well, there's an American student in my Canadian politics course, and I don't know how he hopes to pass the course when he's that ignorant to begin with.

9. Those of us who grew up in rural and small-town Idaho in the 1940s and 1950s never met or heard of any local communists or even communist sympathizers. If any existed, and according to the press there were a few around, we all believed they must be spies and could be found only in New York, Boston, or Philadelphia. But now we are told that during this period one of the largest and most powerful trade unions in northern Idaho was controlled by communist sympathizers. Well, I for one simply don't believe it. I lived through that period, and I should know.

10. Last year both Frances and Rhonda spent six hours a day training with T.J. Davis and followed his special diet, and both made the US national swim team. This year I'm training just as hard with the same coach and following the same diet. So I bet I'll make the team.

11. The Student Union conducted a telephone poll of students to see how much support there was for a fee increase to help pay for new athletic facilities. Every twentieth name in the student directory was telephoned last weekend. The results showed that only 44 per cent supported the proposal.

12. Perhaps we cannot know for certain that many animals feel pain, but there are three reasons for holding that they do. First, they exhibit behavior that in humans is invariably associated with feeling pain. Second, they

have a central nervous system that is similar to that of humans. And third, the ability to feel pain would have the same kind of evolutionary advantage for many animals that it does for humans.

10.7 QUESTIONS FOR DISCUSSION

Answer the questions accompanying the following passages in light of the appropriate criteria for the kind of argument found in each passage.

1. Ann Landers once asked the women readers of her newspaper column to send her a card stating which they would prefer: "to be held close and treated tenderly," or to have sex. Of the 90,000 people who replied, 72 per cent said they would prefer the former. She concluded that most women preferred being held close and treated tenderly to having sex. How strong is this inductive generalization?

2. Fifty one per cent of the popular vote in the 2012 presidential election went to the Democratic candidate, presumably because voters wanted a Democratic government. Many people concluded from this that 51 per cent of all Americans wanted a Democratic government. Is this a reasonable conclusion?

3. It is sometimes suggested that racism is caused by two types of bad inductive reasoning. First, it is argued that racial stereotypes are caused by weak inductive generalizations: racial stereotypes arise because people tend to notice individuals who stand out from the crowd, and then they use this sample as the basis for their generalizations about race as a whole. But such a sample is necessarily unrepresentative since it is based only on those few individuals who stand out, that is, who are different. Second, it is argued that individual members of other races are discriminated against because of weak statistical syllogisms: all evidence that an individual does not fit the generalization is ignored. Is this a plausible explanation for racism?

4. It is clearly unreasonable to argue as follows: *I have known three Irishmen in my life, and all were drunkards with violent tempers; therefore, all Irishmen are drunkards with violent tempers.* Why then is it not equally unreasonable to argue as follows: *I have read three Harlequin Romance novels, and all had uninteresting characters and predictable plots; therefore, all Harlequin Romance novels have uninteresting characters and predictable plots?*

5. The following passage comes from a seventeenth-century author whose information about other planets in the solar system was much more limited than ours. Even so, what problems might one of his contemporaries have spotted in the argument? *We may observe a very great similitude between this earth which we inhabit, and other planets, Saturn, Jupiter, Mars, Venus, and Mercury. They all revolve round the sun, as the earth does, although at different distances and in different periods. They borrow all their light from the sun, as the earth does. Several of them are known to revolve around their axis like the earth and, by that means, must have a like succession of day and night. Some of them have moons that serve to give them light in the absence of the sun, as our moon does to us. They are all, in their motions, subject to the same law of gravitation, as the earth is. From all this similitude, it is not unreasonable to think that those planets may, like our earth, be the habitation of various orders of living creatures. There is some probability in this conclusion from analogy.*

6. When medical treatment is unsuccessful and the patient dies or is permanently incapacitated, many people feel that the doctor must be guilty of negligence, and the patient or the family often launches a suit for medical malpractice. Is this reasonable, given that the reasoning that lies behind all treatment decisions must be inductive in nature?

7. Are there any inconsistent assumptions in the following argument that are exposed by schematizing it? *I am conscious of a series of facts connected by a uniform sequence, of which the beginning is modifications of my body, the middle is feelings, and the end is outward demeanour. In the case of other human beings I have the evidence of my senses for the first and last links of the series, but not for the intermediate link. I find, however, that the sequence between the first and last is as regular and constant in those other cases as it is in mine. In my own case I know that the first link produces the last through the intermediate link and could not produce it without. Experience, therefore, obliges me to conclude that there must be an intermediate link; which must either be the same in others as in myself, or a different one;... by supposing the link to be of the same nature ... I conform to the legitimate rules of experimental enquiry* (J.S. Mill, *An Examination of Sir William Hamilton's Philosophy*, 1867, pp. 237–38).

11. Arguing Back

In debates and other argumentative contexts we are not usually content to remain passive and merely note the weaknesses in another person's arguments. Usually we want to argue back or at least diagnose the weakness in their arguments for them. We may want to help our interlocutor to see the truth (as we understand it). Or, if we do not know what the truth of the matter is, we may want to pursue the argument in hopes of increasing our understanding and perhaps getting closer to the truth. Or, we may simply want to persuade someone of the error of their ways because we don't want them to get away with weak arguments. Whatever the reason, we all want to be able to respond effectively to the arguments other people present to us. In this chapter we examine several helpful strategies for responding to other people's arguments and positions in a focused and critical manner.

11.1 EXPLAINING THE WEAKNESS

In Chapters 5 to 8 we examined the criteria a sound argument must satisfy and the kinds of weaknesses arguments may be subject to. In Chapters 9 and 10 we examined specific types of arguments and their weaknesses. These chapters provide us with some tactics for arguing back in informal contexts. When we detect a weakness in someone's arguments we can point it out, and hope that they see what is weak in their argument. Unfortunately, not everyone we are likely to debate with has studied critical thinking. If we accuse them of relying upon an unacceptable empirical premise or committing the post hoc fallacy, they may not know what we are talking about. If we are trying to convince someone who is not familiar with logical terminology, it is usually necessary to explain, and not merely name, the weakness, even in the informal context of a conversation.

A full explanation involves two stages. First, we need to explain the nature of the weakness we think we've identified. It is usually best to begin by explaining the relevant criteria for a sound argument. If a fallacy is diagnosed, it is best to name it only after the relevant criteria have been explained. The purpose of this part of the explanation is to ensure that the person understands what we are concerned about. We should always ensure that they understand the nature of a weakness before we try to persuade them that our diagnosis is correct. If an interlocutor disputes our diagnosis, we should immediately attempt to determine whether he or she fails to understand the nature of the diagnosis or understands it but believes we cannot back it up.

The second stage of a full explanation is backing up our diagnosis. This involves reconstructing the argument, supplying missing premises, identifying the logical structure, and so on, in the way described in previous chapters. If done properly, our explanation should convince our interlocutor that his or her argument does indeed contain a weakness. Someone who is unwilling to respond to a full explanation of a weakness in his or her argument is probably not interested in serious discussion, and we should (politely, of course) change the topic of conversation.

We should note here that sometimes it is difficult to decide whether a particular weakness results from violating the criterion of relevance or the criterion of adequacy. We have seen that sometimes an appeal to authority may be irrelevant (for example, when a strict proof is called for) and sometimes it may be relevant but inadequate. Appeals to ignorance are also sometimes difficult to classify. This can be a problem with other types of weak arguments as well. All we can do when faced with this problem is to make the best judgment we can as to which criterion will most clearly explain the weakness of the argument to this person.

11.2 COUNTER-EXAMPLES

Fully explaining a weakness is a laborious method of arguing back. The *METHOD OF COUNTER-EXAMPLES* is a short-cut method that is easy to use and can sometimes be remarkably effective. Its use is limited, however, to arguments that rely upon a generalization in the premises that can be challenged as being unacceptable. The method consists simply of presenting an exception to the generalization that shows that it should not be relied upon in the way the original argument does. For example:

> Mike: *You should try the wine cooler I just bought. It's really good. It is a new product, just put on the market by the producers, so it's bound to be better than their old ones.*
> Elaine: *Just like the new Coke, eh?*

Elaine attacks the missing premise of Mike's argument, that a new product is always better than existing products, by citing an example of a new product that was (or was commonly believed to be) inferior to the product it replaced. In this respect, counter-examples are logically adequate. In the face of a generalization, a single counter-example is all that we need to identify a flaw (see 8.3).

Here is another example:

> John: *I've decided to invest most of my savings in gold and gold-mine stocks. I read a book that came out a couple of months ago, written by a business professor at Harvard, and he strongly recommends gold as the best investment for the next few years.*
>
> Peter: *A few years ago my cousin followed the advice in a book written by a business professor. She invested her life savings in an oil-exploration company and lost the bundle.*

Peter's counter-example responds to the missing premise in John's argument—that all business professors are good investment advisors. The counter-example shows that there are exceptions to this generalization. As long as John gets the point of the counter-example, this is a more effective method of challenging his appeal to authority than a detailed explanation of why his appeal has failed to meet the criteria for accepting an appeal to authority.

There is a natural reply that can be made when we cite a counter-example to someone's generalization. Since most generalizations admit of some exceptions, an interlocutor can concede the counter-example but argue that, generally speaking, the generalization still holds. Even if it is not universally true that "All Fs are G," it is generally true that "Fs tend to be G" or that "Fs of a specific type are G" or that "All Fs are G in specific circumstances." For example, Mike might argue that since most new products are better than existing ones, the new wine cooler is likely to be better than the old coolers. And John might claim that most business professors are likely to understand the investment market better than he does. If Mike and John respond in this way, we may need to concede that our counter-examples have failed to show the weakness. But, equally, we may need to undertake the slower process of explaining the weakness, or the generalization may need to be reformulated so that it is more precise and accurate.

Here are some examples of the use of counter-examples with differing degrees of effectiveness:

> Fred: *I don't see that there is anything really wrong with an occasional extra-marital fling. Everybody needs some variety in their lives. It's like food. I mean, if we had to eat the same thing for dinner every night, we'd soon come to hate it.*
>
> Alice: *Does that mean you want to trade in the children for a couple of new teenagers?*

Son: *But, Dad, everybody I know is going to the concert. You say it might be dangerous, but it's not. How can it be dangerous if everybody else's parents are letting them go?*
Father: *What about that concert last summer where there was a riot and three teenagers were killed? I'm sure their parents let them go because they thought it wouldn't be dangerous.*

Bruce: *I don't see anything wrong with the school board firing teachers whose moral standards are different from those of the community. After all, the members of the school board are democratically elected in free elections and represent the will of the people.*
Margaret: *That is exactly what they said in Nazi Germany. Don't forget that Hitler was democratically elected in a free election.*

11.3 ABSURD EXAMPLES

A more effective way of displaying a fallacy is the *METHOD OF ABSURD EXAMPLES*. It is similar to the method of counter-examples but can be used against a broader range of weaknesses, often very effectively. It involves constructing an argument that is parallel to the weak argument, but which has true or plausible premises and an obviously false or absurd conclusion. For example:

Bob: *As far as I'm concerned, people who are against teaching scientific creationism in the schools are communists. They are all atheists, after all, and all communists are atheists.*
Carol: *Don't be silly, Bob. That's like arguing that since all men have two eyes and all women have two eyes, all men are really women.*

Carol's reply shows the weakness in Bob's argument by challenging its structure. Both arguments have an identical structure:

All As are Bs.
All Cs are Bs.
Therefore, all As are Cs.

Carol is in effect saying to Bob that if his argument is a good one, then so is hers; if he is going to believe that all opponents of scientific creationism are communists, then he must also believe that all men are women. Since Bob is presumably unwilling to accept Carol's conclusion, he must either reject his own conclusion or develop another argument to support it.

To be effective, an absurd example must be closely similar to the original argument. The similarity must always involve an identical structure, but it often involves similarity of content as well. In general, the more closely an absurd example resembles the original argument, the more effective it will be in showing a weakness. The above example relies on an absurd example with the same logical structure as the fallacious argument. Here is an example that relies mainly upon similarity of content:

> Walter: *I think the government should ban all pornographic publications. It really bothers me to think of all those people reading all that mindless stuff.*
> Will: *Great argument, Walt. And I think the government should ban the* Toronto Sun. *It really bothers me to think of all those people reading all that mindless stuff.*

Will's absurd example is structurally identical to Walter's argument, but its success as an absurd example depends not so much on this similarity as on the similarity of content.

The practical effectiveness of an absurd example depends on more than similarity of structure and content. To be effective the absurd example should use premises that are obviously true and uncontroversial, so that someone cannot reject it on the ground that it relies on unacceptable premises. Sometimes, we can get away with hypothetical premises. Will, for example, may not be bothered at all by the thought of people reading the *Sun*, but pretends to be in order to make his point. Of course, Walter might miss the point and respond by arguing that Will is not really bothered by people reading the *Toronto Sun*, in which case Will's absurd example has failed in its purpose.

The main drawback to the absurd example method is that it is often difficult to invent a good absurd example on the spur of the moment. If we use a poor absurd example we give our interlocutors a plausible excuse to ignore the serious point we are trying to make, on the ground that we have missed the point of their argument. The greatest strength of the absurd example method, on the other hand, is that it places this person on the horns of a very sharply defined dilemma: either they must accept our absurd conclusion, or they must admit that their argument fails to support their conclusion.

Here are two more absurd example arguments:

> Sadie: *One of the primary responsibilities of parents is to provide their children with a sound moral education. Religion provides a solid foundation for morality. Therefore, any parent who cares about their children's moral education should give their children a religious upbringing.*
> Tamsen: *Sorry, Sadie, your argument is no good. It is just like the following argument: It is a responsibility of architects to design safe and sound buildings.*

Granite provides a solid foundation for a safe building. Therefore, any architect who wants to design safe buildings should design buildings with granite foundations.

Audrey: *The main reason I think abortion is wrong is that you can't draw a sharp line between a fetus that is 39 weeks old (i.e., one ready to be born) and one at any earlier stage of its development. Obviously, it would be wrong to kill a baby while its mother is in labor. But if it's alright to kill it at some earlier stage, then there must be some point at which you can say, "Up to this point it was not a person, but at this point it becomes a person." But no one can do this. Fetal development is absolutely gradual from beginning to end. So if you can't justify killing a fetus at the end of its development, you can't justify killing it at the beginning.*

Betty: *There is something wrong with your argument. You are arguing as follows: You cannot draw a sharp line between when something is hot and when it isn't. When you boil water, it starts out cold and gradually becomes hot. There is no point at which you can say, "Up to this point it is cold, but at this point it becomes hot." Bringing water to a boil is absolutely gradual from beginning to end. So if it is hot at the end of the process, then it must be hot at the beginning. So cold water is really hot.*

11.4 COUNTER-ARGUMENTS

The final method of arguing back goes beyond the intent of the first three. They attempt to display the weakness of another person's argument not by attacking the conclusion directly, but by attacking the way the conclusion is defended. A *COUNTER-ARGUMENT*, on the other hand, attempts to show that someone's conclusion is false or problematic by constructing a different argument altogether to support a conclusion that is inconsistent with the original conclusion. For example:

Roy: *The state must retain the right to apply the death penalty in extreme cases. I believe that any person who commits cold-blooded, premeditated murder is unfit to remain a member of any civilized community. By their act of denying another's right to life, they have renounced their own right to life, and the state is therefore entitled to put them to death.*

Dale: *The trouble with your position is that it brings the state down to the level of the murderer. If the right to life is so important, then don't you think the state ought to show how important it is by refusing to execute anyone, no matter how heinous his or her crime? The real question is whether you want to live in a society where the government from time to time kills some of its citizens.*

Notice that Dale makes no attempt to challenge any of Roy's premises and does not even suggest that Roy's conclusion does not follow from his premises. In fact, she is actually in partial agreement with one of Roy's premises: that there is a right to life. But she ignores Roy's argument and attempts instead to show that the state ought not to inflict the death penalty by appealing to a different set of premises. Every genuine counter-argument has this feature: it ignores the premises of the original argument and presents an independent set of reasons in support of a contrary conclusion.

Every weak argument is therefore open to a counter-argument. In fact, counter-arguments can often be developed against arguments whose weakness we are unable to identify. If we are presented with an argument whose conclusion we are reluctant to accept, there are two possible explanations for our reluctance: (a) the argument is weak, or (b) we are being irrational about the matter. If the argument really is weak, then we ought to be able to describe the weakness in such a way as to persuade our interlocutor. But if, as sometimes happens, we cannot do so, we would have to concede that our refusal to accept it may be irrational. In these circumstances it can be very useful to attempt to develop a counter-argument. If we can develop a plausible one, then we have a good reason to believe that the argument is weak and that we are not being irrational.

In addition, a good counter-argument can often suggest what is weak about the original argument. In the above example, Dale's counter-argument does suggest a line of criticism for Roy's argument. Roy appeals to the fact that murderers have denied the right to life of their victims as a reason for claiming that murderers have renounced their own right to life. Dale's argument relies on the premise that the right to life cannot be lost by anyone, which suggests a way of attacking this sub-argument: she could argue that it violates the criterion of adequacy. We do not as a rule hold that if A violates some right of B's, the state should deny A the same right; that if I, for example, violate your freedom of religion, the state should force me to become a Baptist. Consequently, Roy's sub-argument needs more support in order to be acceptable.

To develop good counter-arguments we have to be familiar with the subject matter under discussion, and we have to care about the issue as well. Counter-arguments cannot be developed merely as a reaction against an argument that looks weak. There are no logical rules for producing a good counter-argument. We have to be skeptical about another person's conclusion, which means we should have reasons for our skepticism. It is only on the basis of the reasons that lead us to be skeptical that we can develop a good counter-argument.

Counter-arguments are often found in debates over controversial issues. In fact, in controversial contexts we can most easily see the chief drawback to the method of counter-argument. We are all aware that in debates over controversial matters both sides often seem to pay no attention to the arguments of the other side. The participants have defined themselves in opposition to each other, and each sees the other as an opponent in a competition. Both sides seem content to repeat, over and over again, their arguments (along with their slogans and, usually, a great deal of invective and frequent ad hominems), all the while ignoring the arguments of their opponents. To avoid such juvenile behavior, we should use counter-arguments not as an excuse to stop thinking rationally about the issue but as a useful tool for carrying forward a rational inquiry. Not only can they suggest weaknesses in our opponents' arguments, but they can give us a better understanding of the issue. A serious attempt to develop a counter-argument against a given argument, and then to examine the two as dispassionately as we can, will give us a deeper understanding of any complex issue.

11.5 SELF-TEST NO. 17

I. Suggest a counter-example that shows the weakness in each of the following generalizations:

1. Wealth always increases human happiness, since it removes one of the major barriers to achieving what we want out of life.

2. The function of law is to force people to do what they would otherwise choose not to do.

3. All humor is cruel: people never find anything funny unless it is at someone else's expense.

4. Women have still not been able to achieve real political power anywhere in the world.

5. Religion has always been a force for good in the world.

II. Suggest an absurd example that shows the weakness in each of the following arguments:

1. You might as well save your breath and go peddle your pamphlets somewhere else. I've been a Republican all my life. I was raised a Republican by my father, and if it was good enough for him, then it is good enough for me.

2. I don't think that taking things like pencils and paperclips from the company is really stealing because the company has never threatened to punish anyone for it.

3. If Jim had a steady job, then he'd be able to afford a new car; well, he has just bought a new car, so he must have a steady job now.

4. You shouldn't eat any of that stuff. It's deadly. They've proven that it kills laboratory animals when they give them a steady diet of it.

5. My wife always gets my breakfast for me. She's been doing it every morning for 14 years, so I'm positive she'll get my breakfast tomorrow.

11.6 QUESTIONS FOR DISCUSSION

Suggest a plausible counter-argument against each of the following arguments.

1. The capitalist economic system is superior to any other system. Western civilization has advanced more since capitalism emerged in the late seventeenth century than in the previous 2,000 years, and these advances could not have occurred except for the tremendous explosion of productivity brought about by capitalism. It may not be perfect, but it is clearly superior to all its rivals.

2. By the late 1950s suicide had been decriminalized in most states: a serious blunder. Until then it had been a criminal offense in most states for anyone to attempt to commit suicide. The value of the old law was not that it made it possible for the courts to punish those who were so disturbed or depressed that they wanted to end their lives. Its value was that it gave the police the right to apprehend someone who was threatening to take his or her own life. The way things are now, if the police find someone threatening suicide, they cannot interfere, for the person is doing nothing illegal. And since most people who threaten suicide are really pleading for help, we should have a law that permits the police to interfere first and ask questions later.

3. Teachers in primary and secondary schools should avoid introducing any controversial political or ethical issues into the classroom. Such discussions tend to be divisive and to create friction among students. They lead many parents to feel that the school is subverting their authority as parents. And they allow teachers to abuse their authority and to impose their values upon their students.

4. Each year, *Maclean's* magazine publishes a ranking of Canadian universities.

One of the criteria used is the percentage of alumni who contribute to the college. This is an absurd criterion when used as a basis for determining the quality of a university. It is like determining the quality of a judge on the basis of her or his income. The quality of a university should depend not on the contributions of alumni, but on what happens to students while they are there.

5. Most Western governments are willing to negotiate with terrorists to obtain the release of hostages or to achieve other goals. This is an ill-advised policy. What governments should do is to announce that their policy will always be to refuse to negotiate with terrorists under any circumstances and then to adhere rigorously to this policy. They should inform all their citizens that this is their new policy and that those who travel abroad should not expect the government to negotiate for their release should they be taken hostage by terrorists. Once terrorist groups realized that a government was serious about its refusal to negotiate under any circumstances, they would realize that their terrorist acts were useless or even counter-productive. They would be forced to cease their terrorist acts, and fewer people would suffer as a result.

6. Government spending on the arts is wasteful and should be abolished. If some particular artists or poets or singers are recognized as good by enough of the public, they will be able to make a decent living by selling their books or giving concerts, in which case they don't need government hand-outs. But if they can't make a decent living it must be because not enough people think they are good enough to buy their books or go to their concerts. In this case, there is no justification for subsidizing artists who are regarded as second best. So all support programs like the National Endowment for the Arts should be eliminated.

12. Irrational Techniques of Persuasion

In this chapter we consider a variety of irrational devices that are commonly used as persuasive techniques. Several of these have already been touched on earlier but are repeated here in order to give a more complete picture of these techniques. Some logicians treat these devices as fallacies, on the ground that they are used in attempts to persuade us of something and thus at least pretend to supply a reason for us to accept it. However, if we treat them as fallacies, we would be obliged to reconstruct an argument from the passages in which they occur, which is often difficult and usually violates the principle of charity. It is usually better to treat them not as arguments at all, but merely as irrational techniques of persuasion. In fact, their success frequently depends upon their not being used in an explicit argument, since once the argument is spelled out, the weakness becomes glaringly obvious.

12.1 LOADED TERMS

We saw in section 3.6 that many words have both a descriptive and an evaluative meaning. A group of rebels may be called freedom fighters, or terrorists, or just plain rebels. All three terms have more or less the same descriptive meaning, but their evaluative meanings are quite different: *freedom fighter* has a positive evaluative meaning, *terrorist* has a negative evaluative meaning, while *rebel* has no (or a neutral) evaluative meaning. The first two of these—*freedom fighter* and *terrorist*— are frequently used as loaded terms. A *LOADED TERM* is any term with a clear descriptive meaning and a positive or negative evaluative meaning, which is used in an attempt to persuade us to accept the evaluation conveyed by the term. Thus, anyone who wants to create support for a group of rebels can do so by always referring to them as freedom fighters, just as anyone who wants to create opposition to them can do so by always referring to them as terrorists.

Loaded terms are most effective in a context where the audience is not already committed to accepting or rejecting the evaluation carried by the loaded term and where this question is not being discussed explicitly. In such situations people can more easily accept the loaded term because it sounds like it is a purely descriptive term. How many terrorists are there? How well-armed are the terrorists? Do the terrorists have support from outside the country in which they operate? These are all empirical questions that do not explicitly raise the ethical question of whether or not the rebels should be supported. But after a discussion of such factual questions through which we become accustomed to referring to the rebels as terrorists, when the ethical question is finally raised, we can easily find ourselves placed in a position where we *seem* to be committed to opposing the rebels. After all, terrorism *is* the kind of thing one ought to oppose, so the ethical question already seems to have been answered. In the same way, had we become accustomed to referring to the rebels as freedom fighters, then, when the ethical question is finally raised, we *seem* to be committed to supporting the rebels. After all, freedom *is* the kind of thing one ought to support. In this way loaded terms can prevent us from making explicit value judgments, because the loaded term makes the judgment for us without our realizing it.

Advertisers are well aware of the fact that loaded terms can force value judgments upon the unwary. American Airlines announces that it is celebrating 65 years of service and commitment to Mexico; the fact that the company has been in business for 65 years means that it is not a fly-by-night outfit, but the phrase "Service to Mexico" suggests an affinity with service organizations such as the Red Cross. A blatant use of loaded terms sometimes occurs in naming certain products or even companies. A detergent is called *Joy* in an attempt to make us think we enjoy it. A car rental company is called *Budget* to suggest that it has low rates. But loaded terms are used in many contexts besides business. We are all aware of the impact of racist terms (e.g., *wop, kike, nigger, chink*) and of other derogatory terms (*pinko, fascist, nerd, shyster, egg-head, bleeding heart, yuppie, book-worm, jock*). Fortunately, most of these terms are so blatantly evaluative that they are unlikely to persuade anyone who is not already prone to accept the evaluation carried by them.

A loaded term must have both a clear evaluative meaning (positive or negative) and a fairly specific descriptive meaning. It is the *descriptive* adequacy of the use of the term that makes it possible to insinuate the *evaluative* meaning. Once we accept the descriptive adequacy of the term, we are more likely to accept its evaluative meaning as well. It should be noted, however, that some evaluative terms, such as *good, evil, right,* and *wrong,* lack a descriptive meaning and therefore cannot function as loaded terms. They are pure evaluative terms (i.e., they have no specific descriptive meaning) and thus can be used in almost any context, since there is no descriptive meaning to determine their correct use.

12.2 VAGUE TERMS

In section 3.2.1 we distinguished vagueness from ambiguity on the basis that a vague sentence lacks a precise meaning, whereas an ambiguous sentence has two or more different but usually quite precise meanings. We noted that although vagueness is often acceptable, it should sometimes be criticized; in particular, it should be criticized in contexts where greater precision is needed. The fact that a vague sentence lacks a precise meaning makes it possible for vague language to be quite misleading. A vague sentence has a large number of possible meanings, and often some of these possible meanings will make the sentence true while others will make it false. As a result we usually recognize that a vague sentence is true on at least one possible interpretation (i.e., that it is partly, or in some sense, true), and if we are not careful we can be led to think that it is also true on other interpretations, when in fact it is false. For example:

> *What I admired most about Ernest Hemingway was that he broke the mold.*

The phrase *broke the mold* is exceedingly vague. There are several different meanings we might give to it. It might mean that Hemingway was unconventional in his personal life. In this sense the claim would be true. On the other hand, it might mean that he was a creative genius or that his prose style is entirely unique. But on these interpretations the claim may well be false.

Vague language can thus be used to persuade us to accept something that is either false or problematic. This technique is much used by advertisers, politicians, and others who want to persuade us to do something that we would be reluctant to do if we thought carefully about it. It is commonly used in slogans of all sorts. For example:

> *Vote Jones—The People's Choice.*

> *Coke Is The Real Thing.*

> *Canadians want a leader who is human, who knows what it is to struggle, to have ups and downs, and who has compassion for the tribulations of ordinary people.*

12.3 LOADED QUESTIONS

A question is not an argument and not even a statement, so it may be difficult to imagine how a question can be a technique of persuasion. Nevertheless, because questions presuppose and imply statements in order to be intelligible, they can sometimes suggest something in a way that may be persuasive. A real question attempts to elicit from a respondent information or opinions, and, presumably, the questioner leaves it up to the respondent to answer it. *OPEN QUESTIONS* leave it up to the respondent to structure and organize an answer however the respondent thinks best, and sometimes even the content is left entirely undetermined. For example, we may ask an acquaintance, "How are you?" Respondents are free to talk about their health, state of mind, mood, or anything else that occurs to them. *RESTRICTED QUESTIONS* narrow the options available to a respondent to a limited range of possibilities. For example, a restaurant server may ask a customer, "Do you prefer your coffee black, with sugar, with cream, or with cream and sugar?" Restricted questions are the point of reference for the old adage "a well-asked question is half answered." Such questions are half answered because the options are laid out in the question itself. *LOADED QUESTIONS*, by contrast, are not genuinely interrogative. Either they are allusions to the presuppositions and implications that make them intelligible, or they are really disguised claims.

Sometimes the persuasive suggestion is explicitly contained in the question itself. For example:

Have you stopped beating your wife?

The form of the question requires a yes or no answer, but both answers presuppose the admission that you used to beat your wife. If you answer *yes*, you are admitting that you used to beat your wife but no longer do so. If you answer *no*, you are admitting that you used to beat your wife and still do so. In either case you have admitted to beating your wife. This question cannot elicit an answer without impaling you on either horn of a dilemma. Such questions are called *COMPLEX QUESTIONS* because they contain an assumption that any possible answer will confirm. Complex questions thus are a way of making a claim without appearing to do so. The only way to respond to a complex question containing a false assumption is to refuse to answer it in the form in which it has been asked and to challenge the assumption directly. Here are some more complex questions:

Is your sister still as moody as she used to be?

Will Republicans ever recover from their bitterness over losing the presidential election?

Has the United States lost its reputation as guardian of the free world?

There are other more subtle ways in which questions can mislead us. *RHETORIC-AL QUESTIONS* appear on the surface to elicit new information from a respondent just as a real question does, but they are really disguised statements. Such questions are formulated to suggest that there is only one reasonable answer, and the question presupposes that answer rather than eliciting anything new from the audience. The questioner counts on agreement with the presupposed answer, and this can win an audience's approval by tapping into its sympathies rather than presenting it with statements and evidence. When politicians ask, "Is there anything more important for the future of society than child welfare?" they expect listeners to say "no, nothing." Having gained an audience's implicit assent to the point that child welfare is of paramount importance, they can introduce a new policy or law as a measure that purports to uphold this principle; other commitments or principles need not be considered, because everyone implicitly and uncritically agrees that child welfare is the only one that is relevant. The speaker can then proceed as if he or she has asserted, "There is nothing more important to the future of a society than child welfare, not the rule of law, not economic stability, not world peace, and so on." Put this way, as a statement with a host of logical implications, the same point looks less like an indubitable axiom, and more like a premise in an argument that requires further support. In short, rhetorical questions presuppose many of the claims that a good argument will articulate and defend. Rhetorical questions thus bypass the arguments that critical thinking helps us to assess. They can be very effective oratorical devices, so when a rhetorical question is posed we must be careful not to nod in assent and neglect to analyze the statements they disguise. Here are some more rhetorical questions:

Who would deny that all human life is precious?

Shouldn't the person who messed up the house be the one to clean it up?

Do you want to feel safe and secure in your own home at night?

Should you pay more of your hard-earned money for health insurance just so other people can get cheap health care?

Finally, sometimes merely asking a question can raise possibilities in the absence of evidence. The context in which legitimate questions are asked normally suggests that the questioner believes there to be no obvious answer. As a result, if someone asks a question, the audience will tend to assume that the questioner has plausible grounds to raise the issue. When a question is introduced as a way to raise a possibility in the absence of evidence, we can call these *FRAMING QUESTIONS.* Suppose a newspaper prints an article under the headline *Does the Senator Have a Secret Swiss Bank Account?* Even if the article cites no evidence but merely describes how the reporter, despite a thorough investigation, failed to turn up any hard evidence that the Senator does have a secret Swiss bank account, the unwary reader will suspect that the newspaper had some grounds for asking the question. Simply by asking this question the article suggests that the Senator is the sort of politician who would do that sort of thing. The fact that no proof was found may only show that the reporter has not found it yet, or that a cleverly designed cover-up has been orchestrated. In this case, the question itself suggests the possibility of a scandal without evidence of any wrongdoing. Similarly, a mayoral candidate might ask voters, "Can you afford four more years of high taxes brought on by the current mayor's policies?" In this case, the question presupposes that (a) taxes are higher than they need to be, and (b) that the incumbent is responsible for this purported state of affairs. It is possible to argue for such claims, but the question encourages us to believe both of them without argument. Whereas rhetorical questions are disguised statements or even implicit arguments, framing questions are disguised allegations of wrongdoing without evidence. ·

Any allegation can be turned into a question, and even if the answer is *no*, a suspicion that the allegation is true will remain. After all, if someone thought the question was worth asking, it is natural to assume there must have been some reason to think that the implied allegation might have been true, even if it turns out to be false. In some situations, the taint of suspicion will remain no matter how much evidence is produced to refute the implied allegation. Public figures are especially vulnerable to suspicions created through the adroit use of loaded questions, but the technique can be applied to anyone. Here are some more examples of framing questions:

Do you suppose he tries so hard to be macho because he is secretly afraid of impotence?

Was that excellent essay really your own work?

Did the government lose the election because they were incompetent or because they were arrogant?

Is that really just tobacco in the professor's pipe?

When will you learn to take some responsibility for your actions?

12.4 FALSE CONFIDENCE

People are often willing to accept a claim if the speaker presents it with great confidence. The confidence can be conveyed both by the choice of words and by the manner in which they are expressed. If the speaker is genuinely confident of the truth of the claim, then presenting it with confidence is quite appropriate. But if a questionable claim is presented with confidence, the audience can be misled into thinking that it cannot seriously be questioned. For example:

> *I certainly don't want to suggest that all adopted children are miserable, but the fact is that a majority of adopted children do suffer from a serious problem of self-identity and that the problem is most serious during their teenage years.*

Is this claim true? It is certainly plausible, but in the absence of solid empirical evidence one could just as plausibly claim that it is false. But if it is asserted in a confident tone of voice, and in a way that suggests that everyone who knows anything about adoption would know that it is true, most people will be inclined not to challenge the speaker. They will believe that it is probably true.

FALSE CONFIDENCE is different from deliberately telling a lie. Of course, if a lie is to be convincing, the liar must tell it with confidence, so in a sense lying does require that the liar present false confidence. But we are here describing a different technique, one used by those who believe that what they are saying is true, but who want their audience to accept the claim without critical scrutiny. It is a way of suggesting, rather than saying, to the audience that there is no need to ask for the evidence. It suggests that anyone who did ask for evidence would only reveal their ignorance or naivety.

The effectiveness of false confidence in persuading an audience to accept a claim depends in large part upon the plausibility of the claim being made. No amount of false confidence would persuade most of us to accept a claim that flies in the face of common sense or is inconsistent with what we strongly believe to be true. For example:

> *Mongolian peasants use a method of predicting the sex of unborn children that is accurate more than 95 per cent of the time. On a night when there is a full moon, the father spits into a cup of the mother's urine and leaves it on the doorstep of their hut overnight. If the spit is still floating the next morning, the baby will be a boy.*

No matter how confidently such an assertion is made, most of us will refuse to believe the accuracy of this method of predicting the sex of unborn children. We have good reasons for believing that such a claim is inherently problematic and are unlikely to accept it without strong evidence. But if the claim is one we think could well be true, and especially if we think the speaker just might know something we don't, we can be taken in by the speaker's confidence.

It is not clear why so many people seem willing to accept any plausible claim if the speaker presents it confidently. It may be out of a sense of politeness: not to accept the claim is to suggest that the speaker is ignorant or dishonest. It may be that many people are afraid they may be called upon to present evidence and arguments to defend their skepticism, which they may be unwilling or unable to do. Or it may be a naive belief that most people never seek deliberately to mislead others. Whatever the reason, false confidence can frequently be very effective in persuading people to accept something without supporting reasons.

12.5 SELECTIVITY

Many judgments rest upon a complex body of evidence. Inductive generalizations, as we saw in section 10.2, rest upon a number of particular instances, and their strength depends upon these instances being a representative sample of the entire population; since populations are not usually homogeneous, we can be misled by an unrepresentative sample. This fact makes it possible for someone to create a misleading impression by bringing unrepresentative examples to our attention. Suppose, for example, we disapprove of the National Endowment for the Arts' policy of giving grants to artists. Without presenting arguments against the policy, we can attempt to discredit it by looking for examples where the grants have been abused and mentioning them to anyone who will listen. We say nothing that is false, we make no claim that grants are always or usually abused, we present no arguments against the policy; we merely point out every abuse whenever we find one.

Presenting unrepresentative facts will mislead only when the audience is not aware of all the evidence. It may be that in 99 per cent of cases there is no abuse and that the policy is achieving its goal, but most people are unlikely to know this and will gain the impression that the grants are systematically abused. A rational response to such *SELECTIVITY* would be to ask for evidence that would show what percentage of grants are abused and how the abusers are dealt with, as well as to ask for evidence of the social and cultural benefits produced by the grants, for this is the kind of evidence we would need to pass judgment on the policy. But people who are deliberately selective in the facts they present usually want to avoid presenting such evidence, which is why they are usually careful to avoid even the appearance of presenting an argument. If they say, *Here is my evidence and here is my conclusion*, someone is sure to challenge the evidence, which will defeat the purpose of being selective.

The news media are frequently criticized for being selective in their approach to the news. Often the criticism is deserved, especially when the particular newspaper or television station has a strong political or ideological commitment. Stories that reflect favorably upon their cause are given prominence, and those that do not are ignored or relegated to the back pages.

Of course, if selectivity occurs in an argument, the argument would violate the criterion of adequacy. Most often it would involve both of the weaknesses discussed in section 10.2.

12.6 MISLEADING STATISTICS

One of the more insidious types of selectivity involves the selective use of statistics. An extensive knowledge of statistics would be needed to be able to recognize the many different ways in which statistics can mislead, and we can here describe only a few of the more common types of misleading statistics.

It is often useful to know the average value of something. We may, for example, want to know the average grade for a course, the average grade of a student, the average wage paid by a company, the average rent for a one-bedroom apartment, or the average summer temperature in Australia. But averages can be quite misleading. Suppose we are told that the employees of a company earn an average of $1,000 per week. This is a quite respectable wage, and we would not have a great deal of sympathy if the employees complained of being seriously underpaid, since we would assume that most employees must be receiving around $1,000 per week. But this need not be so. Suppose the company has 11 employees who are paid as follows:

General manager:	$2,400
Sales manager:	$2,000
Production manager:	$2,000
Office manager:	$1,800
Bookkeeper 1:	$440
Bookkeeper 2:	$420
Shipper:	$410
Driver:	$390
Salesperson:	$390
Salesperson:	$390
Receptionist:	$360
Total:	$11,000

The average weekly pay is $1,000, but everyone except the managers receives much less. In such a case most people will be misled by references to the average wage.

To avoid such misleading averages, statisticians make use of two related concepts that help to give a more accurate picture than a *SIMPLE AVERAGE*. The *MEDIAN* is the middle point in the range: half the individual cases will be above it and half below it. In the above example, the median is $420. The *MODE* is the particular value that occurs most frequently. In the above example, the mode is $390. The median and the mode are quite different from the simple average, or *MEAN*, as it is called by statisticians.

A second way in which statistics can mislead is when they are used to describe quantitative changes, such as increases or decreases in prices, productivity, crime rates, and so on. The problem lies in an ambiguity in the way such changes are described. If a merchant buys an item for $6 and sells it for $10, what, in percentage terms, is the merchant's profit? Calculated as a percentage of the merchant's *buying* price, the profit is 66.6 per cent. But calculated as a percentage of the *selling* price, the profit is only 40 per cent. Both methods of calculating the merchant's profit are legitimate (even if one method is unconventional), but they are different and mean different things. If we are told that the mark-up used by a merchant is 50 per cent, we can be misled unless we know which method is being used. Similar problems can arise in a variety of other contexts. If a landlord says the rent on a $600 apartment has increased only 25 per cent in the last five years, does this mean the rent went from $480 to $600 (because the rent has increased by 25 per cent of the original rent of $480) or from $450 to $600 (because the rent has increased by 25 per cent of $600 from the original rent of $450)? If a friend brags about having increased his or her semester average 10 per cent last semester, did it jump from 60 per cent to 70 per cent or from 60 per cent to 66 per cent? In each case, in order not to be misled we should ask, *Percentage of what?*

A third way in which statistical information can be misleading is when it is presented as a graph. Once again, the actual statistical information is not false: the problem is that it can easily be misunderstood if we do not pay careful attention to how it is being presented. The two graphs shown below present identical information about the increase in the price of a commodity over a one-year period.

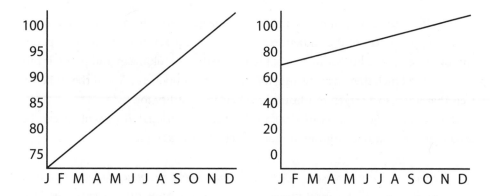

The graph on the left makes it appear that there has been a much more dramatic price increase than the graph on the right, even though both present *the same information*. The graph on the left suggests a greater increase because the bottom three-quarters of the graph have been cut off. The line looks different only because the vertical axis is drawn to a different scale. When interpreting any graph, we should always take the scale into account.

12.7 HUMOR

There is nothing wrong with using humor in a discussion. In fact, if a discussion starts to become boring, a little humor can be a very good thing. Every good public speaker knows the value of a good joke or a witty comment. For example:

> *You've heard of the definition of a philosopher as a blind person in a dark room searching for a black cat that isn't there? Well, a theologian is the person who finds the cat.*

> *When I read what drama critics have to say about my work, I am reminded of Brendan Behan's comment that critics are like eunuchs in a harem: they know how it's done, they've seen it done every day, but they're unable to do it themselves.*

There are, however, limits to the purposes for which humor can legitimately be used. In particular, it should not be used as a substitute for rational argument. In argumentative contexts, any use of humor functions *independently* of reasons in favor of the argument's conclusion. When we use humor to divert attention from a weakness in our argument or to have some fun at the expense of our opponents, no reasons have been provided to believe that our position is stronger than that of our opponent. If our argument was weak before we added some humor, it will be just as weak after.

The effectiveness of humor as a persuasive device depends, of course, upon the views and prejudices of the audience. If the audience is sympathetic to our opponent, our attempts at humor may backfire and make us look mean and petty. If our jokes are too cruel, they may create sympathy for our opponent. And if the audience feels that it is also a target, our humor may create hostility toward us.

But humor is not always used as a substitute for rational argument. It can be used to make a rational argument more effective. For example:

> *The Governor is still refusing to act on the unanimous recommendations of his own committee as well as several independent experts regarding the leakage at the PCB dump in my constituency. Everyone who has examined the situation agrees it constitutes a serious health hazard to the 20,000 people living nearby. But when asked by a reporter yesterday what he was going to do about it, the Governor talked at great length about consulting all the interested parties. This is a totally inadequate response. As usual, the Governor's mouth is in high gear and his brain is in neutral.*

In the face of unanimous recommendations regarding what to do about a serious health hazard, the Governor's response certainly seems totally inadequate. The humor helps to make this point in a more effective manner, even though it adds no logical or rational strength to the argument.

12.8 RED HERRING

When responding to a criticism of some position we hold, it is often tempting to ignore the criticism and launch a counter-attack on our opponent by raising a different issue altogether. When we do this we have introduced a *RED HERRING*. (The label probably derives from fugitives trying to prevent dogs from tracking their scent by rubbing a stinky red herring across their path.) We are attempting to avoid a criticism by shifting the discussion to a new topic on which we can attack the critic. This device is regularly used by politicians when responding to attacks by opponents. For example:

> Representative: *Will the Governor explain why nothing has been done to clean up the mercury poisoning in his state, 18 months after it was brought to his attention?*
> Governor: *The speaker sounds like a broken record with his constant carping about health hazards. The fact is that my administration has been extremely successful in reducing, and in many cases eliminating, environmental pollution across this state. Our record is vastly better than the previous administration's record.*

The Governor has clearly not responded to the question at all but has attempted to shift the discussion to the government's record of pollution control in general to avoid having to answer the question that was asked.

It is important to realize that there is nothing wrong with attempting to shift a discussion from one topic to another. Many discussions ramble naturally from topic to topic; as we get tired of one topic we move on to something else that is more interesting. Shifting topics is only illegitimate when the shift is introduced in an attempt to avoid a criticism.

Here is another example of a red herring:

> *Critics of the automobile industry frequently claim that our cars are not as safe as they could be. One critic has even suggested that we are criminally negligent because of our failure to produce safe cars. What these critics so conveniently forget is that cars do not cause accidents. Accidents are caused by bad drivers. We co-operate with governments in promoting safe driving and have taken numerous initiatives ourselves. We are not sure why our campaigns have been so ineffective. If we thought that spending more money on promoting safe driving would help, we would gladly do so, but no one knows what type of campaign would be most effective. This is where the critics could actually do some good, if they were to help us discover how to promote safe driving habits.*

12.9 GUILT BY ASSOCIATION

One way of attacking an opponent or an opponent's position is by suggesting a similarity with another person or position that the audience regards in an unfavorable light. In a debate on the government's policy of attempting to create a sense of national unity, for example, someone might say:

> *So what you are really advocating is a system like they had in Nazi Germany where the Propaganda Ministry attempted to foster a national ideology.*

Such a comment is an attempt to create the same kind of hostility towards the government's policy that people feel towards Nazi Germany. It suggests that the policy is a totalitarian or fascist idea that ought to be rejected out of hand.

GUILT BY ASSOCIATION involves a faulty analogy. In fact, the analogy is usually so faulty that, if it were presented as a serious argument, its weaknesses would be immediately apparent and the purpose of drawing the analogy would be defeated. Here are some more examples of attempts to establish guilt by association:

We should never forget that the politicians who gave us Medicare borrowed the idea from the communists, who first introduced socialized medical care in the 1920s.

So, you are driving a BMW now. I guess you will soon be sending your children to private schools, like all the other yuppies.

12.10 PERSUASIVE REDEFINITION

An especially effective device for changing attitudes is what is called *PERSUASIVE REDEFINITION*: the redefinition of a familiar term or phrase that has both a descriptive and an evaluative meaning in such a way as to change its descriptive meaning while keeping its evaluative meaning the same. Consider the term *poet*. The dictionary gives as one definition of a poet *a writer of verse*. This gives the term's descriptive meaning. The word can also be used with a strong positive evaluative meaning: to describe someone as a poet is normally to praise him or her. If we wanted to capitalize on this evaluative meaning, we might try a persuasive redefinition that involves dropping the requirement that a poet actually has to write verse: *a poet is a person with a deep and vivid imagination*. Given this definition, we could describe someone as a poet (and hence praiseworthy) who has never actually written a poem. If we are challenged, we could claim that we are not using the word in its ordinary or vulgar sense, according to which anybody who can scribble a rhyme would count as a poet, but rather in the true sense of the term. The essence of being a poet, we might say, is having a deep and vivid imagination. In other words, we attempt to justify shifting the descriptive meaning by claiming that our new definition is superior because it is truer. In fact, of course, such definitions are not usually superior at all but only different and, if judged as reportive definitions, wildly inaccurate.

To be effective, a persuasive redefinition must not change the descriptive meaning too much or else the audience will see the trick and not be fooled by it. If someone tried to redefine the term *intelligence* to mean the ability to use words of more than two syllables, no one would take the attempt seriously. But where the change preserves some of the original descriptive meaning, it may be harder to detect. A definition of intelligence as the ability to perform mental calculations quickly is closer to the original descriptive meaning and hence could be more successful as a persuasive redefinition. People who are good at doing mental calculations might well want to redefine intelligence in this way in order to attract the admiration that intelligence usually evokes.

Persuasive redefinitions are always stipulative, since the new descriptive meaning always differs from the original descriptive meaning to a certain extent. What distinguishes a persuasive definition from an ordinary stipulative definition is its purpose, for it always seeks to retain the original evaluative meaning. Most stipulative definitions are indifferent to the evaluative meaning of the term.

To illustrate the process of persuasive redefinition, let us consider an historical example. In the 1920s the term *fascist* came into use as a name for a political movement in Italy. It was strongly nationalistic and anti-communist and placed great emphasis on the role of a leader in expressing the spirit of the people and furthering the traditional values of the society. Similar movements in Germany and elsewhere also came to be referred to as fascist. Originally, the term lacked any clear evaluative meaning: people in many countries considered fascism as a serious political alternative, and many well-meaning people adopted a number of fascist views. The events of World War II, however, gave the term a strongly negative evaluative meaning. With the defeat of fascist regimes in Germany and Italy, one might have expected the term to fall into disuse. In fact, it has become an accepted part of our political vocabulary, probably because a number of influential political writers wanted to preserve it as a term of abuse. To do so, however, its original descriptive meaning had to be revised to take account of the fact that the original fascist movements no longer exist, and it now refers to any government with totalitarian or racist policies. The original descriptive meaning has largely, although not entirely, disappeared.

12.11 SELF-TEST NO. 18

Identify the irrational techniques of persuasion used in the following passages.

1. So the city of Edmonton has launched an advertising campaign to attract tourists. It reminds me of the time when a Calgary newspaper had some kind of contest: first prize was a weekend in Edmonton, and second prize was a whole week in Edmonton.

2. We take great pride in our products. We've had over 80 years of experience making furniture and we've learned how to balance the highest standards of craftsmanship with a range of styles to suit the tastes of the modern consumer.

    And our customers agree. When people walk into our showrooms the words we hear most frequently are, *Ah, that's what I've been looking for!*

    Pardon us if we're smug. We are the best and can't see why we shouldn't brag about it.

3. Frankly, I don't think it matters whether pornography is harmful to women or not. We live in a pluralistic society in which there are many different voices,

all of which are entitled to be heard. Silencing opinions and points of view that some group doesn't agree with goes against what this country stands for.

4. What is Adam like? Well, he's kind of hard to describe. He's basically just a neat guy: lots of personality, sort of laid back, the kind of person you would like.

5. If you are one of the majority of wage earners over 30 who doesn't have the protection a retirement savings plan provides, you should be asking yourself, *Why do I keep putting it off?*

6. A thriving economy is essential for the country. It is, after all, the source of our collective prosperity and happiness. And is not the best society the one that generates the greatest happiness for everyone?

7. Remember, the next time you're in the market for a new lawn-mower, try a Titan. They've got what it takes.

8. I'm fed up with those people who keep insisting that we shouldn't violate the rights of criminals. What I want to know is, what are they prepared to do for the victims of violent crimes?

9. He's not really a scientist. Sure, he has a Ph.D. in chemistry and works in a research laboratory, but all he does is try to find cheaper ways of making soaps and cosmetics. Real scientists are dedicated to making discoveries, take pride in what they are doing, and care deeply about the progress of the whole discipline. He is nothing more than a glorified lab technician.

10. There sure is a lot of talk these days about the free trade deal, and it's probably going to get a lot worse before it gets better. I don't know about you, but I'm having a helluva time figuring out who's right and who's wrong. You've got the union leaders bleating about the loss of jobs, and the business types telling us we're all going to get rich. So it is difficult to know who to believe. One thing I want to know is, is there any reason to think that this time the government isn't just serving the interests of its tycoon friends in corporate boardrooms?

11. Did you see that, Doris? That car went right through the stop sign without even slowing down. And it was a woman driver too, just like the one that rear-ended Ken last month.

12. Isn't the morally right action in every situation the one that is consistent with duty?

12.12 QUESTIONS FOR DISCUSSION

Some, although not all, of the following passages present real arguments. However, all rely in part on one or more irrational techniques of persuasion to attempt to put their point across. How might these arguments be improved with modifications?

1. Religious cults are extremely dangerous, and we must do everything possible to warn people against them. They always prey upon the young, who are at that vulnerable age when they still retain their idealism but are beginning to learn that the world is a less moral place than it should be. Once they have ensnared a victim they completely take over his or her life. Cult members become slaves: they do exactly what they are told and any questioning or criticism is severely discouraged. They are forbidden all contact with their families and former friends. Their dependency is so complete that it is virtually impossible to rescue them without the risk of doing serious psychological damage.

2. Communism always presented itself as a scientific theory of history and politics, but the reality was that it was essentially a religion. Like religion, its claim to an objective basis was more apparent than real and rested more upon faith than anything else. And it offered its adherents personal salvation: the assurance that they were right and that in the fullness of time they would be seen to have been right. It also offered an evil enemy that had to be opposed at every turn and whose ultimate overthrow would produce a new Jerusalem where at last the lion would lie down with the lamb.

3. For years many of us have regarded the Green Party as an interesting and worthwhile third party. It has lots of ideas as to what the government should be doing, and some of those ideas are practical enough to deserve a hearing. And they're a decent bunch of folks; they often take themselves too seriously, but basically they're honest and concerned people. But now that the polls suggest that they might actually win the next election, we have to ask whether the Greens have the competence—the ability to make tough economic decisions, for example—to govern a country as complex as the United States. How Americans answer this question may well determine whether or not the United States will soon have its first environmentalist Congress representative.

4. There can be no doubt whatever about the fundamental correctness of the government's fiscal and monetary policies, for we absolutely must get the deficit under control or else face economic disaster within 10 years. There

is, quite simply, no alternative to what the government is doing. Of course, the Opposition pretends that it has some magic wand that it can wave at the deficit and make it disappear. The reality, however, is that while the ship of state is in danger of sinking, the Opposition has only a sardine can to bail with. It would be funny if it were not so tragic.

5. During the twentieth century, humankind, at least in the industrialized world, achieved a standard of living that would have astonished people only a century ago. The average person today has more money, more comfort, and better health than ever before. The average person has a better job, has better-educated children, travels more widely and more often, has a better home with more possessions, and can retire at age 55 to enjoy another 25 years of comfortable living.

Appendix: Answers to Self-Tests

The self-tests are designed not to test your comprehension of concepts and principles directly, but to test the critical thinking skills that are based on them. Most of the questions are quite straightforward. If you get more than one or two wrong answers in any test, you should review the preceding material in order to discover why you are having difficulty. Usually it will be because you have misunderstood some concept or principle and not because of any difficulty in the questions themselves.

The fact that the questions are quite straightforward, however, creates a hazard that you should beware of. If you look up the answers without trying to work out an answer of your own, you will usually think that the answer given is quite obvious. This may lead you to conclude that you do not need to do the self-tests. Resist this conclusion, for it is deceptive. The answers given here should all be obvious *after* you read them, but this does not mean that they would have been obvious *before* you read them.

It may be that some of these answers are not as plausible as others that might have been given. I hope this is not the case, but my hopes are no guarantee that I have not missed some better answers. If you are occasionally convinced that your answer is better than the one you find here, you may well be correct. If your critical thinking skills have been well developed by this book, your judgment should not lead you astray.

SELF-TEST NO. 1
I.

1. This is an argument.
   Premise: *You promised your parents you would go home this weekend.*
   Conclusion: *You should go home next weekend.*

2. This is probably not an argument. However, it is possible, although unlikely, that the speaker means that a reason for going home would be to have a good time. On this interpretation, the passage would be an argument.

3. This is an argument.

Premise 1: *Peter took first place in the championships last year.*
Premise 2: *He has been training hard ever since.*
Conclusion: *He should win the championships this year.*

4. Most likely, this is an argument.

Premise 1: *The doctor told me that a second operation won't be necessary.*
Premise 2: *I will be able to go home this Friday.*
Conclusion: *I will be able to visit you next month.*

However, it is possible to interpret this passage in a way that it does not attempt to *prove* that the speaker can make the visit. Rather, it could well be an explanation of how it has become possible for the speaker to make the visit after all. Which interpretation is more plausible would depend on the context in which these things are said.

5. This is not an argument. It is merely a description of an event.

6. This is not an argument. It is merely a statement that is unsupported by any reasons or evidence.

7. This is an argument.

Premise: *The company's sales declined by 23 per cent in the last three months.*
Conclusion: *The company was justified in laying off 250 assembly line workers.*

8. This is not an argument. It is merely a claim.

9. This is not an argument. It is merely a description.

10. This is an argument, although the premises and conclusion need to be rewritten to make explicit what the argument implies.

Premise 1: *Last year Van and Patti both took a full course load while working 20 hours a week.*
Premise 2: *Last year Van and Patti both failed their semesters.*
Conclusion: If you take a full course load while working 20 hours a week, *you will fail your semester.*

11. This is an argument.

Premise 1: *My purse with my cash, my watch, and my necklace are missing from my hotel room.*
Premise 2: *The door of the room was locked while I was out.*
Premise 3: *There's no sign of forced entry into the room.*
Premise 4: *Only someone working in the hotel could have entered the room*

without breaking in.

Conclusion: *It looks like someone on staff at the hotel stole these items.*

12. This is not an argument. It is merely a narrative description of a journey.

II.

1. Sound. However, if you did not know that Albany is in New York, or that New York is in the United States, you should have answered that it is merely a logically strong argument.

2. Merely logically strong. However, if you really thought that Beaver Creek is larger than Vancouver, you should have answered that it is a sound argument.

3. Logically strong, but if you know enough about the people named in the argument to believe that the two premises are true, then you should say that the argument is sound.

4. Merely logically strong. Even if you knew that the first premise is true, since you don't know who Katherine is, it would be incorrect to say that the argument is sound

5. Sound, assuming that hockey is Canada's national sport. Otherwise it is a merely logically strong argument.

6. Sound. However, if you did not know that both premises are true, you should have answered that it is merely a logically strong argument.

7. Merely logically strong. Since the context indicates that the word *cat* is being used in a very broad sense, the first premise is obviously false.

8. Sound. It is not necessary to know who the President is in order to know that he or she is a human being.

9. Merely logically strong. First, while the second premise may be true of the New York Yankees in North American major league baseball, it may well be that there is an amateur team somewhere or a professional team outside North America that has won more games. In addition, it is not true that everybody loves a winner: some people detest winners.

10. Sound. However, if you did not interpret *I* as referring to yourself, the correct answer would be that it is merely a logically strong argument.

11. Merely logically strong. All the ships named in this passage are fictional, and it's not possible to compare how fast or slow they are in relation to each other.

12. Merely logically strong. Not all dogs are excellent companions, and this claim seems to be implicit in the first premise.

SELF-TEST NO. 2

1. Persuasive

2. Descriptive

3. Persuasive

4. Emotive

5. Descriptive

6. Recreational

7. Directive

8. Performative

9. Directive. Note, however, that although it appears to be addressed to all pedestrians, it is really a directive only for those pedestrians who want to cross the street.

10. Emotive and evocative. It is likely that the author has both purposes in mind.

11. Directive

12. Performative

SELF-TEST NO. 3

1. Too narrow, because the defining phrase (*the highest court in the United States*) applies only to the Supreme Court of the United States, and excludes the Supreme Courts of other countries.

2. Too broad, because the defining phrase (*art form that uses words to communicate ideas and images*) includes other art forms that use words to communicate ideas and images, such as novels and plays.

3. Too broad, because the defining phrase (*implement designed to remove snow*) includes other implements designed to remove snow, such as snow shovels and snow blowers. It is also circular, which would make the definition useless for anyone who does not know what snow is.

4. Circular.

5. Obscure. This definition would only be informative to someone who already has extensive knowledge of music theory.

6. Too broad, since the defining phrase includes several other devices that are used to fasten pages together, such as paper clips and binders. It is also too narrow, since the defining phrase excludes staplers that are designed for use in construction and for other industrial uses.

7. Too narrow, because the defining phrase excludes male nurses. It is also too broad, because it includes other health care professionals, such as doctors and chiropractors.

8. Too broad, since the defining phrase includes other kinds of one-story buildings such as garages and shops.

9. Too broad, since the defining phrase also refers to other international organizations, such as the European Community, the Olympics, NATO, and the International Civil Aviation Organization.

10. Too broad, since the defining phrase also includes such competitive activities as operating a business, playing chess, and competing in music festivals, none of which are sports. It is also too narrow, since the defining phrase excludes such individual sports as sport fishing, surf boarding, and sky diving, which are not normally competitive.

SELF-TEST NO. 4

1. There is a referential ambiguity here since it is unclear whether the term *his sisters* is being used collectively or distributively. If it is used distributively, the sentence means that Billy gave two boxes of candy, one to each sister. If it is being used collectively, the sentence means that Billy gave his sisters one box of candy to be shared between them.

2. Because *chicken* can be used metaphorically to characterize a cowardly person or literally to refer to a kind of bird, this sentence is referentially ambiguous.

3. There is a grammatical ambiguity in this sentence. Literally, the sentence means that Melissa has nothing else in the world besides her one dress. If the location of the word *only* is changed to make the sentence read *Melissa has only one dress*, it means that although she may have many possessions, she has only one dress. This is the more likely meaning.

4. The term *General* is referentially ambiguous. It could refer to a local hospital, in which case the sentence means that the nurses won their strike with the hospital. Or it could refer to a specific military officer, in which case the sentence means that the officer was beaten by the nurses in some kind of contest or struggle. In a town that has a local hospital that is routinely called *The General*, however, it will usually be clear which interpretation is best.

5. If the term *Conversational German* is being merely mentioned, then it refers to a textbook or a course, and the sentence means that it is a difficult book or course. If the term is being used, then the sentence means that it is difficult to learn how to speak conversational German.

6. The term *discipline* is referentially ambiguous. It could refer simply to corporal punishment, which is how some people use the term. But it could refer to a set of rules imposed by adults that children are expected to follow. It could also refer to self-discipline, that is, to a set of rules that children learn to develop for themselves. The meaning of the sentence is quite different depending upon which reference we choose.

7. This is grammatically ambiguous. It is likely that the speaker is promising to drop this subject after the condition has been met, that is, if the person thinks over once again the plan to drop out of school. However, if we read the passage according to its literal meaning, there is another claim on the surface: the speaker promises he or she will never speak to the person again if the condition is met. In most contexts, the principle of charity would require us to interpret the speaker as meaning ... *I won't say another word to you about dropping out of school.*

8. The term *instructors* is referentially ambiguous. If it is being used collectively, the sentence means that the instructors, as a group, are free to choose whatever text they can all agree on. If the term is being used distributively, the sentence means that each instructor is free to choose whatever text he or she wishes.

9. The sentence is grammatically ambiguous. If *illegally* modifies *tested* the sentence means that the stores were illegally tested. If *illegally* modifies *sell* it means that the stores were illegally selling cigarettes.

10. This sentence is grammatically ambiguous. If *with a bright red hood* modifies *limousine* the sentence means that the limousine has a bright red

hood. But if *with a bright red hood* completes *she arrived* the sentence means that she was wearing a bright red hood.

11. This sentence is grammatically ambiguous. Literally, it says that the noise the superintendent complained about was coming from *his own pyjamas*. However, the principle of charity encourages us to interpret the speaker as saying that the superintendent was wearing his pyjamas when he was complaining about noise coming from *the apartment*. The comic effect of the sentence depends on seeing the literal meaning and recognizing that the speaker intends us to interpret it as the principle of charity suggests.

12. This sentence is referentially ambiguous. The speaker could be asking about *where* on the person's body he or she was struck, or the speaker could be asking about *where* the person was at the time he or she was struck.

SELF-TEST NO. 5

1. Analytic. If you know what a full deck of cards is, you know that it must have 52 cards. (Of course, a few card games require players to use the jokers, but this is a special case that would be cleared up by the speakers sorting out what is meant by *full deck*, not by counting cards.)

2. Analytic. Since a foot is defined as one-third of a yard, a foot is by definition shorter than a yard.

3. Synthetic. There is nothing about the meanings of the words in this sentence that guarantees its truth or falsity.

4. Synthetic. The truth or falsity of this sentence can only be determined by checking a reference book on sports records. The meaning of the sentence leaves its truth or falsity an open question.

5. Synthetic. As far as we know, this is a true statement. But its truth is something we have learned and is not determined by the meaning of the sentence.

6. Contradictory. The first clause in the sentence is contradicted by the last clause.

7. Synthetic. Assuming that the speaker correctly understands the meanings of the words in this sentence, he or she could only be proven wrong by sending him or her to the southern hemisphere with a compass.

8. Synthetic. Observations would be needed to determine the truth of this statement.

9. Synthetic, on both the literal and metaphorical interpretation. In both cases, the truth of the sentence could only be determined by investigating the facts.

10. On a literal interpretation this is an analytic statement. However, it would normally be used to mean something like *You should not adopt romantic or highly speculative interpretations of ordinary things*, which is synthetic.

11. On the usual interpretation of this cliché, it is analytic. According to the analytic interpretation, *fit* is understood to mean that the peg sits snugly in the hole.

12. Contradictory. Usually, *excellent condition* means that a bicycle does not have any problems and that it does not require the kind of extensive repair work described in the second part of the sentence. (Of course, one might charitably read this sentence to mean that *after* all the repairs are completed, the bike *will be* in excellent condition, but in the present tense it is contradictory.)

SELF-TEST NO. 6

1. The evaluative meaning is negative. Descriptively, *vicious competition* means that the usual aspects of competitiveness (such as wanting to be better than others, complaining when others do well, trying to place others at a disadvantage) are carried to extreme lengths. A good descriptive synonym would be *fierce*.

2. The evaluative meaning is negative. Descriptively, a *compulsively tidy person* is unavoidably uncomfortable with even minor untidiness, and is driven by an irresistible inner force to tidy up. A good descriptive synonym would be *extremely*.

3. The evaluative meaning is positive. Descriptively, *responsible student* means that Mark gets his homework done, submits his assignments on time, pays attention in class, follows the school rules, and so on. Perhaps the best descriptive equivalent phrase would be *hard working* and *thorough*.

4. The evaluative meaning is negative, since a decline in moral standards means that they have changed by becoming more permissive. The

descriptive meaning of *declined* in this context is that moral standards have been enforced less strictly. A good descriptive synonym is *relaxed*.

5. The evaluative meaning is negative. Descriptively, *greed* refers to a desire for money and material goods. A good descriptive equivalent would be *a* substantial *desire for money and material goods*.

6. The evaluative meaning is negative, because it suggests that the budget reduction has been ruthless or excessive. Descriptively, *slashed* means reduced, and *reduced substantially* is the best descriptive synonym.

7. The evaluative meaning is negative. *Very, extremely,* and *highly* all capture the descriptive meaning of *excessively* and would be good descriptive synonyms.

8. The evaluative meaning is negative. Descriptively, *suckered* means being persuaded to do something by underhanded or dishonest means. The best descriptive synonym is *persuaded*.

9. The evaluative meaning is positive since *mature* suggests the opposite of inexperienced. Descriptively, *mature years* means that he was middle-aged or older. *Old age* would be the best descriptive synonym.

10. The evaluative meaning is negative, since referring to an adult woman as a *girl* denigrates her. A better descriptive synonym is *assistant*.

SELF-TEST NO. 7

1. A sufficient condition, since this is only one of several ways to bring down a fever. If interpreted as a necessary condition, it would mean that this is the only way of bringing down a fever, which is false.

2. The two conditions stated are jointly sufficient conditions for being required to withdraw from the university. If interpreted as a necessary condition for being required to withdraw, the statement would mean that this is the only way of being required to withdraw, which is false since one can be required to withdraw for other reasons, such as failing too many courses.

3. Almost always a necessary condition, since while no applicants will be admitted unless they meet the stated conditions, not every student who meets these conditions can expect to be admitted. If the sentence is interpreted as stating a sufficient condition it means that every student

who meets these conditions will be admitted, which is a highly implausible interpretation (although not impossible).

4. Probably a necessary condition, since working hard throughout the term is not the only thing most students have to do to get an A average. If interpreted as a sufficient condition, it means that working hard will always produce an A average. This is an unlikely interpretation, since even students who work hard throughout the whole term would probably not get an A if they failed to hand in their term assignments.

5. A sufficient condition, since there are normally other defects that may lead to an essay's being returned ungraded, for example, if it is illegible or submitted late.

6. This statement gives both the necessary and sufficient conditions for winning the prize. If interpreted merely as a necessary condition, it would mean that, although every winner would have the highest average, some years the student with the highest average might not be awarded the prize. If interpreted merely as a sufficient condition, it would mean that, although each year the student with the highest average would receive the prize, another student who failed to achieve the highest average might also receive the prize, perhaps with the money divided between them.

7. A necessary condition. If interpreted as a sufficient condition, it would mean that every US citizen could become president which is false since (among other things) one must be US-born to become president.

8. A necessary condition, since presumably if interest rates do not come down, the confidence of the business community will not be restored. It might also be a sufficient condition, if reducing interest rates is the only thing necessary to restore confidence in the economy, but this would only make sense if it is assumed that all the other factors necessary to restore confidence (such as stable international markets, acceptable exchange rates, reasonable taxes) are already present and are unlikely to change.

9. A necessary condition, since good physical coordination is necessary for becoming a good skier. But it is not a sufficient condition, or else anyone with good physical coordination who had never skied before would already be a good skier, which is absurd.

10. A necessary condition. If it were a sufficient condition, it would mean that everyone with a Ph.D. could become a university professor, which isn't

true, as there are other prerequisites to being a university professor (public speaking skills, etc.).

11. Two necessary conditions, which are probably jointly sufficient. Both completing the homework and having a bath are necessary conditions for Sarah being allowed to watch television. Presumably, permission is automatically granted once these conditions are satisfied.

12. The condition is both necessary and sufficient. The *only if* means that it is a necessary condition, and the *if* means that it is also a sufficient condition.

SELF-TEST NO. 8

1. Missing premise: *My car (van, truck, or motorcycle) doesn't have enough gas to drive you home.*

2. Missing premise: *Your car is flooded.*

3. Missing conclusion: *You should attend (or make an effort to attend) church at Easter.*

4. Missing premise: *Jennifer has been living in a small town.*

5. Missing premise: *Students who do not attend class regularly are likely to do poorly in the course.*

6. Missing conclusion: *Todd is a teenage rebel.*

7. Missing premise: *It won't be possible to repair my hearing aid.*

8. Missing premise: *School boards have a responsibility to achieve a low drop-out rate.*

9. Missing premise: *Students who work hard on an assignment deserve a high grade.*

10. Missing premise: *Animals deserve the same kind of legal protection as humans enjoy.*

SELF-TEST NO. 9

1. This is an explanation. The speaker is offering an explanation for his or her stage fright.

2. This is not an argument. It is a description of an event, but it includes an explanation of David's behavior (i.e., that David was upset at what he thought was his fault and felt responsible for Michael).

3. This is an argument. It states a conclusion (*We'd better watch Mary closely for the next 24 hours*) and gives reasons to support it.

4. This is merely a general explanation of the form *X may be caused by a, b, or c.*

5. This is an explanation of why local taxes increase. By adding the comment *That is how the system works*, the speaker makes it clear that he or she is merely explaining the system.

6. This is a report of an argument. In a context where it was clear that the speaker approved of the court's practice, it could legitimately be regarded as an argument.

7. This is an argument. The conclusion is *Never turn off your computer without following the exit procedure for your software program.* The reason given in support of this conclusion consists of an explanation of what the consequences will be if the exit procedure is not followed.

8. This is probably best interpreted as an argument with a missing conclusion: *You ought to refund the entire purchase price.* The advice received from the speaker's lawyer is the reason the speaker gives for this conclusion.

9. This is an argument. It includes an explanation of why the jury system allegedly works to the advantage of criminals, but this explanation is merely a premise used to support the conclusion that the jury system should be abolished.

10. This is probably best interpreted as an explanation. In most contexts it would likely be an explanation of why Americans fail to understand how Canadian political parties operate.

SELF-TEST NO. 10

1. [Anyone who has brains and ambition will go far in this world.](P1) [Carla has certainly got plenty of both.](P2) <u>So she will go far.</u>

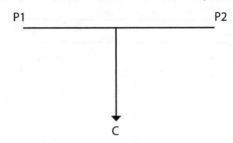

2. [I have never had any problems with the last four Fords I've bought,](P1) <u>so I don't think I'll have any problems this time.</u> Note that there is a missing premise in this argument: [A company that has made good products in the past is likely to continue to make good products.](MP2)

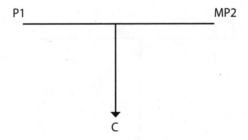

3. <u>The Mets should win the National League pennant this year.</u> [They have solid depth in their pitching staff,](P1) [their hitting has been consistently good this year,](P2) [their coaching is excellent,](P3) and [there is a good team spirit.](P4)

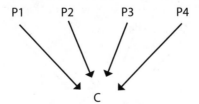

4. [A recent public opinion poll showed that more than two-thirds of Canadians believed that most politicians are dishonest.](P1) Clearly, <u>there is a crisis of confidence in Canadian politics</u>. There is a missing premise: [Widespread belief that most politicians are dishonest constitutes a crisis of confidence.](MP2)

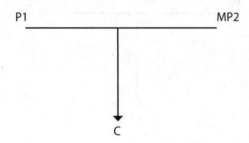

5. There is a missing conclusion: [<u>In the last 70 years there has been a tremendous increase in the percentage of Americans that have graduated high school or higher.</u>] (MC) [As of 2009, 80% of Americans are graduates of high school or higher,](P1) compared with [25% in 1940.] (P2)

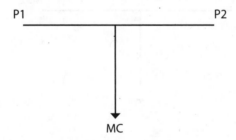

6. [Laura gets pretty good grades,](P1) [she is the best gymnast in the school,] (P2) [she has a lot of friends,](P3) and [she organized the campaign last year that forced the school to start a recycling program.](P4) I think <u>she will probably win the election for president of the Student Council.</u>

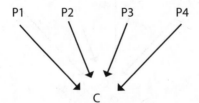

7. [If he tells his teacher he cheated, he will be punished by the principal.] (P1) But [if he doesn't tell his teacher he cheated, he will be punished by his parents.](P2) Either way he is going to be punished.

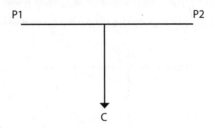

8. Since [angle CAB is 60 degrees,](P1) and [angle ACB is 40 degrees,](P2) then angle ABC must be 80 degrees. There are two missing premises in this argument: [Figure ABC is a triangle](MP3) and [The angles of a triangle always add up to 180 degrees.](MP4)

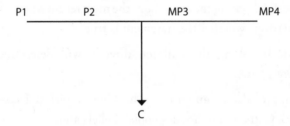

9. Any reporter who says that good reporters never slant their stories but simply report the objective facts must be either stupid or dishonest, since [it is obvious that one cannot write anything without an element of interpretation creeping in.](P1) There is a missing premise: [Someone who denies something that is obvious is either stupid or dishonest.](MP2)

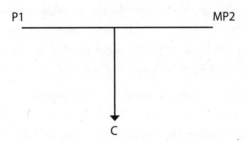

10. [That reporter is obviously not stupid.](P1) So <u>he must be dishonest</u>. There are two missing premises: [Any reporter who says that good reporters never slant their stories but simply report the objective facts must be either stupid or dishonest](MP2) and [That reporter said that good reporters never slant their stories but simply report the objective facts.](MP3)

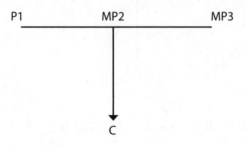

SELF-TEST NO. 11

1. Empirical. Checking the facts about the most recent Massachusetts election will determine whether the statement is true.

2. Empirical. Asking the children directly will determine whether the statement is true.

3. Non-empirical. No amount of checking empirical facts—either about St. Paul's Cathedral or about people's beliefs about it—will determine the truth or falsity of this statement. It is an evaluation.

4. Empirical. The empirical facts that will determine whether this statement is true or false are not easy to obtain, although scientists claim that there is clear and mounting evidence that it is true. But nothing other than empirical evidence could determine the truth or falsity of this claim.

5. Non-empirical. This is an analytic statement that states one of the essential features of a triangle. If you thought you could determine its truth value by measuring the angles of a triangle with a protractor, you would be treating this as an empirical statement. But as any mathematics teacher would tell you, doing this would not get you any marks on a mathematics examination.

6. Empirical. This statement should be interpreted as meaning something like *It's certain that the Toronto Maple Leafs will not win the Stanley Cup this year,* and whether this prediction is true will be determined by what

happens at the end of the season. Even if it is taken literally, however, it would still be an empirical statement whose truth would be determined by whether the speaker eats his or her hat if the team wins the Cup.

7. Empirical. This is a hypothetical statement. Some evidence right now can be obtained through complex analysis of a wide range of economic and political information; later on, if the federal government did indeed eliminate the debt, there would be more direct evidence.

8. Empirical. Despite the fact that the award is given to the best student in the school, this statement does not endorse the fact that Paula received the award. It is a simple statement of an empirical fact.

9. Non-empirical. Although the statement includes the empirical claim that suicide rates are highest around Christmas, the primary purpose of the statement is most likely to make an evaluation of this fact.

10. Empirical. This is a claim about the effects of the policy of banning the sale of ivory. Its truth would be determined by an examination of the facts regarding the ivory market and the decline in the illegal killing of elephants in Africa.

11. Non-empirical. Because *3 out of 4 people* is arithmetically equivalent to *75 per cent of the population* the sentence makes no empirical claim about facts.

12. Empirical. Although evaluative claims are not in themselves empirical, a report of an evaluative claim is a description of empirical fact.

SELF-TEST NO. 12

1. The conclusion of the argument is:

   If we want economic prosperity, we should be looking for even more wars to get involved in.

   The weakness in the argument is that the premise *Every nation that has fought a major war in the last century emerged from the war economically stronger than it was before* is false. Many nations, such as Britain, the USSR, Vietnam, Japan, and Iran, among others, have suffered great economic losses as a result of wars they have been involved in. This is, or should be, a matter of common knowledge.

2. The conclusion of the argument is:

The government has no right to force me and others who think the way I do to pay school taxes.

The argument commits the fallacy of equivocation. The word *governed* is used collectively in the first premise but distributively in the second premise.

3. The conclusion of the argument is:

There is nothing I can do about the fact that the outboard motor I bought last year turned out to be a real lemon.

The weakness of the argument is that it relies upon a false dichotomy in the premises. The speaker assumes that there are only two possibilities open to him or her: (1) sue the company and (2) do nothing. But there are other things that could be done: for example, (3) write to the president of the company, asking for compensation, or (4) make a public stink by writing letters to the press or mounting a sign on the boat that says *Evinrudes are Lemons.*

4. The conclusion of the argument is:

Only in democracies does the human spirit flourish.

The weakness in the argument is that it begs the question. Does the human spirit flourish only in democratic societies? Yes, says the author, because undemocratic societies prevent the human spirit from flourishing. The "evidence" is just another way of stating the conclusion.

5. The conclusion of the argument is:

He should be found not guilty.

This argument commits the fallacy of inconsistency. The lawyer cannot have it both ways: if either one of the two "compelling" reasons is true, then the other must be false. They cannot consistently be asserted together.

6. The conclusion of the argument is:

People are much more interested in local issues than they are in state and national political issues.

The weakness in the argument is that in recent years the premise is false in the United States.

7. The conclusion of the argument is:

Scientists should accept that biblical miracles actually occurred.

The premises of the argument, however, use the word *miracle* in a quite different sense from the way the author uses it in the conclusion. The argument therefore commits the fallacy of equivocation.

8. The conclusion of the argument is:

We should adopt a non-aligned foreign policy.

The author, however, is presupposing that the two alternatives presented are the only possibilities. This is unacceptable, since it ignores the possibility of a foreign policy that does not rely upon the threat of nuclear annihilation but rejects a non-aligned foreign policy. The argument commits the fallacy of false dichotomy.

9. The conclusion of the argument is:

Professor Smith's new course will be a great course.

The weakness in the argument is that it fails to recognize the difference between being a member of a team that developed and taught a great course and developing and teaching a course by oneself. What is true of the three professors as a team may not be true of them individually. Thus, the argument relies upon a fallacy of equivocation between the collective and distributive senses of the phrase *excellent teachers*.

10. The conclusion of the argument is:

I am almost halfway through this book.

The premise *There are 13 chapters in this book* is false, as you could discover by checking the Table of Contents. Even though the conclusion is true, and the premise is relevant, the argument is weak.

SELF-TEST NO. 13

1. There is no direct reason to think that the fact that someone's father has been convicted for fraud means that the person is completely untrustworthy. The premise is thus irrelevant. This is similar to an ad hominem, although it is the personal qualities of the speaker's father that are being attacked rather than those of the speaker. Alternatively, we could read *Like father, like son* as a second premise. This might make the first premise relevant, but it's often not true.

2. Unless one is prepared to argue that the popularity of a television show is a good indicator of the quality of the show, this argument commits an irrelevant appeal to popularity.

3. This is a legitimate appeal to authority, at least if presented by someone who knows who Gödel is and knows he meets the criteria for a reliable authority. If you did not know that Gödel meets these criteria, you should refuse to accept the appeal until you have reason to believe that the criteria are satisfied.

4. This argument commits the straw man fallacy. Evolutionary theory does not claim that humans are just monkeys with less hair or that our ancestors were apes.

5. This argument commits the ad hominem fallacy. It attacks the views of feminists on the ground that feminists are selfish. It also commits the straw man fallacy, since feminists are characterized in a false way, that is, as a group that is seeking all the good jobs for women.

6. This argument appeals to *the wisdom of history* as the reason for condemning the view that mothers and fathers can be equal partners as head of the family unit. History is thus treated as a kind of authority on how the family should be organized. This is clearly an irrelevant appeal.

7. This is an example of the kind of irrelevant things we say when we are pressed to defend an irrational position. Obviously, the fact that Janine hates flying has nothing to do with whether or not the speaker is being silly.

8. This argument probably commits the straw man fallacy, since it is unlikely that the son actually believes, as his father claims he does, that everybody should be free to do whatever they want in life. Perhaps the son actually said what his father attributes to him, but in this case the father has violated the principle of charity, since the son probably meant something much more reasonable, namely, that everybody should be free to seek whatever career they want. The father's attempted rebuttal, of course, is relevant only against the unreasonable interpretation of the son's beliefs.

9. Ralph commits the fallacy of tu quoque. Rather than respond to Ed's complaint, Ralph deflects responsibility for the noise he is responsible for by noting that Ed is responsible for late night noise too. His complaint about Ed's dog may be justifiable, but voiced at this time, without responding to Ed's complaint, it is fallacious.

10. This argument is the tu quoque fallacy, since it argues that the fact that Anglophones treated Spanish speakers unfairly in the past is a good reason for Spanish speakers to treat Anglophones unfairly in the present. The only way to avoid the tu quoque charge here would be to argue that revenge of this sort is morally justified.

11. This argument is a blatant ad hominem. There is not even a pretence that the schoolteacher's charges against the principal have been investigated and found to be invalid on the basis of relevant evidence.

12. This argument is both ad hominem and question begging. It is ad hominem because the Senator implies that the opposing party member's objection to the new program is the result of her own stubbornness rather than the government's management of the program. At the same time, it is question begging; instead of defending the stimulus program on any matters of substance or responding to the opponents objections, it merely asserts that the program is valuable.

13. This argument is a straw man. The speaker implies that infrastructure development was promoted for purposes other than stimulating the economy and improving the standard of living for the poor. But if this development was not pursued as a means to improve international trade, reduce taxes, or reduce the national debt, then these are irrelevant complaints.

SELF-TEST NO. 14

1. This is a post hoc fallacy, since the only evidence offered to show that the nuclear power plant caused the miscarriage is that the miscarriage occurred after the plant was built. There may be a causal connection, but this argument does nothing to establish it. Also, presumably the people who say that there is no proof that it is dangerous to live near a nuclear power plant have assessed the evidence and found it to be inconclusive. The speaker takes this dearth of conclusive evidence as an opportunity to assert something that cannot be disproven. So there is an appeal to ignorance here too.

2. This argument probably commits the fallacy of common cause. Those who have not worked very hard during the term (a) tend to cram immediately before examinations and (b) tend to get lower marks than the average. It is more likely that both (a) and (b) are caused by not working hard during the term than that (a) causes (b).

3. This is a slippery slope fallacy. The intermediate steps in the chain of predictions are only sketched, but even if they were spelled out in detail, the final predicted outcome (complete loss of job security for Americans) would probably not be well supported. Without the intermediate steps being explicitly stated, the premises are clearly inadequate.

4. There are two post hoc fallacies in this argument. (1) The stomach cramps started shortly after the fluoridation program was introduced; therefore, the fluoridation caused the cramps. (2) The stomach cramps disappeared

shortly after the speaker started drinking bottled water; therefore, the bottled water cured the cramps.

5. Perhaps there is no causal relationship whatever between high-school drop-out rates and the incidence of juvenile delinquency. However, there might be a common cause of the two phenomena: both might be caused by underlying social conditions. This is at least a plausible assertion. But if there is a common cause, it would not support the suggestion that improving the drop-out rate will reduce juvenile delinquency.

6. This is a fallacious appeal to authority. In particular, it seems to violate rule #4 concerning whether the subject is one of genuine expertise and rule #5 concerning whether there is a genuine consensus among experts in the field. The pope's scholarly credentials and undeniable concern for the welfare of the Catholic Church are not adequate grounds for accepting his judgment about what *is* best for the church.

7. The evidence cited by the politician is clearly inadequate to support the conclusion of the argument. There could be a number of plausible explanations for the fact that the politician has received no phone calls supporting the proposal: he or she may have a reputation for being unsympathetic to the poor; there may have been no publicity given to the proposal, so the voters may not know about it; and so on. The appeal to the absence of contrary evidence is illegitimate in this case.

8. Even if everyone knows how low the President's approval ratings are, the conclusion of this argument is not adequately supported by the evidence. First, disapproval for one person in office does not translate into disapproval for that person's party; in fact, voters may disapprove of the President because they think he no longer represents Democrat principles or ideals. Second, even in the likely case that disapproval for the President does hurt the party's popularity, the particular incumbent Senators and Congressional representatives up for re-election may be so popular that disapproval for the President or the party does not reduce their individual chances. Third, even if voters no longer approve of incumbent Democrat Senators and Congress representatives, they may still vote for them for a variety of reasons. Perhaps candidates from other parties are less popular than the Democrat incumbents, or perhaps voters believe that this is a bad time to change the government (due to economic uncertainty, for example).

9. This is an appeal to anecdotal evidence. The weakness of this argument derives from the fact that most people regard the right to hold demonstrations on public property as an important democratic right, one not to be restricted unless there is a very strong reason for doing so. Clearly, the author does not agree with this view, since he or she wants demonstrations banned simply because they are an inconvenience to some people. But the argument violates the criterion of adequacy because it fails to address the reasons most people have for tolerating the inconvenience of public demonstrations.

10. This argument probably commits the slippery slope fallacy. The policy of releasing very poor countries from their debts is not refuted directly; rather, it is said that this policy entails other policies that are clearly problematic. Much of the problem in this argument can be traced to vagueness about who the original policy applies to—that is, *some of the poorest developing nations*. What counts as being among the poorest developing nations is not specified, and this vagueness becomes more problematic because only *some* of these nations are being considered (but no criteria are provided to tell us which ones).

11. This is a fallacious appeal to authority. While the medical efficacy of marijuana is something about which a physician might have some expertise, his expertise does not include the motivation behind people who support decriminalizing it for medical purposes. Moreover, even if the doctor confined his opinions to medical matters, the therapeutic value of marijuana is not an area of medicine about which there is consensus among experts.

12. This passage commits the slippery slope fallacy. It makes *no* claim about the bill in question. Instead, it suggests without argument that, if passed, the bill will lead to inevitable, unacceptable consequences.

SELF-TEST NO. 15

In some of the passages found in this self-test, it is possible to analyze the English sentences in more detail to uncover implied premises and sub-arguments, and in a symbolic logic course these steps would be important. However, for these exercises it is sufficient to identify the overall structure of the arguments.

1. p = You buy a new coat.

   q = You won't be able to buy your textbooks for next term.

   r = Your grades will suffer.

   If p then q.

   If q then r.

   Therefore, if p then r.

   This is a chain argument and, thus, is a valid argument.

2. p = Ellen violated the confidentiality of the committee.

   q = Ellen would have harmed herself more than anyone else.

   If p then q.

   Not-q.

   Therefore, not-p.

   This is a denial of the consequent and, thus, is a valid argument.

3. p = My doctor wants me to have surgery.

   q = My doctor wants me to have a long program of physiotherapy.

   Either p or q.

   Not-p.

   Therefore, q.

   This is a disjunctive syllogism and, thus, is a valid argument.

4. p = It will rain during the game.

   q = The team will lose.

   If p then q.

   Not-p.

   Therefore, not-q.

   This is a denial of the antecedent and, thus, is fallacious.

5. p = The Republicans won more than 50 per cent of the votes in the 2008 election.

   q = The Republicans have a mandate to implement the Marriage Protection Act.

   If p then q.

   Not-p.

   Therefore, not-q.

   This is a denial of the antecedent and, thus, is fallacious.

6. p = Chris wins the election.

q = Chris is well known to a lot of students.

If p then q.

Not-q.

Therefore, not-p.

This is a denial of the consequent and, thus, is a valid argument.

7. p = Chris is well known to a lot of students.

q = Chris wins the election.

If p then q.

Not-p.

Therefore, not-q.

This is a denial of the antecedent and, thus, is fallacious.

Had we let p and q stand for the same statements as in question 6, the form
of the argument would still be the same:

If q then p.

Not-q.

Therefore, not-p.

8. p = Left-wing radicals are really committed to freedom of speech.

q = Left-wing radicals would defend freedom of speech whenever and
wherever it comes under attack.

If p then q.

Not-q.

Therefore, not-p.

This is a denial of the consequent and, thus, is a valid argument.

9. p = This is question 5.

q = I am losing my mind.

If p then q.

Not-p.

Therefore, not-q.

This is a denial of the antecedent and, thus, is fallacious.

10. p = I have not lost my mind.

q = This is question 10.

If p then q.

q.

Therefore, p.

This is an affirmation of the consequent and, thus, is fallacious. If we let p
stand for *I have lost my mind*, then we have the following form:

If not-p then q.

q.

Therefore, not-p.

This is still an affirmation of the consequent. By letting p stand for the
negative statement, it is easier to identify the form, but there is nothing
wrong with using not-p instead of p as long as we do so consistently.

SELF-TEST NO. 16

1. This is an inductive generalization.

Z = 80 per cent

F = people who live in the City

G = people who are satisfied with the recreational facilities provided by the City

There is no information on the number of questionnaires returned, so we
cannot tell whether the sample is large enough. But the sample is not a
representative one, for the responses will have come only from those who
pay their municipal taxes directly, and this excludes all tenants and almost
all young people. The argument is therefore quite weak. There is another
possible weakness in the argument. Taxpayers were asked whether they
were satisfied with the recreational facilities provided by the city at the
same time as they were presented with their tax bills. It is likely that some
people who were in fact not satisfied with the current facilities would state
that they were satisfied because they were unwilling to pay higher taxes
for new facilities. This would also bias the sample and further weaken the
argument.

2. This is an analogical argument by relations.

x = relative cost of the current policy in Sweden

y = percentage of Swedish men who use the program

R = 12 per cent

a = relative cost of the prospective policy in the US

b = percentage of American men who use the program

The subject case is a prospective policy of paid leave for new fathers. The
analogue case is an actual policy of paid leave in Sweden. The relevance of
the analogy depends on further details that are not included in the argument,

which weakens the strength of the argument. Most importantly, we would want to know how similar the two policies themselves are. If the prospective US policy is more generous than the present Swedish policy, then we would expect more than 12 per cent of American fathers to take paid leave, and it will cost more per father to finance the leave. Finally, we would want to know how similar the United States and Sweden are socially. If social values are markedly different, then the program will not be received by Americans in the same way it was received in Sweden. So while the argument is not very strong as it is stated, it is possible that it could be improved with more information.

3. This is an inductive generalization.

Z = 70 per cent

F = tourists who visit Washington State

G = people who are satisfied with tourist facilities

The sample is certainly large enough, but is clearly not representative, for several reasons. (a) American tourists from other states are under-represented, since unless they were going on from Washington into Canada they would not be included. (b) Overseas tourists are under-represented, since most of them travel by air. (c) Canadian non-tourists such as business people, workers, and so on are included since they were given questionnaires and may have responded even though they were not tourists. The argument is therefore weak.

4. This is a statistical syllogism.

Z = 90 per cent

x = my roommate

F = members of this year's graduating class

G = students who will find a job within three months of graduating

It is a weak argument because some obviously relevant information is ignored: the roommate is taking a non-specialized program, it is in arts rather than in science or engineering, and he has only a D average. All these factors make it likely that his chances of finding a job within three months of graduation are somewhat less than 90 per cent.

5. This is an analogical argument by relations.

x = Those who can easily save a drowning person with a life preserver

y = Those who refuse to throw a drowning person a life preserver

R = sick or immoral

a = Those who live in nations that can send emergency aid to a Third World country suffering from famine b = Those who oppose providing aid to Third World nations in need

The subject case is people who oppose aid to Third World countries, and the analogue case is people who would refuse to throw a life preserver to a drowning person. This argument ignores some potentially important dissimilarities between the two cases. One can readily see how to cast a preserver to someone in the water directly in front of them, whereas few people know what programs might provide effective forms of aid. Many people oppose aid because they have legitimate concerns about the organizations that provide aid. Many other people oppose aid because they believe trade programs would be more effective. This argument may commit the ad hominem fallacy as well, attacking the people who oppose aid rather than attempting to refute the arguments against aid.

6. This is an inductive generalization.

Z = 88 per cent

F = students at the university

G = students who think that a university education will improve their communication skills

If introductory philosophy is an elective and not a required course, it is possible that the sample may be unrepresentative, since the kind of students who choose introductory philosophy as an elective course may be more likely to expect a university education to improve their communication skills than those who would avoid philosophy as an elective. The sample in this case is self-selected, so it is difficult to know whether it might be unrepresentative.

7. This is an analogical argument by relations.

x = prohibition of alcohol

y = reduction of drunkenness

R = an ineffectual measure for

a = gun control legislation

b = reduction in the number of murders

The subject case is gun control legislation and the analogue case is alcohol prohibition in the United States between World War I and 1933. This is a weak analogy and, therefore, a weak argument. First, gun control legislation, unlike the prohibition of alcohol, is not aimed at eliminating guns from society. Second, gun legislation is intended to reduce the incidence of something that is already illegal in itself, namely, murder, whereas drunkenness is not in itself illegal (even if public drunkenness, drinking under age, and drinking and driving are).

8. This is a statistical syllogism.

Z = 90 per cent

x = the American who is in my Canadian politics course

F = Americans

G = people who know very little about Canadian politics

It is weak for two reasons. It ignores the fact that the American is sufficiently interested in Canadian politics to take a course in it. It also ignores the fact that he or she is, presumably, attending a Canadian university and thus is living in Canada. Both these factors make it likely that he or she will know more about Canadian politics than the average American.

9. This is an inductive generalization, to whatever extent it is an inductive argument at all.

Z = highly improbable (no exact percentage is given, but something very low is implied)

F = people in Idaho in the 1940s and 1950s

G = communist sympathizers

It is extremely weak, because the sample is far too small and clearly unrepresentative. This example illustrates the weaknesses of relying on anecdotal evidence. Because the speaker seems incapable of imagining that communist sympathizers might exist outside of major eastern cities, he or she does not want to examine evidence that an Idaho trade union may have been organized by such people.

10. This passage may be interpreted in one of two ways.

A) First, it may be interpreted as comprising two arguments. The first argument has a missing conclusion (*Anyone who trains for six hours a day with T.J. Davis and follows his diet is likely to make the national swim team*), which also forms the premise of the second argument. The first argument is:

Last year Frances and Rhonda spent six hours a day training with T.J. Davis and followed his special diet, and made the United States' national swim team.

Therefore, anyone who trains for six hours a day with T.J. Davis and follows his diet is likely to make the national swim team.

This is a very weak inductive generalization.

Z = 100 per cent (it is implied that Frances and Rhonda are the only members of the sample)

F = swimmers who train for six hours a day with T.J. Davis and follow his special diet

G = swimmers who make the national swim team

The sample is certainly too small, and probably biased as well.

The second argument is:

Anyone who trains for six hours a day with T.J. Davis and follows his diet is likely to make the national swim team.

I am training for six hours a day with T.J. Davis and following his special diet.

Therefore, I am likely to make the national swim team.

This is a statistical syllogism.

Z = a high degree of probability (no exact percentage is given)

x = I (the speaker)

F = swimmers who train with T.J. Davis and follow his special diet

G = swimmers who make the national swim team

It is a strong argument as it stands, although there might be important and relevant information about the speaker that would lead us to revise this judgment. If someone is not already an elite swimmer, then it is unlikely that T.J. Davis's supervision will help them make the national swim team. The possible strength of the second argument does not, however, compensate for the weakness of the first argument.

B) Alternatively, it may be interpreted as an argument by an analogy of properties:

x = Frances and Rhonda

y = I [the speaker]

A = training with T.J. Davis

B = training 6 hours per day

C = following T.J. Davis's special diet

D = making the US swim team

The subject case is the speaker, and the analogue cases are Frances and Rhonda. Frances and Rhonda followed a training regimen that led to their being named to the US swim team. The speaker infers that she can make the US swim team by following the same regimen. On its own the analogical argument is not very strong, because we don't know how the speaker's swimming abilities compare with those of Frances and Rhonda. If the speaker is a novice swimmer or has little experience in high-level competition and Frances and Rhonda were already very strong swimmers before training with T.J. Davis, then the analogy is very weak. Also, it may well be that Frances and Rhonda were such strong swimmers that they could have made the team by using another training regimen, in which case the speaker's training strategy may be ineffectual.

11. This is an inductive generalization.

Z = 44 per cent

F = students in the university telephone directory

G = students who support a proposal for a fee increase to pay for new athletic facilities

The sample is large enough, but it may be somewhat unrepresentative. Because the survey was conducted on a weekend, the sample probably under-represents first-year students, who are much more likely to visit their families on weekends than senior students. And senior students are probably less likely to support a fee increase to pay for new athletic facilities that may not be ready until after they graduate. In addition, perhaps those who would be most likely to support new athletic facilities are less likely to be home on a weekend because they are out training or engaged in some sporting activity. We should also want to know how the question put to the students was framed. If the question was stated in a way that doesn't inflame student resentment about the proposed increase (*do you approve of a small fee increase as part of the school's fundraising efforts for a new athletic complex?*), then 44 per cent seems surprisingly low. But if the question was stated in a way that could inflame their resentment (*do you approve of making students pay for a new athletic complex by adding a new fee to existing fees?*), then it may be unduly biased to say that *only* 44 per cent approved of it.

12. This is an analogical argument by properties.

x = human beings

y = non-human animals

A = exhibiting behavior associated with feeling pain

B = having a central nervous system

C = getting an evolutionary advantage from feeling pain

D = feels pain

The subject case is animal pain, and the analogue case is human pain. Human pain is associated with three features (behavior, a central nervous system, and its evolutionary advantage), and all three of these features are evident in non-human animals. This is a strong analogy, and therefore a strong argument. Certainly, if we remain in doubt about whether non-human animals feel pain, then we have almost as much reason to doubt whether other humans feel pain too. Of course, we cannot decisively eliminate these doubts; however, this argument gives us good inductive grounds to set them aside.

SELF-TEST NO. 17

I.

1. There are many examples of wealthy people whose lives are obviously miserable (for example, through drug addiction or alcoholism). Others, such as Kurt Cobain and Christina Onassis, have died by suicide.

2. This certainly applies to the criminal law, but there are important areas of law in which coercion is either absent or very remote. For example, some laws lay down the conditions for making a valid will, and it is difficult to see how the function of these laws is coercive. Other examples of non-coercive laws are laws establishing courts, various aspects of constitutional law, and laws establishing the right of an individual to run for political office.

3. The only real counter-example would consist of telling a joke that is not at the expense of someone else, such as a joke at one's own expense or at nobody's expense. So, for example: A grasshopper walks into a bar, and the bartender says, "Hey, we have a drink named after you!" The grasshopper replies, "Really, you have a drink named Dave?" To be effective, however, it needs to be funny.

4. The following women have become leaders of their countries: Angela Merkel, Margaret Thatcher, Golda Meir, Benazir Bhutto, Indira Gandhi, Kim Campbell, and Gro Harlem Brundtland. There have been numerous others.

5. The Spanish Inquisition, the Crusades, religious fanaticism in Northern Ireland, the Taliban regime in Afghanistan, Arab-Israeli hostility, and so on.

II.

1. Well, I've been a sex pervert all my life. I was raised as a sex pervert by my father, and if it was good enough for him then it is good enough for me.

2. I don't think that stealing my roommate's chemistry notes is really stealing, because he has never threatened to punish me for it.

3. And if Jim had found $20,000 lying in the street he'd be able to afford a new car; well, he has just bought a new car so he must have found $20,000 lying in the street.

4. Yes, and you shouldn't eat any salt either. It's deadly. They've proven that it kills laboratory animals when they give them a steady dose of it.

5. That's what my uncle said the day my aunt left him for good. Or, That's what the turkey said about the farmer the day before Thanksgiving.

SELF-TEST NO. 18

1. Humor.

2. Vague terms: *the highest standards of craftsmanship* and *range of styles to suit the tastes of the modern consumer* have no clear meaning. False confidence: *We are the best ...*

3. If the speaker has been challenged to defend his or her earlier claim that pornography is not harmful to women, this would be a red herring. In some contexts, however, this attempt to change the topic might be legitimate.

4. Vague terms: the entire passage is vague, but *neat guy, laid back,* and *lots of personality* are especially vague.

5. Loaded question: This complex question assumes that we need protection of the sort being advocated or that we have been putting off seeking this protection.

6. Loaded question: this is a rhetorical question. Actually, many people have argued that generating the greatest happiness is not essential to the best society. A non-consequentialist, such as Immanuel Kant, might say that happiness was morally irrelevant, and that the answer to this question should be "no." And Plato would have claimed that justice is essential to a good society. Mill, however, would have answered "yes" to the question, but even he understood how important it was to analyze happiness and to formulate arguments in defense of the principle.

7. Vague terms: *got what it takes.*

8. If the speaker has been challenged to defend his or her earlier claim

regarding how criminals should be treated, this would be a red herring. In other contexts, however, this statement might be legitimate.

9. Persuasive redefinition: the term *scientist* is being redefined in a way that changes its normal descriptive meaning.

10. Loaded question: This framing question presupposes that normally the government serves the interests of its tycoon friends.

    Loaded terms: *bleating, tycoon.*

11. Selectivity: focuses attention on an unrepresentative sample of events.

12. Loaded question: This is a rhetorical question. Even Kant, who championed duty as the central feature of moral action argued that acting *consistently* with duty was insufficient; someone who seeks selfish ends might act consistently with duty and their actions would have no moral worth. Rather, a morally right action must be performed *out of a sense of duty alone.* So there is at least one person who would answer this rhetorical question by denying what the speaker presupposes.

Glossary

Numbers in brackets indicate section numbers where discussion of item occurs in text.

absurd examples, method of: See **method of absurd examples**.

acceptability of the premises: Premises are acceptable when they can reasonably be accepted as true. This is the first criterion for good arguments. (5.2.1)

ad hominem: A fallacious argument that substitutes irrelevant information discrediting the author of a statement for genuine evidence that the statement is false. Latin for "against the man." (7.4.1)

adequacy of support provided by the premises: The support the premises give is strong enough for the purposes of the argument. This is the third criterion for good arguments. (5.2.1)

affirming the antecedent: An argument of the form *If p then q; p; therefore q.* Any argument of this form is formally valid. (9.4)

affirming the consequent: An invalid argument of the form *If p then q; q; therefore p.* Any argument of this form is formally invalid. (9.5)

alternatives, exclusive: See **exclusive alternatives**.

alternatives, exhaustive: See **exhaustive alternatives**.

ambiguity, grammatical: See **grammatical ambiguity**.

ambiguity, referential: See **referential ambiguity**.

ambiguous sentence: A sentence that has two or more different but possibly quite precise meanings. (3.2.1)

analogical argument by properties: Reasoning by analogy based on a comparison of the properties of the subject case and those of the analogy case. This has the form *x has A, B, C; y has A, B; It is probable, therefore, that y has C.* (10.5)

analogical argument by relations: Reasoning by analogy based on a comparison between relations that obtain in the subject case and those of the analogue case. This has the form *x is to y as a is to b; x is R to y; It is probable, therefore, that a is R to b.* (10.5)

analogue case: The case with which we are more familiar, which is supposed to be relevantly similar to the subject case, and which is used to draw the conclusion in an analogical argument. (10.5)

analogy, reasoning by: See **reasoning by analogy**.

analytic statement: A statement that is true by definition. (3.4)

antecedent: The component *p* of an implication *if p then q*. Note that this may come second in an English sentence; for example, in "The picnic is off if it's raining," the antecedent is "it's raining." (9.2)

antecedent, affirming the: See **affirming the antecedent**.

antecedent, denying the: See **denying the antecedent**.

appeal to authority: A fallacious argument which cites the (irrelevant) testimony of someone who is not a reliable authority on the matter at issue. (7.3)

appeal to force: A fallacious argument which substitutes an irrelevant threat of force or other kind of pressure for genuine evidence for the conclusion. (7.2)

appeal to ignorance: A fallacious argument which appeals to the fact that there is no evidence for a claim, to show that it is false. (8.4)

appeal to pity: A fallacious argument which substitutes an irrelevant attempt to elicit pity or sympathy for the presentation of genuine evidence for the conclusion. (7.2)

appeal to popularity: A fallacious argument which substitutes an irrelevant attempt to base a claim's acceptability on the fact that it is widely believed. (7.2)

argument: A set of statements that claims that one or more of those statements supports another. (1.1)

average, simple: See **simple average**.

begging the question: The fallacy committed by an argument when its premises presuppose, directly or indirectly, the truth of its conclusion. (Also known by its Latin name, *petitio principii*.) (6.7.1)

causal fallacies: A group of fallacies that misidentify the cause of something. See *post hoc*, **confusing cause and effect**, and **common cause**. (8.5)

cause and effect, confusing: See **confusing cause and effect**.

cause, common: See **common cause**.

chain argument: An argument of the form *If p then q; if q then r; therefore if p then r*. Any argument of this form is formally valid. (9.4)

charity, principle of: See **principle of charity**.

circular definition: A definition that includes the term being defined (or its cognate) in the definition. (2.9.4)

coherence theory of truth: A theory that holds that a particular statement is true when it is part of a coherent set of mutually supporting statements. (6.1.2)

collective use of a term: Occurs in a statement that says something about the class as a whole. (3.2.2)

common cause: A fallacy committed when it is claimed that there is a causal relation between A and B when in fact both A and B are caused by a third factor, C. (8.6.3)

complex question: See **loaded question**.

complex statement: A statement that contains one or more other statements as component parts. (9.2)

conclusion: The statement in an argument that its premises are supposed to support. (1.1)

confirmation, induction by: See **induction by confirmation**.

confirming instance: An actual observation showing that an observation statement is true. (10.4)

confusing cause and effect: Fallacious reasoning in which an effect is identified as a cause and the cause is identified as the effect. (8.6.2)

conjunct: Each of the two components of a conjunction. (9.2)

conjunction: A truth-functional statement (written *p and q*) with two components (*p*, *q*); its logical operator corresponds to the English *and*. The statement is true only when *p* is true and *q* is true; it is false when *p* is false, or when *q* is false, or when both *p* and *q* are false. (9.2)

connotation: See **sense of a word**.

consequent: The component *q* of an implication *if p then q*. Note that this may come first in an English sentence; for example, in "The picnic is off if it's raining," the consequent is "the picnic is off." (9.2)

consequent, affirming the: See **affirming the consequent**.

consequent, denying the: See **denying the consequent**.

contextual definition: Definition that conveys the meaning by using the word in a standard context and by providing a different sentence with the same meaning but without the word. (2.8.5)

correspondence theory of truth: A theory that holds that the truth of a statement is its correspondence to a fact. (6.1.1)

counter-argument, method of: See **method of counter-argument**.

counter-example: A particular exception to a generalization, used to show that the generalization relied upon in the argument is not universally true. (11.2)

counter-examples, method of: See **method of counter-examples**.

counterfactual argument: An argument whose premises are known or assumed to be false. Used to explore the consequences of these premises. (1.3)

criteria: Standards. (5.2)

criterial approach: An approach to the theory of argument assessment which proceeds mainly by examination of the standards that a good argument must meet. This is the central approach of this text. (5.2)

critical thinking skills: A set of capacities that are used to analyze and assess arguments or lines of reasoning. (1.4)

deductive argument: An argument whose premises, if true, guarantee the truth of the conclusion. (1.2)

definition by synonym: Defining a word by providing a precise synonym. (2.8)

denotation: See **reference of a word**.

denying the antecedent: An invalid argument of the form *If p then q; not-p; therefore not-q*. Any argument of this form is formally invalid. (9.5)

denying the consequent: An argument of the form *If p then q; not-q; therefore not-p*. Any argument of this form is formally valid. (9.4)

descriptive function of language: Language's use to convey factual information. (2.3)

descriptive meaning: The information communicated by a term. (3.6)

dichotomy, false: See **false dichotomy**.

directive function of language: Language's use to command others to do something or to provide advice. (2.3)

disconfirming instance: An actual observation showing that an observation statement is false. (10.4)

disjunct: Each of the two components of a disjunction. (9.2)

disjunction: A truth-functional statement (written *either p or q*) with two components (*p, q*); its logical operator corresponds (roughly) to the English *either ... or*. The statement is false only when *p* and *q* are both false; it is true otherwise—that is, when one or both of the components are true. (9.2)

disjunctive syllogism: An argument of the form *either p or q; not-p; therefore q*. Any argument of this form is formally valid. (9.4)

distributive use of a term: This occurs in a statement that says something about each and every member of the class named by that term. (3.2.2)

emotive function of language: Language's use to express feelings or emotions. (2.3)

empirical fact: A fact that is observable in principle—that is, if one were in the right place at the right time, under the right conditions. (6.1.1)

empirical statement: A statement that asserts an empirical fact, or a set of empirical facts. (6.1.1)

equivocation: The fallacy committed by an argument when a premise has two interpretations, one acceptable and one unacceptable, and when it is the unacceptable interpretation that is required by the conclusion. (6.7.3)

essentialist definition: A definition that attempts to report the real nature of what is being defined. (2.7.3)

evaluative function of language: Language's use to make value judgments—to evaluate things. (2.3)

evaluative meaning: The positive or negative value judgment communicated by a term. (3.6)

evocative function of language: Language's use to evoke feelings or emotions in an audience. (2.3)

exclusive alternatives: Alternatives that cannot both (or all) be true: when one is true, the other(s) must be false. (6.7.4)

exhaustive alternatives: Alternatives that cover all the possibilities. (6.7.4)

explanation: An attempt to show why or how something happens (or has happened). It is taken for granted that the event happened—which is in contrast to an argument attempting to prove that some event happened. (4.4.2)

extension: See **reference of a word**.

fallacies approach: An approach to the theory of argument assessment which proceeds mainly by attempting to describe the main types of fallacious argument—the common mistakes one must guard against. (5.1)

fallacy: An error or weakness in an argument that detracts from its soundness, but is disguised so that it may look like the conclusion is supported. (5.1)

false confidence: When a questionable claim is presented with great confidence, attempting to mislead the audience into thinking it cannot seriously be questioned. Another irrational technique of persuasion. (12.4)

false dichotomy: The fallacy committed by an argument when a premise presents us with a choice between two alternatives and assumes that they are exhaustive or exclusive or both, when in fact they are not. (6.7.4)

falsified truth-claim: A truth-claim that has been shown to be false. (6.2)

force, appeal to: See **appeal to force**.

formal invalidity: Describes an argument that is not formally valid; that is, it is such that if its premises are true, then its conclusion may nevertheless be false. (9.5)

formal validity: Describes an argument such that if its premises are true, then its conclusion must also be true. (9.3)

foundational principles: Statements that underlie a practice or body of knowledge, such as the law of causality in science, which cannot be doubted without undermining everything else associated with that practice or body of knowledge. (6.2.2)

framing question: The use of a question to suggest that something is possible without any evidence. See **loaded question** and **rhetorical question**. (12.3)

general empirical statement: A statement the truth-value of which depends on experience and concerns a wide range of particulars within the same class. See **universal empirical statements** and **statistical empirical statements**. (6.2.1)

genus-species definition: A definition that mentions a larger category (a genus) to which that kind of thing belongs, and then specifies what makes that particular kind (that species) different from the other species in that genus. (2.8.1)

grammatical ambiguity: An ambiguity that arises when the grammatical structure of a sentence allows two interpretations, each of which gives rise to a different meaning. (3.2.3)

guilt by association: The technique of attacking an opponent or an opponent's position by suggesting a similarity with another person or position that the audience regards in an unfavorable light. This is a technique of irrational persuasion when this is a faulty analogy. (12.9)

hypothesis: A principle or statement that, if true, would explain the event(s) or situation(s) to which it applies. See **rival hypotheses**. (10.4)

idea theory of meaning: The view that the meaning of a word consists of the idea or mental image that is associated with the word. (2.2.2)

ignorance, appeal to: See **appeal to ignorance**.

implication: A truth-functional statement (written *if p then q*) with two components (*p, q*); its logical operator corresponds (roughly) to the English *if ... then*. The statement is false only when *p* is true and *q* is false; it is true otherwise—that is, when *p* is false, or when *q* is true, or both. (9.2)

inconsistency: The fallacy committed by an argument when it contains, implicitly or explicitly, a contradiction, usually between two premises. (6.7.2)

induction by confirmation: A form of inductive reasoning in which confirming instances, and the lack of disconfirming instances, are used as evidence to support a hypothesis. (10.4)

inductive argument: An argument whose premises, if true, make it reasonable to conclude that the conclusion is true, but do not provide an absolute guarantee. (1.2)

inference: The process of reasoning from one thought A, to another, B, when we believe that A *supports* or *justifies* or *makes it reasonable to believe* in the truth of B. (1.1)

inference indicators: Words that indicate that one thought is intended to support (i.e., to justify, provide a reason for, provide evidence for, or entail) another thought. Examples include *therefore, since, thus, implies, consequently, because, it follows that, given that.* (1.1)

intension: See **sense of a word**.

interpretive skills: A set of capacities that are used to discern the meaning of something; in the context of this book, usually something written or said. (1.4)

interrogative function of language: Language's use to elicit information. (2.3)

invalidity, formal: See **formal invalidity**.

jointly sufficient conditions: A collection of conditions which are not individually sufficient, but which are sufficient as a group when all occur. (3.8)

loaded question (also called **complex question**): A question containing an assumption that any possible answer would confirm. These are used as an irrational technique of persuasion. See **framing question** and **rhetorical question**. (12.3)

loaded term: A term with a clear descriptive meaning and a positive or negative evaluative meaning, which is used in an attempt to persuade us to accept the evaluation conveyed by the term. This is an irrational technique of persuasion. (12.1)

logic: The study of inferential connections between premises and conclusions in arguments with a view to determining whether the premises really do support the conclusion in any given argument. (1.5)

logical operator: An element of a truth-functional statement connecting (or, in the case of negation, modifying) the component sentences and determining how the truth or falsity of the whole statement is related to the truth or falsity of the components. (9.2)

logical strength: An argument is said to have logical strength when its premises, *if true*, actually provide support for its conclusion. (1.2)

mean: See **simple average**.

meaning as use: The approach that explains meaning of linguistic items—primarily sentences, but, derivatively, words—in terms of their use. (2.2.3)

meaning, theories of: See **reference theory of meaning**, **idea theory of meaning**, **meaning as use**.

median: The middle point in a range of values: half the cases in the range are above this point, and half below. (12.6)

mention: See **use vs. mention**.

method of absurd examples: A method for arguing back by constructing an argument with a closely parallel structure to the one being criticised, with true premises, and with an obviously false or absurd conclusion. (11.3)

method of counter-arguments: A method for arguing back by constructing a different argument attempting to show that the conclusion under criticism is false or problematic. (11.4)

method of counter-examples: A method for arguing back involving presentation of a counter-example showing that the generalization cannot be relied on the way the argument does. (11.2)

mode: The particular value that occurs most frequently in a range of values. (12.6)

necessary condition: A condition without which something wouldn't happen. In other words, X is a necessary condition for Y if, and only if, when X is false Y must also be false (or, when X is absent Y cannot occur). (3.8)

negation: A truth-functional statement (written *not-p*) with one component (*p*), its logical operator corresponds to the English "not" or "it is false that." The statement is true when the component is false, and false when the component is true. (9.2)

non sequitur: An argument with irrelevant premises. Latin for *it does not follow*. (7.2)

normative principles: Rules that regulate a practice by serving as its standards of proper operation. (1.5)

observation statement: An empirical prediction deduced from a hypothesis. (10.4)

open question: A genuine attempt to elicit information in which the formulation of the question does not delimit the range of possible answers. See **restricted question**. (12.3)

operational definition: Definition made by specifying a rule or operation. (2.8.4)

operator, logical: See **logical operator**.

ostensive definition: A definition that conveys the meaning by giving examples. (2.8)

performative function of language: Language's use to perform actions, such as can be performed merely by saying a sentence; for example, when one says "I hereby promise / find the accused guilty / christen this boat / resign." (2.3)

persuasive function of language: Language's use to persuade people to accept something or to act in a certain way. (2.3)

persuasive redefinition: The redefinition of a familiar term or phrase that has both a descriptive and an evaluative meaning in such a way as to change its descriptive meaning while keeping its evaluative meaning the same. (12.10)

petitio principii: See **begging the question**.

pity, appeal to: See **appeal to pity**.

post hoc: The fallacious argument that because something comes before an event, it must therefore be the cause of that event. Short for the Latin *post hoc ergo propter hoc*, which means "after this therefore because of this." (8.5.1)

pragmatic theory of truth: A theory that holds that the truth of a statement consists in the fact that it leads to the successful solution of a real problem. (6.1.3)

premise (plural: **premises**): A statement in an argument that is supposed to provide support for the conclusion. (1.1)

premises, acceptability of: See **acceptability of the premises**.

premises, adequacy of support provided by: See **adequacy of support provided by the premises**.

premises, relevance of: See **relevance of the premises**.

presupposition: A premise that is a general principle the speaker takes to be important in the connection between the other premises and the conclusion, but that is missing (unstated) in the argument. (4.2)

principle of charity: A principle for interpreting someone's words according to which one should, when faced with various possible interpretations, always adopt the one that interprets those words as expressing views that are as reasonable, plausible, or defensible as possible. (3.1)

probative arguments: Arguments that purport to prove a claim (the conclusion) to be true (as distinct from explanations, which are not proofs). (4.4.2)

properties, analogical argument by: See **analogical argument by properties**.

property: A feature that is attributable to a thing considered on its own. (10.5)

reasoning by analogy: A form of inductive reasoning in which there is an attempt to support a conclusion by pointing to a separate case supposed to be similar. (10.5)

reasoning skills: A set of capacities that are used to construct arguments and lines of reasoning. (1.4)

reconstructing an argument: The process of identifying and extracting the premises and conclusion (including spelling them out when they are unstated but implied), and making explicit the connection between them (i.e., the structure of the argument). (4.1)

recreational function of language: Language's use merely to amuse ourselves and others: puns, word-games, songs, etc. (2.3)

red herring: An irrelevant issue introduced to distract hearers and shift the topic to one about which the speaker is on firmer ground. An irrational technique of persuasion. (12.8)

redefinition, persuasive: See **persuasive redefinition**.

reductio ad absurdum: An argument in which a statement is proven to be true by assuming it to be false and then deriving a contradiction from that assumption. A species of counterfactual argument. (1.3)

reference of a word: The class of things to which the word refers (also known as its **denotation** or **extension**). (2.6)

reference theory of meaning: The view that the meaning of a word consists in what it refers to. (2.2.1)

referential ambiguity: An ambiguity that arises when a word or phrase could, in the context of a particular sentence, refer to two or more properties or things. (3.2.2)

relation: A feature that is attributable to the relationship between two or more things. (10.5)

relations, analogical argument by: See **analogical argument by relations**.

relevance of the premises: Premises are relevant when they provide support for the conclusion. Relevance of the premises is the second criterion for good arguments. (5.2.1)

report of an argument: The attribution of an argument to somebody other than the speaker; the speaker does not necessarily endorse the argument. (4.4.1)

reportive definition: A definition intended to convey the information needed to use a word correctly in its standard use. (2.7.1)

restricted question: A genuine attempt to elicit information in which the question is formulated to delimit the range of possible answers. See **open question**. (12.3)

rhetorical question: A disguised statement in the form of a question; it attempts to induce assent to the disguised statement rather than elicit information from whomever the question is addressed to. See **framing question**. (12.3)

sampling: A form of inductive reasoning in which observations of a portion of a group are used to justify a conclusion about the whole group. (10.2)

selectivity: An irrational technique of persuasion which attempts to mislead an audience into a generalization by producing an unrepresentative sample. (12.5)

sense of a word: What we understand when we understand its meaning (also known as its **connotation** or **intension**). (2.6)

simple argument: An argument with a single premise and a single conclusion. (4.6.1)

simple average (also called **mean**): The value obtained by adding all the values in a range, and dividing the sum by the number of values. (12.6)

simple statement: A statement that does not contain any other statement as a part. (9.2)

slippery slope: A fallacious argument which attempts to justify a negative assessment of a policy by appealing to a chain of consequences, each one causing the next, ending with an undesirable result. This is fallacious when it is not likely that the policy will really result in this outcome. (8.4)

sound argument: An argument that has both logical strength and true premises. (1.3)

statement: A sentence (i.e., a set of words) that is used to make a claim that is capable of being true or false. (1.1)

statement, analytic: See **analytic statement**.

statement, complex: See **complex statement**.

statement, contradictory: See **contradictory statement**.

statement, empirical: See **empirical statement**.

statement, observation: See **observation statement**.

statement, simple: See **simple statement**.

statement, synthetic: See **synthetic statement**.

statement, truth-functional: See **truth-functional statement**.

statistical empirical statement: A qualified general statement the truth-value of which depends on experience; it asserts something about a proportion of a class of things; see **universal empirical statements** and **general empirical statements**. (6.2.1)

statistical syllogism: A form of inductive reasoning in which a generalization stating that a percentage Z of a group has a certain property is used to justify a conclusion that it is probable to degree Z that a particular item in that group has that property. (10.3)

stipulative definition: A definition that creates a new precise meaning. (2.7.2)

straw man: A fallacious argument which irrelevantly attacks a position that appears similar to, but is actually different from, an opponent's position, and concludes that the opponent's real position has thereby been refuted. (7.4.3)

strict proof: The most stringent standard of acceptability that can be made for a claim because the possibility of error has been eliminated (either in its use of empirical evidence or its support in a theorem). (6.3)

subject case: The case about which one is trying to draw a conclusion in an analogical argument. (10.5)

sufficient condition: A condition such that if it happens, something will follow. In other words, X is a sufficient condition for Y if, and only if, when X is true Y must also be true (or, when X is present Y must occur). (3.8)

synonym, definition by: See **definition by synonym**.

synthetic statement: A statement whose truth or falsity is not solely dependent upon the definitions—the meanings—of the words involved. (3.4)

T argument: An argument with two or more premises, none of which offers significant support for the conclusion by itself; but all the premises do support the conclusion when working together, in combination. This argument is so-called because the lines in the tree diagram joining the premises to the conclusion form a T. (4.6.2)

target feature: The feature of the subject case in an analogue argument about which the conclusion is being drawn. (10.5)

tree diagram: A schematic representation of the structure of an argument using letters (P1, P2, MP3, C, etc.) to represent the premises and conclusion, and an arrow to represent *therefore*. (4.6)

truth: See **coherence theory of truth, correspondence theory of truth, pragmatic theory of truth**.

truth-claim: See **falsified truth-claim, undetermined truth-claim, verified truth-claim**.

truth-functional statement: A complex statement whose truth or falsity is entirely determined by the truth or falsity of the component statements. (9.2)

tu quoque: A fallacious argument which attempts to show that a criticism directed at the speaker is irrelevant by claiming that the accuser is open to the same criticism. Latin for "you too." (7.4.2)

undetermined truth-claim: A truth-claim that has been neither shown to be true nor shown to be false. (6.2)

universal empirical statement: An unrestricted general statement about a class of things the truth-value of which depends on experience; it asserts something about the entire class. See **statistical empirical statements** and **general empirical statements**. (6.2.1)

use vs. mention: Usually, sentences use words, referring to their reference. But sentences may merely mention words, referring to the word itself. (Careful writers put words intended this way inside quotation marks, or in italics.) (3.2.4)

V argument: An argument with two or more premises, each of which offers some support for the conclusion by itself; in combination, the support of each is added. This argument is so-called because the lines in a tree diagram joining two premises to the conclusion form a V (though not when there are more than two). (4.6.3)

vague sentence: A sentence that lacks a precise meaning. (3.2.1)

validity, formal: See **formal validity**.

verification: The process of determining whether a truth-claim is true. (6.2)

verification skills: A set of capacities that are used to determine the truth or falsity of statements. (1.4)

verified truth-claim: A truth-claim that has been shown to be true. (6.2)

INDEX